The Young Fed

MARKETS AND GOVERNMENTS IN ECONOMIC HISTORY

A series edited by Price Fishback

Also in the series:

The Young Fed

*The Banking Crises of the 1920s and the
Making of a Lender of Last Resort*

MARK CARLSON

THE UNIVERSITY OF CHICAGO PRESS   CHICAGO AND LONDON

The University of Chicago Press, Chicago 60637
The University of Chicago Press, Ltd., London
Cover design and text design © 2025 by The University of Chicago
The University of Chicago claims no copyright to the content of this book. Quotes and
illustrations from previously published works cited in the text may be copyright protected.
Published 2025
Printed in the United States of America

34 33 32 31 30 29 28 27 26 25   1 2 3 4 5

ISBN-13: 978-0-226-83782-6 (cloth)
ISBN-13: 978-0-226-83783-3 (e-book)
DOI: https://doi.org/10.7208/chicago/9780226837833.001.0001

Library of Congress Cataloging-in-Publication Data

Names: Carlson, Mark, author.
Title: The young Fed : the banking crises of the 1920s and the making of a lender
    of last resort / Mark Carlson.
Other titles: Markets and governments in economic history.
Description: Chicago : The University of Chicago, 2025. | Series: Markets and governments
    in economic history | Includes bibliographical references and index.
Identifiers: LCCN 2024021800 | ISBN 9780226837826 (cloth) | ISBN 9780226837833 (ebook)
Subjects: LCSH: United States. Federal Reserve Board. | Banks and banking—
    United States—History.
Classification: LCC HG2563 .C37 2025 | DDC 332.1/1097309042—dc23/eng/20240614
LC record available at https://lccn.loc.gov/2024021800

To my parents,
my wife,
and my children

Contents

Figures and Tables

Tables

Acknowledgments

I have long been intrigued by how policymakers have responded to financial crises, but writing a book on the subject was a daunting task. I thank my colleagues for their support for this endeavor and for the helpful conversations and valuable comments that were essential in moving it forward. I am particularly indebted to Jim Clouse, Will Roberds, and David Wheelock for reading the earliest drafts and enthusiastically encouraging me to pursue this project. My thanks also to the many others who diligently read different versions and offered valuable feedback, including Michael Bordo, Kris Mitchener, Bill English, Jonathan Rose, Maylis Avaro, Eugene White, Charlie Calomiris, Clemens Jobst, Barry Eichengreen, Haelim Anderson, Matt Jaremski, and Kilian Rieder. While these colleagues provided many helpful thoughts, the standard disclaimer applies; the views presented in this book are my own and do not necessarily reflect the views of anyone who provided comments, the Board of Governors of the Federal Reserve System and members of its staff, or anyone else within the Federal Reserve System.

To understand more about what motivated policymakers to act and why they took the particular actions they did, and more importantly to help the reader understand, I have relied extensively on policymakers' own words and the reports that informed them. Tracking down those words and reports was challenging at times, and I am indebted to the librarians and archivists who spent copious amounts of time helping me locate the materials, ensuring I had the necessary access, and finding innovative ways to share historical documents long-distance. Without them, this book would not have nearly the depth that it does. Among them are Christina Horak, Magda Morales, Anne Hall, Krista Box, Helen Keil-Losch, Mark Miller, Katrina Stierholz, Susan Illis, Meredith Rector, Pat Hilleman, Shawne Osborne, Cindy Edwards, LuAnne Pederson, and Jennifer Steinhardt.

I am also grateful for the support of the University of Chicago Press and the people who helped transform the raw manuscript into a finished book. There are many steps in that process and I appreciate the work of Chad Zimmerman, Rosemary Frehe, Michaela Rae Luckey, and Tamara Ghattas to make that happen.

Finally, and most importantly, I thank my family. My parents for their unwavering encouragement. My wife and children for their immense support and near-endless patience listening as I mused out loud (yet again) about the latest historical document that I'd read and how it fit, or didn't, with the others I had read. They tolerated without complaint the long hours I spent in archives and the even longer subsequent hours spent trying to fit together the material that I'd found there. Their support and encouragement have been truly a gift.

CHAPTER ONE

Introduction

The Roaring 1920s evoke images of a boom—the rise of the automobile and extravagant Gatsby-style parties—that ended in the economic and financial collapse of the Great Depression. However, there was considerable financial turmoil within the decade as well. The start of the 1920s saw the end of an agricultural and commodity boom that had been fueled by World War I. The boom had swept up farmers, miners, and others with promises of prosperity but left them struggling when it turned to bust not long after the war ended. In a regional episode in the middle of the decade, land prices in Florida soared and then plunged, causing havoc among developers and prospective land buyers. Banks that had extended credit into these and other booms faced customers who would be long delayed in repaying loans, if repayment was to come at all, as well as depositors worried whether their bank was one of those that had extended too much credit to troubled borrowers. Amid concerns about the extent of troubles in the banking sector, the spectacular failures of some banks threatened to trigger contagious collapses and the closures of many other banks.

When the Federal Reserve was established by an act of Congress in 1913, a primary purpose was to support the US banking system during times of stress and to prevent financial instability from causing significant damage to the rest of the economy. So when faced with banks experiencing illiquidity, insolvency, or both during the 1920s, Federal Reserve officials had to decide whether and how to respond.

At times, the imperative seemed to be to lend into the crisis. Policymakers viewed doing so and taking the related risks as essential to preserving broader financial and economic stability. This view is apparent in a letter by officials from the Federal Reserve Bank (FRB) of Chicago:

> Our board of directors believed at the time that the very critical situation should be met as far as possible through a broad liberal policy on our own part, even though in pursuing any such policy, we were faced with a possibility of considerable loss. Any other policy at the time would undoubtedly have resulted in an almost complete business collapse in the state of Iowa. . . . We extended very large lines of credit to many individual banks. No doubt in some cases we made mistakes; that was inevitable. We feel, however, that our record is evidence that we were willing to go to the limit to help the general situation as well as the individual member banks, and the communities in which they were located. (FRB Chicago 1927)

At other times, policymakers thought the appropriate policy was to stop lending and close the banks. In these instances, they saw intervention as unhelpful and only likely to exacerbate losses and worsen conditions.

> The whole situation simply resolves itself into the proposition that errors of judgement and unsound policies on the part of the management of a member bank cannot be corrected by continuous extensions of credit by a Federal Reserve Bank or any other creditor. Those extensions of credit simply serve to create further opportunities to make the same mistakes of judgement and to further prosecute the same unsound policies with consequences usually vicious for the bank receiving the credit, for the community which it serves, and for the [Federal Reserve] bank extending the credit. (FRB Dallas 1927)

These contrasting views should not be taken as representing deeply held opposing views of dueling policymakers. Rather, they represent views held by policymakers wrestling with specific situations and weighing trade-offs associated with interventions amid particular conditions. Many policymakers expressed different views when confronted with different settings. Indeed, each of the Reserve Banks cited here also expressed essentially the opposite point of view when facing alternative circumstances.

The purpose of this book is to provide a history of the Federal Reserve's approach to emergency liquidity provision in the 1920s to describe what the policymakers did, what circumstances and considerations led them to make some of the choices they made, and what they learned from the outcomes of those choices. Often they were confronting issues quite similar to those faced by policymakers dealing with financial stresses in modern times. The fact that these issues are still relevant one hundred years later is a valuable reminder of just how difficult they are to deal with. Moreover, policymakers employed a fair bit of experimentation in these early years of the Federal Reserve. By studying the actions taken, we can learn a bit more about what worked and what did not, as well as something about what lessons should be drawn, or not drawn, from the outcomes of interventions to deal with financial crises.

At the heart of the book is a review of Federal Reserve officials' thinking about the best way to provide emergency liquidity support and a set of case studies demonstrating how the tools for liquidity provision were actually deployed during emergencies. Most of the liquidity provision occurred through the discount window, the main policy tool provided in the Federal Reserve Act to address financial instability. This flexible tool enables the Federal Reserve to lend bilaterally to commercial banks on specific types of collateral in times of need.[1] Policymakers also showed their creativity in deploying other tools to respond to stress. For instance, in a few situations, the Federal Reserve shipped and strategically deployed (but did not lend) large amounts of cash to locations experiencing, or expected to experience, stress. The availability of cash provided reassurance and helped calm anxious bank depositors. Using all its tools, the Federal Reserve was able to provide critical liquidity support to banks and alleviate potentially severe episodes of financial instability. A review of these episodes and the rationale for providing liquidity improves our understanding of how the discount window operated in the 1920s and what Federal Reserve policymakers thought about emergency liquidity provision.

Although, as documented in the case studies, policymakers experienced a large number of successes when providing emergency liquidity to banks in the 1920s, they also had concerns with how things played out. Policies of supporting banks during extended periods of stress resulted in some banks becoming highly dependent on Federal Reserve liquidity support. Other banks failed with discount window loans outstanding, which put the Federal Reserve in uncomfortable situations. Consequently, Federal Reserve officials adopted a more cautious approach to lending and increased their efforts to dissuade banks from relying too much on the Federal Reserve for liquidity support. These shifts affected how the Federal Reserve responded to bank distress in the Great Depression and influenced the framework for discount window lending policy for decades afterward. Thus, a review of the experience of the 1920s helps us understand the evolution of thinking at the Federal Reserve regarding how the institution should act as a lender of last resort.

Understanding this evolution of thinking regarding discount window lending policy highlights the challenges that Federal Reserve officials faced in implementing the goals of the authors of the Federal Reserve Act. The United States had long had concerns about the concentration of financial power that might accompany a central bank, but the economic disruptions associated with the Panic of 1907 convinced lawmakers that a central bank was needed to respond to, and to help prevent, the cash hoarding and contagious bank closures that occurred during financial crises. Representative Samuel Beakes put it this way during the congressional debate on the Federal Reserve Act:

> This system increases the safety of banks. No bank can make any money and keep in its vaults money enough to pay all its depositors if they all want their money within a short time. So as times get tight the banks have been in the habit of loaning less and less money and hoarding up more of it to provide for emergencies, thus greatly increasing the very stringency which has caused them alarm. In tight times each bank is looking out for itself and will not rediscount the paper of [lend to] other banks in distress. In the Glass bill [the Federal Reserve Act] we have the regional reserve banks, with means of putting out needed currency, formed for the very purpose of taking care of the local banks in time of stress, where they can quickly turn their good paper into money, and thus can safely loan out more of their deposits. Thus are the bank reserves mobilized for immediate use. When the regional reserve banks get in full operation the member banks will no longer fear runs upon them, and as the depositors will know that their deposits will be paid when wanted, there will be no runs on banks in this system. (Beakes 1913, 4906)

Others in Congress who favored the establishment of the Federal Reserve expressed similar sentiments. Robert Owen (1919), the senator who sponsored the bill in that chamber, expressed it succinctly: "It is the duty of the United States to provide a means by which the periodic panics which shake the American Republic and do it enormous injury shall be stopped."

The statement by Representative Beakes highlights two goals for the central bank. First, the Federal Reserve should promote confidence by standing ready to provide liquidity and respond forcefully to stress. Second, Beakes references "good paper," which implies that the Federal Reserve should not support insolvent banks. The challenge of responding robustly to inspire confidence but being cautious and lending only to solvent banks is one of the key tensions that policymakers grappled with during the 1920s. One interpretation of the shift in policies in the late 1920s is that Federal Reserve officials were rebalancing their approach to meeting these objectives in light of their experiences.

The range of situations discussed in this book concerning lender-of-last-resort actions and emergency lending is quite broad. Some situations involved short-term, intense liquidity needs in which funds were provided to keep banks from having to close amid a bank run or in which funds were pre-positioned to head off potential bank runs. In other situations, longer-term central bank support was needed to help the banks adjust in the wake of local economic dislocations. Finally, in some situations the Federal Reserve provided support to facilitate the orderly resolution of a troubled bank. It is not clear that the liquidity support provided in all these situations would meet all modern definitions of lender-of-last-resort actions.[2] Nevertheless, these interventions are included because Federal Reserve officials in the 1920s viewed their actions in all these situations as emergency lending and the wide assortment of experiences illuminates how these officials viewed the scope of their responsibilities. Moreover, reviewing the full range of experiences is crucial to understanding the lessons that policymakers took from them.

The experiences of the 1920s illustrate the basics of what a lender of last resort can and cannot do. Central banks have the tools to address issues of illiquidity. Lending by the central bank to commercial banks that are experiencing deposit outflows can prevent those banks from having to sell assets at fire-sale prices that would affect their solvency. Moreover, in crises, if commercial banks are concerned that the funding markets will become impaired, those banks may hoard liquidity and thus precipitate the impairment that they were concerned about; a central bank can stop that dynamic by assuring the banks that liquidity will be readily available so that there is no need to hoard funds. By contrast, central banks cannot provide equity capital and thus cannot save an institution that is truly nonviable. In these cases, central bank lending may simply allow some creditors to flee and reduce their exposure to the troubled bank; that in turn can engender moral hazard as creditors have less incentive to monitor the condition and risk-taking of the bank. (However, rapid bank collapses can be quite disruptive and socially costly, and there may be benefits to preventing a disorderly collapse; in the 1920s, balancing that benefit with the costs of supporting troubled banks and letting some creditors leave was a challenge that the Federal Reserve faced on several occasions.)

Through an investigation into the wide range of situations, important concepts for us today become apparent. Most of these ideas are general in nature and are considered in the modern literature (see, for example, Goodhart 1999; Freixas et al. 1999), but it is useful to be reminded just how universal they are.

First, the episodes discussed here frequently involved concerns about both the insolvency and the illiquidity of the institutions at the center of the episode, and the decision to lend often had to be made amid considerable uncertainty about the solvency of the borrower. Sometimes that uncertainty was due to the speed at which events unfolded. In other situations, the uncertainty arose because the solvency of the bank's own customers would only become known with the passage of time but the liquidity need required Federal Reserve officials to make an immediate decision about lending. Taking collateral is one way that the lender of last resort can manage the credit risk when lending in uncertain situations; however, taking substantial amounts of collateral can negatively affect other creditors, which may create a new set of problems.

Second, flexibility and creativity are important. The case studies presented here are a useful reminder of the range of circumstances that may require an intervention by a lender of last resort. Stresses in some episodes appear to have built slowly over time, while in other cases the stress materialized suddenly. Some episodes were truly idiosyncratic, while others were part of more systemic events. Decisions about whether and how to intervene involved balancing the need to preserve financial stability with the need to manage moral hazard and risk shifting. Flexibility and creativity to adapt to the facts of the situation were key to trying to achieve that balance.

Third, publicity surrounding such interventions needs to be managed carefully. In some instances, bold statements or actions that clearly indicated that the Federal Reserve was acting helped promote confidence. These instances tended to be those where runs were already underway and support would help restore confidence or where officials could make it clear that they were providing support without specifying exactly which institutions were benefiting. In other cases, such as when specific institutions required longer-term support, the interventions were kept quiet to avoid creating alarm.

It is also illuminating to consider how Federal Reserve actions compared with contemporary wisdom about lender-of-last-resort interventions.

Probably the most influential articulation of how a lender of last resort should act was set down by Walter Bagehot in 1873 in his book *Lombard Street*. To summarize Bagehot, a lender of last resort should lend freely at a high rate against good collateral to solvent borrowers.[3] Lending freely promotes confidence that liquidity will be available to those that need it. A high rate, relative to normal times, ensures that funds will be used only in an emergency and that borrowing will diminish as conditions in money markets normalize. (At the time when Bagehot was writing, the high rate was also valuable in maintaining the commitment to the gold standard by attracting gold inflows and discouraging outflows.) Lending to solvent borrowers on good collateral mitigates concerns about moral hazard.

Federal Reserve policymakers were certainly aware of his thinking. In his testimony before the Joint Commission of Agricultural Inquiry, Governor Strong of FRB New York responded to a question on emergency liquidity provisions by pointing specifically to Bagehot and the importance of lending freely at a high rate (Joint Commission of Agricultural Inquiry 1921, 2:513). However, the Federal Reserve's approach to emergency lending was not always in line with Bagehot. *Lombard Street* focuses mainly on the central money market and severe stress in that market. The Federal Reserve officials in the Districts discussed here were often interacting with institutions more on the periphery, a number of whom were experiencing more structural issues. Consequently, Federal Reserve officials had a somewhat different approach than the one suggested by Bagehot.

First, Federal Reserve officials had several ways of managing the risks associated with discount window lending. Collateral, just as in Bagehot, was one key aspect of doing so. There appear to have been some variations in the interpretation of eligibility criteria across Reserve Banks, but the sense that the collateral ought to be of good quality was universally shared. Reserve Bank officials also requested extra collateral or personal guarantees from the bank managers when there were concerns about the condition of the bank or the initial collateral. In addition, officials of the Reserve Banks used inside information about the banks from examiners' reports to help assess the risks they were taking. The officials appear to have been particularly attentive to information about the quality of the management. Reserve Bank staff also managed risk by considering the amount of stable funding at the bank relative to the loans it was extending. That ratio helped inform Federal Reserve officials about whether the support they were providing would likely be temporary in nature or might be needed for some time.

Second, the case studies make clear that Federal Reserve officials were attuned to the willingness of shareholders to provide additional equity support to the banks. Solvency was not just a point-in-time concept but had to do with long-term viability and the willingness of shareholders to see the institution through its current difficulties. Equity support and general engagement by shareholders also reassured Federal Reserve officials that moral hazard issues associated with lender-of-last-resort support were being contained and that the Reserve Banks were not merely propping up failing banks.

Third, Federal Reserve officials were quite concerned with the externalities associated with bank closures. They paid particularly close attention to whether the banks seeking support were themselves a source of credit for other banks, as their closure might trigger further closures. They were also attentive to whether the banks were the last in their particular communities, as their closure would significantly impair access to financial services. In the face of potentially large costs from disruptions associated with a bank's failure, Federal Reserve officials appear to have been more willing to provide liquidity support while they worked to resolve uncertainties about the bank's condition.

Finally, Federal Reserve policymakers were aware of some potential downsides to lending. For instance, they knew that lending on a secured basis and facilitating some depositor withdrawals would affect the distribution of losses in the event that the bank failed. Moreover, policymakers were aware that novel actions on their part could set precedent and might generate moral hazard or give rise to increased risk-taking at other institutions.[4]

The Federal Reserve System of the 1920s should not be thought of as a singular institution.[5] While the Federal Reserve Board located in Washington, DC, set broad policies, the twelve Reserve Banks distributed across the country had latitude in implementing these policies, especially with respect to decisions about liquidity provision to member banks. The thinking at the different Reserve Banks was often similar but not necessarily identical, and this book makes an effort to be clear about attributing particular statements to the relevant officials as well as to indicate whether those statements seem broadly representative of thinking throughout the Federal Reserve System.

The economic difficulties in the 1920s and the associated stresses on the banking system were concentrated in the agricultural regions of the country. Consequently, certain Reserve Banks within the Federal Reserve System had more experience with emergency lending, and discussions of financial instability issues feature more frequently in the writings and correspondence of the officials at those institutions. There is much less information about how officials at other Reserve Banks thought about emergency lending or which approach they would have taken to deal with emergencies in this period. Reflecting the locations of the stresses in the banking system and the availability of relevant information, this book deals mainly with the experiences of the Federal Reserve Banks of Atlanta, Chicago, Dallas, Kansas City, Minneapolis, and San Francisco.

The case studies presented in this book focus on how the Federal Reserve responded to financial stress at particular institutions or in fairly small regions. At the same time, a number of these financial stress events occurred in the context of the Federal Reserve's overall response to the collapse of agricultural prices in the early 1920s. White (2015) and White and Roberds (2020) provide a more macroeconomic view of the response, especially of the response in the Atlanta District. The case-level analysis here usefully complements the broader picture described in these other references.

Responding to financial stress was not the Federal Reserve's only concern. Policymakers needed to set policy to maintain the gold standard and ensure the sufficiency of the gold reserve held at the Federal Reserve. Policymakers were also concerned with promoting credit conditions that would foster a business expansion without giving rise to speculative or inflationary conditions. This latter concern was a precursor to more modern monetary policy in that the intent was to shape financial conditions with an eye toward influencing the broader economy.

It is important to bear in mind, though, that Federal Reserve policymakers' approach to using their tools to address financial instability and to acting as a lender of last resort could be different from their approach to credit and monetary policy. For instance, FRB San Francisco responded quite forcefully to several episodes of financial instability and articulated the importance of a central bank responding aggressively to widespread financial distress; however, Chandler (1971) describes this Reserve Bank as having a relatively conservative approach to the conduct of monetary policy. Thus, one should not assume that the approach to one set of policies necessarily provides any insights into the approach to another set of policies.

The focus in this book is on the Federal Reserve's experience with financial instability and emergency lending in the 1920s. Much more well known as a period of financial instability are the years from 1930 to 1933, the early years of the Great Depression, which witnessed some of the most

severe banking panics and highest levels of bank failure in the history of
the United States. The history of that instability and the Federal Reserve's
response has been the subject of considerable study—see, for instance,
the extensive discussion by Friedman and Schwarz (1963), Wicker (1996),
Calomiris and Mason (2003), Richardson and Troost (2009), and many
others. This book does not deal directly with the financial instability that
occurred in these subsequent years.

Nevertheless, a thorough appreciation of the experience of the 1920s is
quite helpful for understanding what followed. In particular, while policymakers generally acted in ways that they thought would prevent disruptive financial instability and support communities, they later became concerned that some actions may have sustained banks that should have been
shut down or may have resulted in greater losses to depositors or to the
Federal Reserve itself. As a consequence, Federal Reserve policymakers
appear to have tightened the rules regarding the provision of credit
through the discount window. These tighter standards may have contributed to the Federal Reserve responding less forcefully to the stresses in
the banking sector in the 1930s than would have been the case had the
experience of the 1920s been different.

Some Notes on Sources

The information presented in this book comes from a range of sources. A
few are worth mentioning specifically.

One exceptionally important resource for understanding the thinking
of Reserve Bank officials was an informal survey of six Reserve Banks
conducted by the Federal Reserve Board in 1927 regarding their approach
to dealing with weak and overextended banks. The precise wording of this
survey, sent by telegram, follows:

> The Board is interested in knowing character of assistance which has been and
> can advisably be extended to member banks in weakened condition and would
> request that for its confidential use you select 4 or 5 banks which were in a
> weakened condition say three or four years ago and follow through to present
> time, or to date of closing in case of such of the selected banks as have failed,
> the trend in the loan portfolio of such banks and state what assistance if any
> was rendered by the reserve bank, also in each case whether in light of present
> knowledge you feel that the assistance given by the reserve bank was helpful

to the bank and to the community served. Also please state the fundamental principles followed by your bank in granting or refusing assistance to member banks in a weakened condition and briefly what constructive policies can be developed from experience with weak and over-extended banks during the past few years. (Board of Governors 1927)

Thoughtful responses were received from the Reserve Banks to which the survey was sent: Atlanta, Chicago, Dallas, Kansas City, Minneapolis, and San Francisco. Indeed, the responses are an important reason that this book focuses on these Reserve Banks. Even though the question asks specifically about banks in a weakened condition, many of the thoughts conveyed by the Reserve Banks cover a broader range of circumstances. References to these responses are labeled as being from the Troubled Bank Survey Response (TBSR). This material is available in the National Archives along with an assortment of other correspondence from Federal Reserve officials and internal staff memorandums that are extremely informative about their actions and thinking.

Other information in the National Archives was valuable as well. The examination reports for banks supervised by the Office of the Comptroller of the Currency (OCC) for the period up to 1930 are publicly available in the archives. These insightful documents provide a considerable amount of objective information on the inner workings of the banks as well as the examiners' subjective assessments of the quality of the banks' managements and assets. For the 1920s, a variety of correspondence from the banks and the examiners to the main office of the OCC is available in the archives alongside the examination reports.

Previous histories of the Reserve Banks were also tremendously helpful. One that is referred to extensively is Herman Kilman's 1961 history of the FRB Dallas; this history was distributed internally within the Federal Reserve System and contained enough inside information that it was originally labeled as confidential. It has since been made generally accessible within the system, and copies are currently available in several Federal Reserve System library reading rooms, including at FRB Dallas and at the Board of Governors as well as online at FRB St. Louis's FRASER historical document repository. Franklin Garrett's 1968 history of the FRB Atlanta is similarly detailed and also cited frequently. This history was never published, but it is also available in the FRASER historical document repository.

Finally, the Federal Reserve Banks of Atlanta, Chicago, Dallas, Minneapolis, and San Francisco granted access to the minutes of their board of directors meetings. These meeting minutes provide critical background about the discussions that policymakers were having and context for the thoughts that appear in the correspondence. Thus, while the minutes of the board meetings are not often quoted in this book, they have been invaluable in making sure that material quoted from correspondence and other more public sources is correctly represented and contextualized.

Of course, this book also draws on a variety of other contemporary sources as well as on the rich modern literature on the history of the Federal Reserve and of the 1920s.

CHAPTER TWO

Background on the 1920s, the Banking System, and the Federal Reserve

The 1920s are often thought of as a period of robust economic growth. Employment and output in the manufacturing and industrial sector surged over the course of the decade. There was a marked expansion in the availability of consumer goods; among these were the automobile and the radio, both of which had a tremendous impact on American households. Households and businesses also benefited from electrification efforts as more and more of the country gained access to stable sources of electric power.

While strong growth characterized much of the 1920s, the decade started out quite differently. In 1920 and 1921, the United States experienced one of the sharpest, though also briefest, recessions in its history. Industrial production contracted by over 25 percent in less than a year, and the number of people employed plunged more than 10 percent. The recovery was also fairly rapid, with production and employment returning to prerecession levels within a few years.

The economic turmoil at the start of the decade was especially pronounced in the agricultural sector, with the collapse of a boom linked to dynamics stemming from World War I. Moreover, while the industrial sector recovered rapidly, the difficulties in agriculture lingered for several years after the recession had ended because it took time to deal with the excesses created by the boom and because droughts, insects, and other issues caused residual challenges for farmers and ranchers. As the agricultural sector represented roughly one-fourth of the country's economic activity, these problems were consequential for a significant portion of the US economy.

These broader trends, especially those related to agriculture, had a pronounced effect on developments in the banking sector. In the decade leading up to the 1920s, the number of banks in the United States had swelled with the addition of thousands of smaller banks, especially in agricultural communities. Leverage in the banking sector rose as these banks lent into the agricultural boom. When the recession occurred at the start of the decade and the postwar agricultural sector suffered, many banks closed. It took some time before the banking sector was able to fully work through the debt issues stemming from the boom and bust (see, for instance, the discussion in Alston, Grove, and Wheelock 1994).

The newly founded Federal Reserve contributed to the broad contours of economic developments. Policymakers learned how to use their tools, both the discount window and open market operations, to shape credit conditions. To combat an inflationary surge after World War I, the Federal Reserve tightened policy notably and likely contributed to the severity of the recession in 1920 and 1921. After that, policy was eased and, in what Friedman and Schwarz (1963) describe as the "high-tide" of the Federal Reserve, fluctuated only moderately for most of the decade against the largely favorable economic backdrop.

The Agricultural Sector

Developments in the agricultural sector of the early 1920s were shaped significantly by World War I. The war severely disrupted European agricultural production, and prices of agricultural commodities soared globally. US farmers bought more land, planted more crops, and raised more livestock amid expectations that the boom would last for some time or that prices might continue to rise (Helm 1939). A significant portion of the expansion of farm activities was financed through borrowing. When European agriculture recovered far more quickly after the war than expected, prices of agricultural commodities collapsed, and farmers struggled to repay debts.

The agricultural boom during World War I was truly impressive. Prices of many crops doubled or tripled relative to the levels that had prevailed for decades. For instance, as shown in figure 2.1, the price of corn had hovered around fifty cents a bushel for most of the period from 1876 to 1913

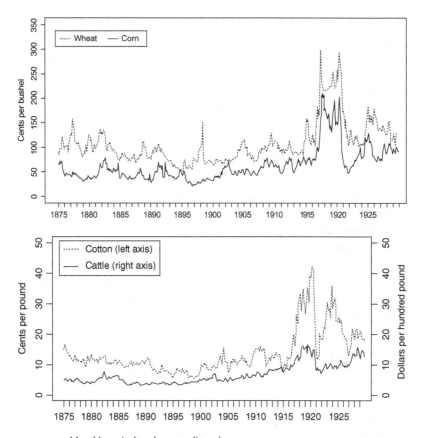

FIGURE 2.1. Monthly agricultural commodity prices

Source: National Bureau of Economic Research, Macrohistory Database. Wholesale prices of wheat (Chicago); corn (Chicago); cotton (New York); and cattle (Chicago).

and then jumped to triple that amount at $1.45 a bushel in 1918. Similarly, cotton had averaged about ten cents a pound from 1876 to 1913 before quadrupling to reach forty cents a pound in 1920. Wheat prices also more than doubled relative to the average level of the previous four decades. Cattle prices, which had been on an upward trend since around the turn of the century, accelerated with the war. Indeed, prices for nearly every agricultural commodity reached record levels.[1]

Farmers sought to take advantage of the surge in prices by expanding production. They bought and cultivated additional acres. With this increased activity, the cost of inputs to farming, such as fertilizer and farm machinery, went up. The price of farmland rose notably. Much of that surge occurred around the peak of the agricultural boom, when land prices in some areas reportedly doubled over the course of a few months (Boyle 1928; Rajan and Ramcharan 2015). Jaremski and Wheelock (2020a) report that the value of farmland rose more than 80 percent in southern states and more than 50 percent in the Great Plains. Helm (1939) reports that the average price per acre of farm real estate in Missouri in 1921 was nearly four times the level that had prevailed in 1897. Some of the rise in prices reflected the demand from farmers, but some also reflected speculative pressures as buyers entered the market in hopes of reselling for a profit; Griswold (1936) reports that in some parts of the Seventh Federal Reserve District (FRB Chicago), farmland was changing hands as often as four times a year.

To purchase the increasingly expensive land, as well as the more expensive seeds and farm implements, farmers needed to borrow (as did many land speculators). Studies of this period document an increase both in the share of farms with a mortgage and in the average size of those mortgage debts (Alston 1983; Alston, Grove, and Wheelock 1994; Jaremski and Wheelock 2020a). This rise in mortgage debt was more pronounced in some areas of the country than others, with some of the largest increases occurring in the South, where mortgage debt more than doubled. During the boom period, with prices increasing, lending standards appear to have been relaxed. Griswold (1936) reports that, amid the rapid run-up in values—lenders—which may not necessarily have been banks—were willing to lend amounts as much as twice the value of the land.

While some clearly hoped that crop prices would remain high for a long time, the agricultural boom did not endure, and the collapse was as dramatic as the run-up had been. Agricultural output in Europe recovered more quickly than expected, and agricultural prices dropped. As is evident in figure 2.1, the prices of many agricultural commodities fell back to levels similar to those that had prevailed before the war. These drops had a devastating effect on farmers, especially those who had borrowed significantly. In some cases, the farmers sought to avoid selling their crops at the fallen prices and instead stored them in hopes of a recovery. The financing needs associated with holding those inventories put an enormous strain on the banking industry, which was asked not only to extend the maturity on existing loans but then to provide additional credit in subsequent years so that farmers could plant the next round of crops (see, for instance, Kilman 1961, 54).

Land values also fell; Jaremski and Wheelock (2020a) report that farmland prices fell by 27 percent, on average, between 1920 and 1925. In many cases, borrowers owed more on their mortgages than the land was worth. If a mortgagee defaulted, lenders could seize the land but faced difficulties selling it at a price that covered the mortgage balance. That in turn undermined the financial condition of the lenders and threatened their solvency.

Amid these struggles, farm foreclosures surged. Alston (1983) reports that the average farm foreclosure rate jumped from about 3.2 percent during the period from 1913 to 1920 to around 10.7 percent from 1921 to 1925. The foreclosure rates remained high for several years thereafter, peaking during the Great Depression before returning to low levels after World War II. Areas where the boom had been the most pronounced, such as the Great Plains and the South, had the highest foreclosure rates.

In some cases, a strategy of waiting paid off. As shown in figure 2.1, crop prices eventually did rebound, if not to their wartime levels, then at least to levels above their postwar lows. This rebound allowed many farmers to get back on their feet and the agricultural sector to work through many of the existing debts.

However, the troubles were not entirely over. Crop prices remained volatile during the rest of the decade, and farmers had to decide whether to store or sell crops. Droughts afflicted parts of the country; while not as severe or widespread as those in the Dust Bowl of the 1930s, these droughts did create considerable hardships for farmers in the affected regions. The combination of volatile prices and drought meant that farmers faced challenging conditions throughout the decade.

The Nonagricultural Sectors

In general, the nonagricultural sectors of the US economy, especially the industrial sector, grew robustly during the 1920s. While manufacturing and industrial activity declined in the 1920–1921 recession, industrial production quickly rebounded and grew at a robust pace during the 1920s. From the trough reached in April 1922, year-over-year changes in industrial production averaged over 9 percent through 1929, a pace not matched in the post–World War II years. Employment gains in this period were also solid, especially outside of the struggling farm sector. Nonagricultural employment in the United States increased nearly 40 percent from 26.6 million in 1921 to 37.1 million in 1929 and came to represent a larger and larger share of total employment. Estimates of the unemployment rate in the

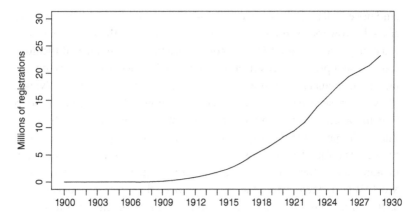

FIGURE 2.2. Annual automobile registrations

Source: National Bureau of Economic Research, Macrohistory Database. Automobile registrations in the United States, passenger cars.

1920s are well below the average rate for the decade preceding the entry of the United States into World War I (Carter et al. 2006).

A notable portion of the expansion in economic activity consisted of the creation of new consumer durables. One of the most visible and important of these durable goods was the automobile. New automobile registrations, an indicator of the number of automobiles added to the economy each year, nearly tripled during the decade, from 8.2 million in 1920 to 23.1 million in 1929 (see fig. 2.2). Automobiles changed the life of the American household by making it considerably more mobile. Moreover, the construction of automobiles involved large amounts of labor and other inputs and hence had a consequential impact on both employment and manufacturing output. With increased electrification, a variety of other consumer products became more widely used during this period, including the radio, washing machine, and vacuum cleaner (see Olney 2013).

The expansion of manufacturing required an increase in financial intermediation to support it, and bond, stock, and banking activity grew robustly. In addition, many consumer durables were purchased on credit, which boosted the financing needs of households; some of those financing needs were met by banks, while others were met by new types of nonbank financial companies, such as sales finance companies. Amid relatively strong growth in business earnings and household wealth, the increased use of credit associated with the production or purchase of consumer durables tended not to be a source of financial stress during the 1920s.[2]

The Banking Sector

In the 1920s, the banking sector consisted predominantly of small local banks, often referred to as country banks, that were deeply connected to their communities. Legal restrictions on the banks' ability to establish branch offices meant that most banks operated a single office in a single town. To be sure, there were large banks with extensive operations in the financial centers, but these were the exceptions. To give a sense of the size, the average (mean) bank in 1920 had assets of $1.7 million and deposits of $1.4 million. Many banks were much smaller than that, with assets of less than $500,000. These banks operated very differently from the large banks located in the financial centers, the biggest of which was National City Bank of New York, which had assets of nearly $850 million.

There were, however, quite a lot of small local banks. The number of banks had been on the upswing for some time and swelled further amid the boom at the start of the decade. The total number of banks in the United States peaked at about thirty-one thousand in 1921, after which, amid more challenging conditions, the count slowly declined.

Bank Lending and Deposits

With the local nature of banking, banks' balance sheets tended to be quite closely tied to local economic activity, and their financial health was closely connected to the health of the local economy. Banks in communities dominated by a single economic activity had loan portfolios that were tied, directly or indirectly, to that activity and did not have much scope to diversify. Loans also tended to be used to finance shorter-term needs. For instance, money could be lent to merchants to finance inventories, farmers to grow crops or raise cattle, or manufacturers to purchase the inputs to production or to finance the shipment of final goods. Loans to finance long-term capital investment were less common but were starting to grow as a share of bank lending. Banks in agricultural areas tended to have loan portfolios that expanded and contracted with the crop or livestock cycles, while banks in urban centers were more likely to see their balance sheets fluctuate with year-end activity.

The local community typically provided the core of the deposit base for the banks. Most depositors were local businesses or households. The majority of these funds took the form of checking deposits. City or county funds were also placed at local banks and in some cases served as a valuable source of funding.

There was some scope for banks experiencing unusual loan demands or deposit withdrawals to raise funds by borrowing from other banks (and from the Federal Reserve, as discussed in depth below). Banks could *rediscount* their loans—essentially obtaining funds by borrowing against the proceeds that would be received from the repayment of a particular loan—or borrow in their own name using specific loans as collateral, referred to as *bills payable*. Rediscounts and bills payable were expensive sources of funding; hence, they were not part of the core funding of banks but were typically available to banks seeking short-term financing.

In the years preceding the 1920s, both lending and deposit taking by banks had been rising briskly. Total loans originated by the banking sector and total deposits held at banks roughly doubled between 1900 and 1910 and then more than doubled again between 1910 and 1920. Most of the growth in this latter period occurred between 1915 and 1920 as loans and deposits grew at, or near, double-digit rates in each year. Loan growth during the war years likely helped businesses and agriculture ramp up production to meet increased demand. However, the fastest loan growth occurred in 1920, as the boom turned to bust, possibly as banks extended loans to their customers to help them weather the trouble.

The role of banks in agricultural finance appears prominently in many of the stress episodes discussed below and so is worth a bit of extra discussion. The harvest or livestock cycle had pronounced effects on the balance sheets of banks located in agricultural communities. The demand for loans was particularly strong during the harvest season. Harvest season was also a period when deposits were drawn down. As a result, banks in agricultural communities needed to make extensive use of nonlocal sources of funding to meet their needs. Kemmerer (1910) and Carlson and Wheelock (2018a) document that, before the founding of the Federal Reserve, there were substantial flows of funds within the banking sector to meet these seasonal dynamics. While key to efficiently distributing banking-sector reserves, these flows also put notable strains on money markets and bank funding markets. Once the Federal Reserve was established, the discount window and loans from the Reserve Banks played an important role in providing funds to enable banks to meet these seasonal needs and to facilitate the harvest and shipment of crops to market.

In addition, banks were important providers of credit for general farm operations. Personal and collateral loans from banks were used to finance the purchase of farm capital goods such as tractors. Wall (1937) estimates that the volume of these loans more than doubled between 1914 and 1920. Commercial banks provided just over half of all farm mortgage credit from institutions in the United States—though informal credit from individuals and others was the largest component of farm mortgages—and this amount increased notably from 1914 to 1920 (Horton, Larsen, and Wall 1942; Rajan and Ramcharan 2015). The dollar amounts of loans on banks' books understate the role played by banks in providing such financing and the linkages of banks to farm credit. Helm (1939) reports that some farm credit companies operated within the offices of the banks and employed the same staff as the banks even though these businesses were legally separate. In such cases, the bank might have been pressed to provide backstop financing for the farm credit company if there were liquidity issues. Such entanglements show up in a few of the case studies discussed in chapter 5.

Interbank Connections

While loans and deposits were mainly local, banks did need to have connections outside their area. Banks enable their customers to make and receive payments and thereby facilitate their customers' ability to engage in commerce. Conducting that business requires a connection to the nationwide payment system. Before the establishment of the Federal Reserve, banks connected to the payment system through an extensive correspondent banking network. This network was largely a hub-and-spoke system with a central hub in New York City and regional hubs scattered throughout the United States. Local banks (referred to as respondent banks) held deposits at the hub banks (referred to as correspondent banks). Shifts in balances in the deposit accounts at the hub banks could be used as part of the payment-clearing process. These deposit balances also serve as high-quality liquid investments (balances held at correspondent banks typically paid a low but positive rate of interest). In addition, these interbank networks helped banks manage their liquidity risk; correspondent banks could lend funds to their respondent banks, through bills payable or rediscounts, for example, when such resources were needed (see James 1978).[3]

Once the Federal Reserve was established, it was integrated into this network. The Federal Reserve System operated a check-clearing system and also provided funds to banks in need. However, not every bank joined the Federal Reserve System, and many country banks found it valuable to maintain at least some of their existing correspondent banks. Indeed, the Federal Reserve Banks were placed in the central hubs and some regional hubs, and they may have reinforced the importance of the banks in these cities, since those banks had ready access to the Federal Reserve (Jaremski and Wheelock 2020b).

Bank Net Worth and Leverage

Bank net worth, which includes equity capital and retained earnings, represents the stake that the owners have in the bank. Greater amounts of net worth ensure that the owners have more invested in the bank and a greater incentive to make sure that the bank is well run: that lending will generate profits and not involve unwarranted risks, that liquidity is managed appropriately, and that the bank is generally operating in a safe and sound manner.[4] Net worth also provides a cushion to protect the liability holders from losses in the event that the bank becomes troubled; when banks fund a greater proportion of their assets using equity, there are more assets whose proceeds can be used to pay off the depositors and other creditors—who are paid before equity holders—if the bank fails. Less net worth, especially relative to the assets of the bank, means that depositors are less well protected.

In this period, net worth consisted of three components (for additional details, see Alcorn 1908). The first component was paid-in capital. Bank equity shares were issued with a particular face value. For example, many banks issued shares where the face value of each share was one hundred dollars. The book value of paid-in capital was the number of shares outstanding multiplied by the face value of those shares. This book value was referenced in a variety of bank regulations. It was also reported on regulatory filings and did not change even if the market price of those shares moved around.

The second component was the surplus. These were funds that the bank retained from its earnings and formally set aside to serve as a buffer that could, for instance, absorb losses on loans that had gone bad or be written down if the bank experienced extraordinary expenses. Most banks were subject to legal requirements that they maintain a surplus of a specified size. Moreover, some banking regulations limited the maximum size of individual loans to some percentage of paid-in capital and surplus, so having a greater surplus provided the bank more latitude in its operations.[5]

The final component of net worth was undivided profits. These were accumulated earnings that the bank could use to write down losses (before tapping the surplus) or to cover operating expenses. If sufficient undivided profits accumulated, they could be formally added to the surplus, which

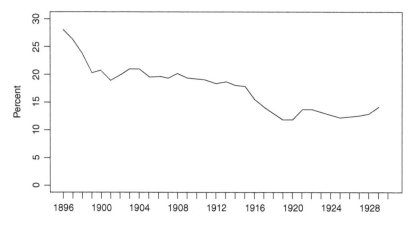

FIGURE 2.3. Aggregate equity-to-asset ratio for commercial banks in the United States

Source: Board of Governors of the Federal Reserve System, *All Bank Statistics, 1896–1955* (1959).

Note: Equity consists of capital, surplus, and other capital accounts.

could then enhance the ability of the bank to make loans. As both surplus and undivided profits reflected the bank's retained earnings, larger amounts of these on the books tended to reflect more profitable institutions.

While the amount of bank net worth increased during the late 1910s and 1920s, it did not keep pace with the rapid expansion of bank assets and bank loans. The resulting decline in the ratios of net worth to assets (and the implied increase in leverage) is apparent in figure 2.3; the fall in this ratio is particularly noticeable around the time of the boom in agricultural prices. As shown in the figure, during the early 1910s, the average ratio of equity (capital, surplus, and undivided profits) to assets was in the neighborhood of 17 percent. By 1920, this ratio had fallen to 11.3 percent. This decline in the net worth relative to assets meant that banks were more vulnerable: equity capital and the loss-absorbing buffers of undivided profits and surplus could be depleted much more quickly for the same loss rate on loans.

Bank Charters and the Number of Banks

As noted above, there were a lot of banks in the 1920s. Bank charters could be granted by both the state governments (state banks) and the federal government (national banks).[6] The requirements for starting a national bank, and the rules about how they operated, tended to be stricter than those for state banks. For instance, in this period, chartering a bank involved

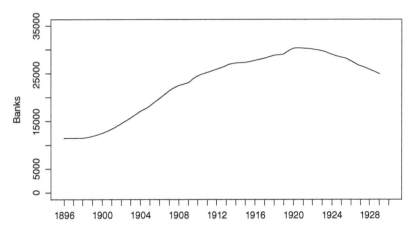

FIGURE 2.4. Number of state and national banks in the continental United States
Source: Board of Governors of the Federal Reserve System, *All Bank Statistics, 1896–1955* (1959).

the initial shareholders paying in a certain amount of capital that varied depending on the size of the town where the bank was being established. Establishing a bank in a larger town required more paid-in capital. For national banks, the minimum required equity to start a bank in the smallest towns was $25,000. For state banks, the minimum in many cases was $10,000—and in one case, North Carolina, $5,000 (White 1983)—as state legislatures sought to ensure that smaller communities might still have access to banks. (There was considerable variation across states; in a few states, the requirements were as high as or higher than those for national banks.)

The number of banks in the United States had been growing since the turn of the century and continued to rise during the wartime boom in agriculture and commodities (fig. 2.4). Between 1900 and 1920, the number of banks in the United States more than doubled from about 12,500 to about 30,500 (Board of Governors 1959). Most of these new banks were state banks. In addition to lower capital requirements in some states, state bank regulations typically provided greater latitude to lend against real estate. Being able to lend against real estate was highly desirable during the boom in agriculture and in the price of agricultural land (though doing so meant that these banks were more directly exposed during the bust). In addition, many of the new banks were smaller banks located in smaller towns that were in turn closer to the agricultural communities to which the new banks were lending. In 1920, over 25 percent of the banks in the United States were operating in towns with less than 500 people, and two-thirds of all banks were operating in towns with less than 2,500 people (Board of Governors 1937, 906).

The peak year for the number of banks was 1921. After that, the number declined year by year and fell to 25,568 by the end of the decade. The role of the agricultural boom in boosting the number of banks is clear in comparisons of states where agriculture was important, such as Kansas and Texas, and states where agriculture played less of a role, such as Massachusetts. In Massachusetts, the number of banks was slightly higher in 1920 than in the preceding years, but not by very much (see fig. 2.5). By contrast, in states like Kansas or Texas, the number of banks roughly tripled or quadrupled between 1900 and 1920. Jaremski and Wheelock (2020a) establish more formally that the boom in agriculture prices strongly contributed to the chartering of new banks.

The decline in the number of banks during the 1920s was partly the result of bank closures as the loans they had extended during the agricultural boom went bad. There was also a wave of banking consolidations. Some of these mergers occurred as banks attempted to avoid failure. Others occurred as banks sought to take advantage of scale. In some urban settings, banks consolidated to more effectively provide services to their corporate customers, as those firms were also increasing in size (White 2009b). Most banks at this time were limited to being unit banks and operating in a single location. However, in a few states, banks were allowed to establish branches in multiple locations. In these states, especially in

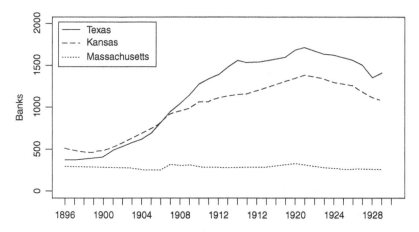

FIGURE 2.5. Number of state and national banks in selected states

Source: Board of Governors of the Federal Reserve System, *All Bank Statistics, 1896–1955* (1959).

California, bank mergers occurred as a few banks sought to establish large branch networks and benefit from an increase in the scale of their operations (Carlson and Mitchener 2009).

Bank Suspensions

Amid the challenging economic environment and the greater vulnerability to shocks, bank closures were elevated in the 1920s. Data are only available on bank suspensions, which included both temporary and permanent closures due to decisions either by the regulators or by the governing boards of the banks themselves. The proportion of the banks that suspended in the early 1920s vastly exceeded that of the preceding couple of decades (see fig. 2.6).[7] One would need to go back to the Panic of 1893 to find even a single year where the share of banks that suspended operations was as high as it was in the 1920s. Moreover, the number of suspensions in the 1920s continued to be high year after year rather than diminishing as some temporary shock receded, as had been the case in the banking panics.

These bank suspensions were concentrated in the areas of the country most affected by the collapse of the boom. For instance, the average annual bank suspension rates for the period from 1921 to 1929 in Kansas and Texas were both about 2 percent. For Texas, the highest single-year sus-

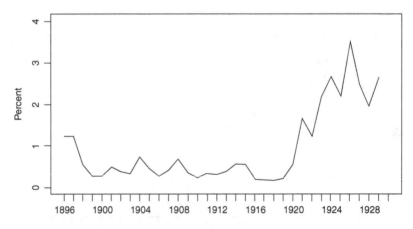

FIGURE 2.6. Bank suspensions as a share of all banks

Source: Board of Governors of the Federal Reserve System, *All Bank Statistics, 1896–1955* (1959), for number of commercial banks; Board of Governors of the Federal Reserve System, *Banking and Monetary Statistics, 1914–1941* (1943) for number of commercial bank suspensions.

pension rate was 3.7 percent, reached in 1921 as the cotton price crashed. For Kansas, the suspension rate peaked in 1926, much later in the decade. The continued challenges in the banking sector partly reflected the ongoing troubles in the agricultural sector. They also reflected the fact that a significant portion of agricultural loans had maturities as long as five years (Helm 1939); loans extended at the height of the boom stayed on banks' books for years, and only when these loans matured were banks forced to recognize the losses.[8] In less agricultural sections of the country, the banks' failure rate was much lower. For instance, in Massachusetts only two banks suspended during the entire decade, so the average annual suspension rate was less than 0.1 percent.

The Early 1920s Boom and Bust and the Banking Sector

Recent scholarship has provided evidence of a feedback loop between banks and agricultural prices on both the upside and the downside. Rajan and Ramcharan (2015) find that, during the boom, counties with more banks had larger increases in farmland prices, acres under cultivation, and farm capital goods. All those developments are also associated with a rise in indebtedness. Rajan and Ramcharan (2016) find evidence that greater indebtedness, especially to banks, mattered on the downside as well, with the failure of one bank in a locality being associated with lower recovery rates on the assets of nearby closed banks. Jaremski and Wheelock (2020a) add to this story and show that more banks were chartered in areas where agricultural prices were rising faster and that these new banks were especially aggressive in growing their balance sheets, though the balance sheets of existing banks also tended to increase faster in areas where agricultural prices were rising more rapidly. The connection was also strong on the downside, as banks that had expanded more rapidly, or were more leveraged, also tended to be more likely to fail during the bust. Completing the loop, Jaremski and Wheelock find that the bank failures appear to have contributed to the declines in farmland values between 1920 and 1925.

Examination and Regulation of the Banking Sector

In the 1920s, as now, banks were visited by examiners who checked on their condition, and the banks were subject to a variety of statutory and

regulatory rules (including, but certainly not limited to, requirements regarding holdings of liquid assets, capital, limits on loan size, the extent to
which loans could be made against real estate, and the banks' ability to
operate a trust business). The examination process provided important
information on the conditions of banks to the authorities, including Federal Reserve Bank officials who oversaw discount window lending. The
various rules also affected the incentives of the bank managers, stockholders, and depositors, as well as the bank regulators themselves. Hence, it is
helpful to have a sense of the examination process and some of the rules.[9]

The particulars of the examination process and the details of the rules
that applied to an individual bank varied depending on whether the bank
had a national or a state charter and, if a state charter, which state the
bank was located in. As national banks constituted the majority of Federal
Reserve member banks and nearly all the case studies described in chapter 5, this section focuses mainly on the rules for national banks.

Supervision and Examination

In general, banks were supervised and examined by the chartering authority. The OCC had been responsible for chartering and examining national
banks since the office was founded in the 1860s. The examination process
became more detailed and thorough over time as the OCC learned about
the aspects of the banks that were most likely to generate problems and
asked the examiners to dig more deeply into those areas. The examiners
themselves seem, on the whole, to have been a relatively knowledgeable
group and to have provided valuable insights into bank operations (see
Calomiris and Carlson 2022). In some cases, state agencies had been examining the state-chartered banks for several decades before the 1920s,
while in other cases, the examining agencies had only been established
after the Panic of 1907 and so had considerably less experience. Moreover,
the rapid growth in the number of banks, particularly of state banks, may
have made it more difficult for the state agencies to keep up. Hence, there
was considerable variation in the extent to which state banks were examined (see Mitchener 2005; White 2013; Jaremski and Mitchener 2015).

When the Federal Reserve was established, it was also given the power
to supervise the banks that opted to become members of the system (all
national banks were required to join, and state banks had the option to
join). This authority gave rise to some complications as those banks were
already being examined by other agencies. The OCC remained the main

examiner for national banks but was expected to share the results of examinations with the Federal Reserve. To facilitate cooperation between the OCC and the Federal Reserve, the OCC was reorganized to create examination districts—each overseen by a chief examiner—that aligned with the Federal Reserve districts. Despite this setup, as discussed by Harding (1925) and White (2013), in the early years there was notable tension about the extent of information sharing. Harding (1925, 7) reports that the reports furnished by Comptroller John Williams during the first years of the Federal Reserve were incomplete. The palpable hostility between (then retired) Comptroller Williams and Governors Benjamin Strong of FRB New York and William Harding of the Federal Reserve Board regarding the supervision and examination of banks, especially those in the Second District, is clearly evident in their testimony before the Joint Commission of Agricultural Inquiry (1921–1922, see, in particular, 2:219–253, 709). Nevertheless, over time, and with some change in personnel, cooperation appeared to improve. In the case studies below, there appears to have been fairly good communication, which suggests that, at least in instances of stress, there was a general willingness to cooperate.

The Federal Reserve Banks had a choice about whether to accept examinations conducted by the state bank authorities. As indicated by the response in Senate hearings (1931), there appears to have been considerable variation in how the Reserve Banks approached interactions with state banking authorities, with some Reserve Banks seeking to do their own examinations on a regular basis and others largely deferring to the state authorities. Over time, the Reserve Banks built up their own capacity to conduct examinations, which enabled them to conduct special examinations for institutions about which they had particular interest or concerns.

The examination process for national banks involved a thorough review of bank operations. The examination reports asked examiners to record detailed information about the balance sheet and especially the loan portfolio by including a listing of, and commentary about, the large loans, insider loans, and loans associated with real estate that had been made by the bank. The examiner was also asked to opine on the quality of the management, the recordkeeping practices, and the bank's efforts to keep track of borrowers' credit quality. One of the most important parts of the examination was the examiner's estimate of the losses that the bank was likely to incur on its assets. That provided the authorities—the comptroller or the Federal Reserve—with an assessment of the bank's health.

The examiner in the field would send a summary of his findings to the chief examiner of the district and the officials at OCC headquarters in Washington, DC. Those officials would then issue a letter to the bank indicating what items needed to be corrected and requesting updates on the bank's progress in accomplishing those items. The actual progress would be checked during the next examination, the timing of which could be expedited if the bank was not sending letters indicating progress or if the concerns about the bank's health were particularly dire.

An additional, and quite important, part of the process of monitoring banks in this period involved public disclosures. Most banks were required to report the condition of their balance sheets to the relevant authorities several times a year (for national banks, these were the call reports or reports of condition). Abbreviated versions of these reports were also required to be printed in local newspapers. That gave the public regular, pertinent information about the health of their local banks.

Liquidity Regulation

A vital part of banks' business involves liquidity and maturity transformation. Banks take deposits that can be withdrawn on demand (such as checking deposits) or on relatively short notice and use those resources to fund loans that have a longer maturity. Historically, the maturity of many loans was not especially long; business financing was often related to inventory or shipping, which tended to have maturities measured in weeks or months. Agricultural finance could involve providing loans that lasted from planting time to harvest sales, but even here loans were typically less than a year. Nevertheless, many customers tended to roll over at least part of the loans they took out, so the effective maturity of some loans could be longer than the apparent contractual maturity.

This liquidity-maturity mismatch means that banks might face withdrawals of deposits well before the loans that those deposits are funding mature. While banks keep cash on hand to meet these withdrawals (and liquid or short-term securities to serve as a secondary reserve), there might be circumstances, such as a bank run, where a bank's typical supply of liquid resources would not be enough. There is a long-standing debate about the extent to which banks should self-insure against the possibility of a shock instead of relying on the government as a backstop.[10] Requirements for self-insurance had historically taken the form of reserve requirements that mandated that banks have a particular supply of cash or other liquid assets on hand. In theory, those liquid assets could be used to meet withdrawals during stress events. Higher reserve requirements meant that banks were insured against bigger shocks but also reduced banks' ability to provide economically valuable lending.

After widespread temporary bank suspensions during the Panic of 1907, the government decided that the reserve requirements were not operating as intended and that a public liquidity backstop was needed.[11] That resulted in the establishment of the Federal Reserve, which could replenish bank liquidity (or bolster it in advance of anticipated withdrawals) by providing funds through the discount window.[12] Reserve requirements, previously used to enforce self-insurance against liquidity shocks, became a device to facilitate the implementation of monetary policy (as discussed below). The intent that the Federal Reserve serve the role of a public liquidity backstop may have affected how Reserve Banks officials approached the provision of funds through the discount window.

Capital Regulation and Dealing with Undercapitalized Banks

As noted above, in this period, establishing a bank involved paying in a particular amount of capital. Once that amount was paid in, however, banks were not required to increase their capital regardless of how large they became. (At least banks with national charters were not required to increase their capital as they grew; as noted by Welldon (1910), some state-chartered banks were required to adjust their capital as their assets or deposits increased.) Moreover, even if the town grew in population such that new banks would need to pay in a greater amount of capital to start, the banks that were already operating in that town did not need to increase their capital. Because the legal requirement focused on the amount of capital needed to be paid in to establish a bank, it functioned importantly as an entry barrier; investors who could not come up with the needed capital were unable to start a bank.

Of course, banks were free to increase their capital beyond the minimum required. The leverage of a bank was determined by the willingness of the liability holders to maintain funds in the bank in proportion to the net worth maintained by shareholders. Risk-averse depositors would presumably be unwilling to let the bank become too leveraged. Thus, banks that wanted to get larger and expand their assets typically needed to increase their net worth to convince depositors that they were safe. Indeed, banks would often advertise the amount of surplus and paid-in capital they had.

All of this did not mean that the capital of the bank was unrelated to prudential regulations. National banks were prohibited from operating with impaired capital. (Here, in particular, the focus is on the rules that applied to national banks. As discussed by Upham and Lamke [1934] and Mitchener [2005], troubled state banks were handled in a range of ways.) In determinations of whether there was an impairment, bank examinations interacted with the capital regulations. As noted above, one of the jobs of the examiner was to estimate the losses the bank was likely to incur on its assets and compare those estimated losses to its surplus and undivided profits. If the estimated losses exceeded the surplus and undivided profits, then the capital was considered to be impaired and corrective action needed to be taken.

One action that the bank could take was a "voluntary assessment" of shareholders. In this case, shareholders would vote to pay in an amount of money sufficient to eliminate the impairment. If the vote was successful, shareholders would be expected to contribute the required amount of money in proportion to the number of shares they held. Shareholders who did not contribute could have their shares seized and sold to cover the contribution.

If there were concerns that the vote to authorize a voluntary assessment would be unsuccessful, or even that a large portion of the shareholders would object and thereby reduce the confidence in the bank, but there was still a core of shareholders committed to keeping the bank going, the comptroller might order a mandatory assessment. Again, shareholders were expected to contribute, and those not doing so might have their shares seized and sold. This approach provided an opportunity for the shareholders who were committed to keeping the bank going to take control of more shares or otherwise reorganize the bank and to make adjustments to the board of directors or other aspects of control. The hope was then that these committed shareholders would point the bank in a more positive direction.

Alternatively, if the vote was not successful (or was not expected to be successful and so was not taken), then, assuming that the bank still had a reasonable amount of equity, the owners could elect to "voluntarily liquidate" the bank and wind down its affairs. In a voluntary liquidation, the owners oversaw the wind-down process. That process might involve paying out the depositors or selling a significant part of the bank to other parties.

If there were concerns that the equity was minimal or completely gone, then the bank could be placed in receivership and wound down by a receiver appointed by the comptroller. The receiver was paid before the shareholders through the proceeds from liquidating the bank. Consequently, the shareholders had an incentive to avoid that expense and deal with the affairs of the bank earlier.[13]

During this period, many banks were subject to double liability.[14] The receiver could require equity holders to contribute an amount up to the face value of the bank shares (typically one hundred dollars per share for national banks) if the proceeds of the liquidation were not sufficient to pay off the bank's liabilities. That was in addition to the loss of whatever funds the investors had paid to acquire the shares in the first place. So shareholder liability was limited but could well exceed the loss of the initial investment. Moreover, putting the bank in receivership was no guarantee that the shareholders would avoid voluntary or mandatory assessments as described above.

Deposit Insurance

One particular regulatory item worth noting, as much for its scarcity as for its presence, is deposit insurance. That insurance in the United States protects bank depositors from losses, up to a specified limit, in the event that the bank fails. That protection reduces the likelihood of bank runs because depositors no longer have an incentive to pull their money out of banks because of concerns about possible losses. Indeed, modern deposit insurance in the United States ensures that bank depositors will maintain ready access to their insured funds in the event of a bank failure so that even depositor concerns about the immediacy of fund availability should not trigger a run.[15]

In the early 1920s, a few states operated deposit insurance programs, but there was no nationwide deposit insurance program. Even in the states in which these programs were offered, national banks were generally not allowed to participate, so the banks included in the case studies were not covered by deposit insurance.[16] There was no protection to assuage depositors' concerns that, in the event of a bank failure, they might experience losses on their deposits and that, perhaps at least as importantly, deposits they might normally expect to have immediate access to would be tied up in the receivership process. Consequently, these depositors would have had strong incentives to withdraw funds from banks about which they had concerns.

While the banks in the case studies were not themselves covered by deposit insurance, several were located in states that had deposit insurance programs. That could have increased the likelihood that, when there were signs of trouble, the depositors might have moved their funds to protected banks. In addition, previous research has found that banks covered by deposit insurance tended to increase their risk-taking. In such cases, economic disruptions associated with the failure of a bank included in the case studies could have had greater potential to cause the failure of additional banks.[17]

The Federal Reserve

The Federal Reserve was established in the wake of the Panic of 1907. One of its important purposes was to promote the stability of the financial system. A key challenge in the period before the establishment of the Federal Reserve was that the money supply was inelastic. Individual banks could lend to one another, and the system proved reasonably effective in moving funds to where they were needed most, but there was not a way to expand the supply of liquidity if there was an overall increase in the demand for money. For example, national banks could issue paper currency, or bank notes, but these notes needed to be secured by US Treasury securities, so the process for expanding the currency supply was not simple. The United States was on the gold standard, so imports of gold or purchases of gold by the Treasury could also expand the money supply, but that also could not be done quickly.

This inelasticity in the money supply was observable in a regular seasonal stringency in money markets during harvest season, when the demand for credit went up and interest rates rose (see Davis, Hanes, and Rhode 2009). Serious stress events, such as banking panics, involved scrambles for funds. Banks could pool their resources to try to accommodate local demands, but that often meant suspending payment flows between cities, which had notable negative economic consequences.[18] The seasonal stringencies and banking panics were thought to be related; during the heightened seasonal demands, the banking system was perceived to be especially vulnerable, so other shocks might result in a panic.

One of the main objectives of the Federal Reserve was to provide an elastic currency that would be responsive to the needs of banks and of business generally for additional liquidity. By expanding the supply of funds available to banks during the harvest season, the Federal Reserve could significantly damp the seasonal swings in interest rates and reduce the extent to which the banking system needed to shift funds throughout the system to accommodate seasonal demands (see Miron 1986; Carlson and Wheelock 2018a).[19] The Federal Reserve could also provide sizable amounts of funds to banks that were experiencing outflows of deposits, such as the large and rapid outflows during a bank run. By providing banks with a liquidity backstop, the Federal Reserve, it was hoped, would promote confidence in the system, prevent a run on one bank from becoming a systemic event, and thus stop panics from developing in the first place (Warburg 1914, 1916; Owen 1919; Bordo and Wheelock 2013; Gorton and Metrick 2013).

The main tool the Federal Reserve was given to establish an elastic currency was the ability to provide loans to banks through the discount window (discussed in more detail in the next chapter). The discount window allowed member commercial banks to borrow funds from the Federal Reserve using as collateral particular commercial and agricultural loans or holdings of government securities. The Federal Reserve could adjust the interest rate charged on the discount window loans to influence the banks' willingness to use the Federal Reserve as a liquidity backstop and hence influence credit conditions more generally.

Early in its existence, the Federal Reserve was also tasked with supporting the efforts to finance World War I. It did so in part by encouraging commercial banks to participate in Liberty loan drives and to buy government securities. The Federal Reserve promoted the purchase of government securities by offering a particularly low rate on discount window loans secured by government securities. This low rate prompted banks to make fairly extensive use of the discount window. Once the war-financing needs had subsided, the lower rate on discount window loans backed by government securities was phased out.

Another objective of the Federal Reserve was to support the US commitment to the gold standard. To do so, the Federal Reserve was required to maintain a legal gold reserve equal to 40 percent of notes in circulation plus 35 percent of its deposit liabilities (the deposits that member banks held at the Federal Reserve). If that requirement had been binding, or close to binding, it would have restrained the ability of the Federal Reserve to implement other policies. This requirement applied at the system level as well as at the level of the individual Reserve Banks. However, if an individual Reserve Bank was getting close to its minimum reserve requirement, it could borrow gold from other districts—for instance, by taking loans or other paper that it had discounted for a member commercial bank and rediscounting it with another Reserve Bank with surplus gold.

During the early 1920s, there was a substantial amount of borrowing between Reserve Banks. Much of that occurred as the Reserve Banks in the
cotton-growing districts lent extensively to their member banks when cotton prices plunged and they needed to borrow gold from other Reserve
Banks to maintain the required ratios.

Money and Credit Policy

In maintaining an elastic currency, the Federal Reserve sought to manage
conditions in money and credit markets. One might think of this today as
broadly akin to monetary policy. As noted earlier, these policies are not
the focus of this book, but it is useful to have them in mind as part of the
larger context in which the efforts to deal with financial stress were occurring. The Federal Reserve Board articulated its approach to managing
conditions in its 1923 *Annual Report*. The policy described seems quite
like countercyclical monetary policy:[20]

> The Federal reserve supplies the needed additions to credit in times of business
> expansion and takes up the slack in times of business recession. . . . When pro-
> duction, trade, and employment are in good volume and the credit resources of
> the commercial banks of the country are approximately all employed and there
> are signs neither of speculative business expansion nor of business reaction,
> Federal reserve bank rates should be neither so low as to invite the use of credit
> for speculative purposes nor so high as to discourage its use for meeting legiti-
> mate productive needs of the business community. It seems clear that if business
> is undergoing a rapid expansion and is in danger of developing an unhealthy
> or speculative boom, it should not be assisted by too easy credit conditions. In
> such circumstances the creation of additional credit by rediscounting at Federal
> reserve banks should be discouraged by increasing the cost of that credit—that
> is, by raising the discount rate. It seems equally obvious that if industry and
> trade are in process of recovery after a period of reaction, they should be given
> the support and encouragement of cheaper credit by the prompt establishment
> at the Federal reserve banks of rates that will invite the use of Federal reserve
> credit to facilitate business recovery. (Board of Governors 1923, 10)

The Federal Reserve influenced conditions in money markets by affecting the availability of balances that banks maintained at the Reserve
Banks, also known as reserves. Commercial banks were required—
through reserve requirements—to hold a certain amount of such balances at the Federal Reserve against their own deposits. Banks also held

reserves for clearing payments with other banks, as this could be done simply by transferring balances from one Federal Reserve account to another. Commercial banks with excess reserves could lend them out, though this was still a developing practice in the 1920s (see Anbil et al. 2021). Banks with insufficient reserves might need to call in loans or sell securities to raise funds, or they could borrow from the Federal Reserve through the discount window. If the total reserves in the banking system were relatively scarce, banks might raise loan rates, especially in money markets, to discourage customers from seeking to obtain the reserves held by the bank, because replacing them could be difficult. If reserves were plentiful, banks might reduce interest rates, especially in money markets, and be more willing to lend funds, as the banks could easily obtain the reserves if needed.

Riefler (1930) and Burgess (1936), for instance, articulated the general approach to managing conditions in money markets through open market operations and the discount rates. The Federal Reserve could affect the quantity of reserves in the banking system through asset purchases or sales. When the Federal Reserve buys Treasury securities, it does so by adding reserves to the account of the bank selling the securities (or, more commonly, if buying from a broker-dealer, by adding reserves to the account of the bank where the broker-dealer maintains an account). Conversely, when the Federal Reserve sells securities, reserves are removed from the system. By making reserves scarce, the Federal Reserve could force banks to turn to the discount window to obtain any reserves they might need. As borrowing at the discount window was more expensive than deposit funding, banks could raise the interest rates on their loans to discourage borrowers and to compensate for the more expensive funding from the Federal Reserve. If the Federal Reserve raised the discount rate when reserves were already scarce, it put even greater pressure on bank loan rates and, consequently, on credit conditions. By lowering the discount rate, the Federal Reserve would reduce the cost of borrowing from the Federal Reserve and make banks more willing to lower their loan rates and make loans.

The general course of policy is shown in figure 2.7. After initially holding policy steady as the economy transitioned from a wartime to peacetime footing, the Federal Reserve began tightening policy rapidly at the end of 1919 by raising discount rates. As noted above, shortly thereafter economic activity contracted sharply. To support a recovery, the Federal Reserve reduced the discount rate and increased its purchases of Treasury securities. There was another, milder tightening and easing cycle in

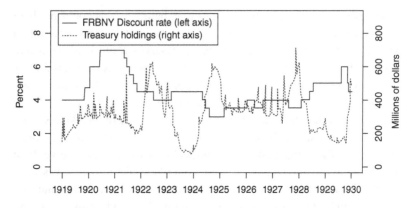

FIGURE 2.7. FRB New York discount rate and system holdings of US Treasury securities

Source: Board of Governors of the Federal Reserve System, *Banking and Monetary Statistics, 1914–1941* (1943);
Factors Affecting Reserve Balances of Depository Institutions and Condition Statement of Federal Reserve Banks
(H.4.1 statistical release). Data are at a weekly frequency.

1923–1924 and another in 1926–1927, when the Federal Reserve adjusted
its holdings of Treasury securities but discount rates were moved only
slightly. Otherwise, policy was not much changed until a serious tightening cycle occurred in 1928. (For considerably more detailed treatments of
shifts in monetary policy during this period, see Friedman and Schwartz
1963; Wheelock 1991; Meltzer 2003.)

Member Banks

Only banks that were members of the Federal Reserve System were eligible to borrow at the discount window in the 1920s (though, as discussed
below, there were some circumstances that allowed nonmembers indirect
access to the discount window).[21] As noted above, banks with national charters were required to join the Federal Reserve System, while state banks
had the option to join. Few state banks did so, in part because they would
have been subject to tighter regulations. However, the state banks that did
join the system tended to be the larger state banks. As a result, a majority
of the assets of the banking system were at Federal Reserve member banks,
even if a majority of banks were not Federal Reserve members.

Structure of the Federal Reserve

At the center of the Federal Reserve System was the Federal Reserve
Board, which was a government institution. The Board set important as-

pects of policy regarding how the system would operate. As a public entity, members of the Federal Reserve Board, referred to at the time simply as Board members (and now as governors), were nominated by the US president and approved by the Senate (just as is the case now). The secretary of the Treasury and the comptroller of the currency (head of the OCC) were ex officio members of the Federal Reserve Board, which connected the Board more closely to the executive branch than is the case today.

The operations of the Federal Reserve and the interactions with the member banks were handled through twelve Reserve Banks. These Reserve Banks were distributed across the United States in regional banking centers and oversaw districts that were designed to be roughly equal in size with respect to banking assets and to broadly align with the existing network relationships among commercial banks (see Jaremski and Wheelock 2020b). Figure 2.8 shows a map of the Federal Reserve districts as they stood in 1920 (there have been some minor revisions to the borders since). The Reserve Banks were owned by the member banks who held nontradable stock in the Reserve Banks. Ownership of this stock provided only limited powers and benefits. Each Reserve Bank was headed by a governor (now referred to as a president), who was elected by a managing board of directors. The majority of the directors at the time were representatives of the banks in the districts.

The chair of the Reserve Banks' board of directors was a representative of the Federal Reserve Board and was also referred to as a Federal Reserve agent. This individual was supposed to oversee certain aspects of the operations of the Reserve Banks, especially with respect to supervision and examinations. The governor of the Reserve Bank was the central figure for setting the policies of the Reserve Bank. However, the importance of the Federal Reserve agent was left ambiguous in the Federal Reserve Act, and the histories of the Reserve Banks suggest that the agents' influence varied depending on the personalities involved.

Policymaking usually involved some interplay between the Federal Reserve Board and the Reserve Banks. In some cases, the Board set the policy parameters and the Reserve Banks operationalized them. For instance, the Federal Reserve Act provides broad guidance about the types of assets that could serve as collateral for discount window loans. It was up to the Federal Reserve Board to establish more specific guidance on what was allowed, and the Reserve Banks decided whether individual pieces of collateral were in line with that guidance and were otherwise acceptable (such as with respect to their quality).

Another example is the rate that was charged on discount window

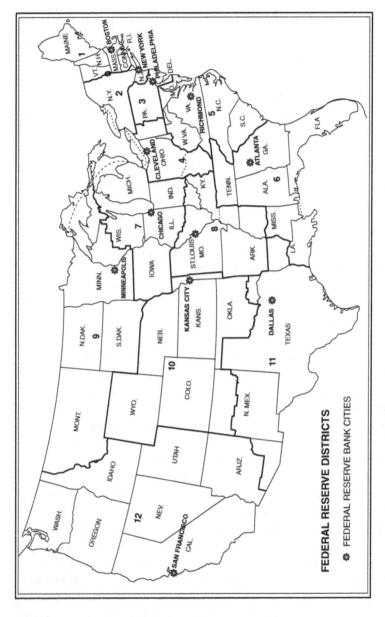

FEDERAL RESERVE DISTRICTS

❋ FEDERAL RESERVE BANK CITIES

FIGURE 2.8. Map of the Federal Reserve Districts as of 1920

Source: Recreated from Board of Governors of the Federal Reserve System (1920b), *Bulletin*, July, back page.

CHAPTER THREE

Tools to Respond to Financial Stress

The Federal Reserve used several tools to respond to financial instability during the 1920s. The principal one was the discount window,
which allowed the Federal Reserve to lend funds to banks. This tool was
important during normal times for influencing credit conditions by affecting the marginal cost of obtaining short-term funding for commercial
banks. It was vital during stress periods as a tool to directly provide liquidity to banks experiencing funding pressures. A second tool built on the
Federal Reserve's role in distributing currency. In particular, the Federal
Reserve devised procedures to warehouse currency at banks in locations
experiencing stress in ways that were publicly observable; the presence of
large volumes of currency on-site could help calm concerned depositors.
Finally, while these are perhaps not quite formal "tools," Federal Reserve
officials were able to exercise moral suasion to encourage cooperation
and coordinate solutions to problems, as well as to use public announcements to promote confidence.

The Discount Window

The discount window enabled the Federal Reserve to provide liquidity
support directly to individual member banks (as opposed to the banking
system as a whole through open market operations) and was the primary
tool used to address emergency liquidity situations. Proceeds from discount

window loans were added to the bank's account at the Federal Reserve as reserves. From there, they could be transferred to other banks to make payments, withdrawn in the form of currency to meet withdrawals, or held to meet reserve requirements.

While this book concerns the use of the discount window in emergency situations, it is important to keep in mind that during the 1920s the discount window was an important regular tool for influencing credit conditions and implementing monetary policy. Borrowing from the discount window was common. Shull (1971) reports that, on average, roughly 60 percent of member banks borrowed in any given year during the 1920s, though the proportion was higher earlier in the decade than later. Banks that used the discount window appear to have viewed it as a regular part of their funding plans; Burgess (1936) reports that banks that borrowed tended to do so multiple times during the year or borrow for relatively longer periods. Use of the discount window was particularly important in addressing seasonal pressures. Borrowing was elevated in the autumn in Federal Reserve districts that were heavily agricultural and around year-end in several more industrial districts (Carlson and Wheelock 2018b). As noted in chapter 2, use of the discount window was sufficiently important to member commercial banks that adjustments to the discount rate affected the banks' general lending decisions; thus, the discount window served as an effective tool the Federal Reserve could use to shape credit conditions.

To understand both the flexibility of this tool and its limitations, it is useful to review the basic legal authority for lending and a variety of operational aspects, such as the rules regarding who was able to borrow, how much credit the Reserve Banks were willing to extend, what rate was charged on discount window loans, and what collateral was associated with the loans. This discussion draws from Hackley (1973), who provides an outstanding review of the legal issues related to the discount window. In addition, this section describes some of the discretion that Reserve Banks had regarding the implementation of discount window policies and, where it was available, some of the ways they used that discretion. It is important to remember that, especially with respect to discretionary actions, each Reserve Bank may have had a slightly different approach. This section also presents some statistics that provide an additional sense of how the discount window was used.

Authority for Lending

In the 1920s, the Federal Reserve had two methods for using the discount window to provide funds to banks: discounting and making advances.[1] The practice of discounting, which gives the discount window its name, involved the Federal Reserve extending credit to a commercial bank against a particular piece of eligible paper—a certain type of loan that the bank had made—or securities that the bank had purchased. The Federal Reserve would provide the bank funds equal to the face value of that eligible paper minus the discount rate. When the eligible paper matured, the associated funds would serve to repay the loan to the Federal Reserve.[2] Thus, the maturity of credit extended through discounting was equal to the remaining maturity of the paper that was discounted. When discounting eligible paper, the Federal Reserve required that the bank to which it was providing funds endorse the paper so that if there were issues obtaining repayment, the bank would be responsible for repaying the Federal Reserve.[3]

Advances were direct loans from the Federal Reserve to a bank. While advances were collateralized, the characteristics of the advance were less clearly tied to the characteristics of the collateral than was the case for discounts. For instance, the maturity of the advance was not tied to the maturity or other characteristics of that collateral. Instead, the maturity of the advance could be set by the Federal Reserve and the bank up to the limits specified in the Federal Reserve Act (as long as the collateral did not mature before the advance matured). Hackley (1973, 85) reports that these features made advances easier for banks to use to manage liquidity, and this authority was added to the Federal Reserve Act to make it more convenient for banks to borrow. When the maturity date of the advance was reached, the Federal Reserve would expect repayment from the bank, and if the bank defaulted, the Federal Reserve would take possession of the collateral that had been provided. The interest rate applied to the advance was the same as the rate applied when discounting loans and securities.

The Federal Reserve was allowed to discount paper with a remaining maturity of ninety days or less. There was a special accommodation for agricultural loans, where the Federal Reserve was able to discount paper with a maturity of up to six months. Advances were shorter term and had a maximum maturity of fifteen days.[4]

The average maturity of the advances and rediscounts extended in June 1927 in each Federal Reserve district is shown in table 3.1. For most Reserve Banks, the average maturity of advances was eight to nine days, and the average maturity of rediscounts was around forty-five to fifty-five days. There were clearly exceptions. Reflecting the importance of agriculture in the Minneapolis and Kansas City Districts, the average maturity of the rediscounts at these Reserve Banks was over the ninety-day limit

TABLE 3.1. **Average maturity of credit extended by Reserve Banks in June 1927 (days)**

	Advances	Rediscounted bills
Boston	7.4	46.0
New York	5.5	53.5
Philadelphia	7.9	47.1
Cleveland	3.4	49.8
Richmond	2.9	57.8
Atlanta	12.3	54.9
Chicago	8.6	45.8
St. Louis	8.5	43.3
Minneapolis	8.5	125.6
Kansas City	8.9	100.1
Dallas	9.2	47.3
San Francisco	9.1	76.3

Source: Board of Governors of the Federal Reserve System, memo, "The Maturity of Bills Discounted by Federal Reserve Banks," Smead (1927).

that applied to most paper eligible for rediscount. FRB Richmond had an average maturity of advances of only 2.9 days, while FRB Atlanta had an average maturity of advances of 12.3 days. It is not clear whether these differences reflected different needs on the part of borrowers or different policies set by the Reserve Banks.

The maturity of paper rediscounted also tended to vary by city size. For instance, in response to an inquiry by the OCC, the Board reported that the average maturity of paper discounted for banks in large cities tended to be less than ten days (for example, 8.3 days in August 1922), on the order of one month in smaller cities (32 days in August 1922), and in the middle in medium-sized cities (22.9 days in August 1922).

In most of the discussion that follows, the term *discount window loan* is used to refer to both discounts and advances. In the few situations where the difference matters, the form of the credit extension is clearly indicated.[5]

Who Could Get Credit and How Much

Borrowing at the discount window was limited to banks that had become members of the Federal Reserve System (national banks and state banks that elected to join the system).[6] The Federal Reserve Act did not limit how much a Reserve Bank could lend to any one member bank. In addition, while commercial banks faced limits on how much they could borrow from other banks, there was no limit on borrowing from the Federal Reserve (see Westerfield 1932, 44).

However, during this period the Federal Reserve articulated the idea of a "basic line." These basic lines did not represent limits on how much banks could borrow, and, indeed, banks on occasion borrowed amounts representing many multiples of their basic lines (though, as discussed below, exceeding the basic line sometimes affected the interest rate at which funds could be obtained from the Federal Reserve). Instead, these basic lines represented a benchmark that affected the amount of scrutiny that banks would face; banks borrowing considerably more than the basic line received more attention from Reserve Bank officials.[7] There was some variation across Reserve Banks and over time in exactly how these lines were calculated, but typically they were related to the bank's capital and surplus, as well as the reserve balances it had been maintaining.[8] Some other adjustments were made as well; for instance, most Reserve Banks did not include borrowing against US Treasury securities when considering how much a member bank was borrowing in comparison to its basic line.

Table 3.2 provides some information about borrowing relative to the basic lines. In most districts, there were considerably more banks borrowing in amounts less than the basic line than in excess of it. Moreover, in many cases in which borrowing exceeded the basic line, it was not by very much. However, as indicated by the ratios of actual borrowing relative to the calculated basic lines in the Richmond and Atlanta Districts, borrowing by some banks must have exceeded the basic line by a considerable amount.

TABLE 3.2. **Member bank borrowing relative to the basic line during the first ten days of November 1920**

	Banks borrowing less than basic line	Banks borrowing in excess of basic line	Calculated basic lines for banks borrowing in excess ($ thousands)	Actual borrowing of banks borrowing in excess ($ thousands)	Ratio of actual borrowing to basic lines for banks exceeding basic line
Boston	396	38	41,415	55,676	1.34
New York	694	88	528,985	756,341	1.43
Philadelphia	590	110	61,373	94,341	1.53
Cleveland	842	29	11,998	20,496	1.71
Richmond	381	230	47,301	115,554	2.44
Atlanta	210	244	58,226	166,845	2.87
Chicago	903	501	214,650	393,874	1.83
St. Louis	417	152	60,375	124,247	2.06
Minneapolis	750	246	39,616	95,413	2.41
Kansas City	712	371	63,526	131,487	2.07
Dallas	477	369	39,133	84,784	2.17
San Francisco	567	257	59,724	127,888	2.14

Source: Board of Governors of the Federal Reserve System, memo regarding member bank borrowing, Smead (1924).

Banks were discouraged from borrowing continuously from the discount window. The Board indicated that discount window credit was expected to be used to meet seasonal and temporary needs, which would be inconsistent with continuous borrowing (Board of Governors 1926a, 4). It was viewed as more appropriate for the banks to adjust their business and possibly increase their capital to repay Federal Reserve credit rather than borrow continuously. In some cases, it was understood that the bank was likely to borrow for quite some time, typically because it was in a locality experiencing a challenging economic situation. In these situations, continuous borrowing was carefully scrutinized.

The Federal Reserve Banks were not obligated to lend, even if the commercial bank seeking a discount window loan had eligible collateral. In some of the cases discussed in the TBSRs, the Reserve Banks indicated that they would not lend because they viewed the bank as being in terrible condition. Several Reserve Banks (including FRB San Francisco and FRB Dallas) cited specific instances where they had declined to provide credit to banks where bad assets were substantial—such as one case where more than half the loans were considered slow, doubtful, or likely to be a loss—and the management was considered incompetent.

Rate at Which Banks Could Borrow

The rate at which banks could borrow from the discount window was one of the main policy instruments the Federal Reserve could use to influence credit conditions. Rates were proposed by the Reserve Banks and approved by the Federal Reserve Board. Each Reserve Bank could have a separate rate, and discount rates differed across Reserve Banks during this period (as shown in fig. 2.9). Policymakers discussed discount rate policy and generally coordinated to determine the overall direction of rate changes across the system to achieve common goals, such as a general easing or tightening of credit conditions. In general, these discussions were collaborative, but, at times, there were pressures on some Reserve Banks—from other Reserve Banks and the Board—to change their discount rates in particular ways.

Very early in the 1920s, the Reserve Banks had multiple rates for their discount window lending, with the applicable rate depending on particular attributes of the extension of funds. For instance, discount rates varied by the maturity of the credit being extended. During World War I, the Reserve Banks maintained preferential rates for loans backed by government securities; this policy was intended to boost demand for the government securities. Once the wartime need had ended, the preferential rate for loans involving government collateral was phased out. The practice of posting multiple discount rates was discontinued as well, so it was not long into the 1920s before each of the Reserve Banks was offering only a single discount rate.

For a few years, from 1920 until 1923, the Federal Reserve Act allowed the Federal Reserve Banks to charge progressive discount rates, where higher rates were charged when banks borrowed greater amounts. Banks that borrowed in amounts up to their basic line could borrow at the posted discount window rate. Loans for more than the basic amount incurred higher interest rates.[9] The progressive rate was intended to discourage banks from borrowing "excessively" large amounts from the window. Four of the Reserve Banks—Atlanta, Kansas City, St. Louis, and Dallas—used this authority for a brief period, though none used it after August 1, 1921 (for additional detail, see Rieder 2020).

Collateral for Discount Window Loans

All discount window loans were required to be collateralized by either government securities or eligible paper.[10] The Federal Reserve Act described eligible paper as "notes, drafts, and bills of exchange issued or drawn for agricultural, industrial, or commercial purposes, or the proceeds of which have been used, or are to be used, for such purposes." That description left room for a fair amount of interpretation, and the work of providing additional clarity about eligibility was left to the Federal Reserve Board. As detailed by Hackley (1973, 36), the Board refined the rules regarding what was eligible over time, but essentially eligible paper consisted of paper that had a short remaining maturity period and that had arisen "out of a commercial transaction, for instance to finance inventories, wholesale goods that would be resold, or agricultural products being shipped to market."

The paper eligible to serve as collateral was intended to be "self-liquidating"; the transaction the paper was supporting would naturally provide the funds necessary for the borrower to repay the loan when the paper matured. That was valuable from a credit risk perspective, as it increased the likelihood that any credit extended by the Federal Reserve would be repaid. Some policymakers also believed that providing credit against such transactions would result in Federal Reserve credit growing along with the needs of business and the "real economy" and that Federal Reserve credit would therefore not support risky or inflationary speculative activities.[11]

The rules articulated by the Board took into consideration the purpose of the loan that had been made by the commercial bank. Hackley (1973, chap. 4) reports that the Federal Reserve Board concluded that paper drawn to finance the carrying of agricultural products pending a higher price was of a speculative nature and was not eligible for discount as agricultural paper. Hence, whether a loan made by a commercial bank to the farmer was considered eligible paper for discount, or eligible to serve as collateral for an advance, depended on whether the loan was used to ship the crop to market (eligible) or to hold the crop while waiting for a higher price (not eligible). That required the Reserve Banks to ask questions and gather information about the collateral they were offered.

The rules on eligibility were fairly detailed yet still offered the Reserve Banks some discretion about what was acceptable. For instance, while the Reserve Banks did need to make sure that the loans offered as collateral were creditworthy, each Reserve Bank appears to have set its own standards regarding the documentation required to prove creditworthiness. Some Reserve Banks required documentation for all paper pledged as collateral, while others required documentation only for paper above a certain dollar amount (Senate Hearings 1931, 708–711). Sometimes Reserve Banks were more expansive in their interpretations of what would be acceptable. Roberts (1927) reports that at least one Reserve Bank was willing to take paper that was considered good quality even if that paper's technical eligibility was questionable. H. Parker Willis (1925a) suggests that some Reserve Banks lent on collateral that was technically eligible but was in reality long-term credit that the commercial banks were regularly rolling over.

Reserve Banks also had the discretion to reject paper that was legally eligible (Board of Governors 1920b, 1303; Hackley 1973, 200). This discretion further allowed the Reserve Banks to limit their exposure to a potential borrowing bank as well as to an entity that had borrowed considerably from multiple commercial banks, all of which were seeking to post the loans to that entity as collateral. At times, concerns about the credit situation led at least some Reserve Banks to shift their rediscounting toward shorter-term paper and to decline to rediscount long-term paper (see FRB Minneapolis 1920–1924, November 8, 1920). The standards appear to have been fairly clear to member banks, as information about rejec-

TABLE 3.3. **Volume of rediscounts by type of paper during October 1922 ($ thousands)**

	Commercial paper	Agricultural paper	Livestock paper	Bankers' or trade acceptances	Percent agricultural or livestock related
Boston	149,888	420	5	120	0.3%
New York	181,973	290	3	670	0.2%
Philadelphia	72.848	273	0	83	0.4%
Cleveland	32,936	289	249	513	1.6%
Richmond	13,615	3,222	75	384	19.1%
Atlanta	23,838	3,365	279	351	13.1%
Chicago	51,893	11,147	0	100	17.7%
St. Louis	14,409	2,028	48	1,031	11.9%
Minneapolis	4,286	3,242	821	4	48.6%
Kansas City	6,903	1,784	5,519	3	51.4%
Dallas	4,424	1,013	1,604	5	37.1%
San Francisco	53,030	1,151	666	171	24.9%

Source: Board of Governors of the Federal Reserve System, *Federal Reserve Bulletin*, December 1922, 1481.

tions of paper suggests that it was relatively rare. For example, Parker B. Willis (1937) reported that less than 5 percent of the paper offered for rediscount to FRB San Francisco was rejected.

The Reserve Banks generally kept the acceptability requirements for the paper offered constant over time and, importantly, did not tighten requirements during periods of stress (Senate Hearings 1931, 711).[12] FRB San Francisco reported that doing so would have inappropriately reduced the availability of credit (FRB San Francisco 1931, 711). Indeed, FRB San Francisco reported that in stressed conditions it would be appropriate to ease the acceptability requirements on collateral: "In a credit stringency (1921, for instance), it becomes necessary to lower the standard, within the bounds of safety, to accommodate commerce" (711).

Typically, in the 1920s, advances were against government securities, and discounts were against private paper. For instance, Burgess (1936, 44) reports that over 85 percent of all advances made from 1921 to 1929 were secured by government obligations. Much of the paper discounted was classified as "commercial," though, as shown in table 3.3, in some districts agricultural or livestock paper was common.

The Federal Reserve Banks were also able to take additional collateral when extending credit. The Reserve Banks offered a variety of reasons for doing so, but a frequently cited reason was the need for additional protection when the Reserve Banks were concerned about the creditworthiness of either the paper being offered or the member bank seeking funds (Senate Hearings 1931, 712–715).[13] Thus, the Reserve Banks differentiated between taking collateral to deal with increasing risks at individual banks and, as noted above, importantly not doing so during systemic events.

FRB Kansas City noted specifically that protecting the Reserve Bank from loss was the main purpose of requiring additional collateral: "We have always endeavored to maintain a reasonably safe position by requiring the pledge of additional collateral from banks in weakened and over-extended condition, and our net losses to date are less than $25,000" (TBSR). FRB Minneapolis noted that it took additional collateral in cases where it was asked to rediscount or make advances against collateral of uncertain quality (Young 1923). Another reason for taking additional collateral was related to the volume of credit that individual member banks might obtain from the Reserve Banks (or other sources). The Reserve Banks were aware that requiring additional collateral would limit the funds that member banks could obtain from the discount window, and, by tying up the collateral, the Reserve Banks would also limit the bank's borrowing from other sources (Senate Hearings 1931, 712–715). Alternatively, Westerfield (1932) notes that some member banks would maintain a stock of excess collateral at their Reserve Bank and use this as a credit line, drawing short-term advances against it as needed to cover temporary shortfalls in reserves.[14] In response to a survey conducted by the US Senate in 1931, all the Reserve Banks indicated that at some point they had required additional collateral in certain cases, and all but FRB San Francisco indicated that they were currently requiring additional collateral from at least one bank at that time (Senate Hearings 1931, 712).

Additional collateral could consist of collateral not eligible to be discounted because, strictly speaking, it was not directly collateralizing the discount window loan (Westerfield 1932, 47; Hackley 1973, 31). Being able to take as additional collateral assets that were sound even though they were not eligible would likely have been quite important during periods of heightened uncertainty, when the value of many assets would have been more questionable.

In response to some questions and criticisms from external parties, FRB Minneapolis sent the Federal Reserve Board information on the eighty-one discount window loans outstanding to member banks in Montana as of November 28, 1923, along with the total amount of collateral held to secure those loans. For about 90 percent of these loans, FRB Minneapolis had collateral exceeding the value of the loan. Indeed, the median ratio of total collateral to loan amount was 1.6. In one case, the Reserve Bank had collateral in excess of three times the loan value; FRB Minneapolis reported that, in this case, it had originally taken excess collateral in the usual proportion and that the bank had repaid part of the loan but had not requested the return of any of its collateral (Young 1923). For this sample of discount window loans, there does not seem to be any relation between the amount of borrowing by the bank and the amount of excess collateral. Indeed there is a slightly negative correlation between the ratio of total collateral to loan amount and the ratio of loan amount to the bank's capital and surplus.

The collateral taken by the Federal Reserve Banks was likely to be among the banks' better collateral, but this does not mean that it was necessarily of very high quality. In the same package of materials, FRB Minneapolis also provided some data on loans outstanding to banks that had closed and the total collateral that it had for these loans. In most of these cases, FRB Minneapolis had excess collateral. Nevertheless, it identified a number of instances in which it was concerned that even this excess collateral would be insufficient to protect it against losses.[15]

In some situations, the Reserve Banks would also request that the discount window loans be endorsed by the bank directors. The directors were usually fairly wealthy individuals, so their guarantee would have provided meaningful protection for the Reserve Banks. More importantly, as noted by FRB Dallas, requiring directors to be personally liable for the repayment of the discount window loans would make sure the directors of the banks "are awake to their duty in shaping the bank's policies along sounder lines" (TBSR). Garrett (1968) reports that FRB Atlanta also urged directors to guarantee their discount window borrowing, especially in cases where the bank was in a strained condition. Governor Harding of the Federal Reserve Board expressed his approval of the practice in his testimony before the Joint Commission of Agricultural Inquiry (1921–1922, 2:417).

Some failing member banks had loans from the Federal Reserve outstanding at the time they closed. In this case, the Reserve Bank had to collect on the collateral, which could have consisted of loans to businesses, farmers, or other clients of the failing bank. Collecting on these loans could be challenging. Moreover, given the number of banks that failed in the early 1920s, the Reserve Banks ended up holding a considerable amount of collateral resulting from situations in which a bank had defaulted on a discount window loan. Several Reserve Banks, such as FRB Dallas and FRB Minneapolis, set up separate departments within the Reserve Banks to handle these assets.

Over time there were changes in the rules regarding the ability of banks to pledge collateral acquired from other banks. These rules mattered for the ability of member banks to pass on liquidity acquired from the Federal Reserve to other banks, especially nonmember banks. To support US government bond drives during World War I, the Board allowed the Reserve Banks to discount for nonmember banks notes that were secured by government securities as long as those notes were endorsed by a member bank. In 1921, during the period of severe strains on the banking system, the Federal Reserve Board gave general authority to Reserve Banks to discount for member banks any eligible paper acquired from nonmember banks (Hackley 1973, 119). This policy allowed for a fairly liberal amount of pass-through of Federal Reserve liquidity, as a member bank could discount paper for a nonmember bank and then rediscount that same paper at the Federal Reserve. This authority was withdrawn in 1923 when the perceived emergency had passed, although the Federal Reserve Board could, and did, allow this type of liquidity pass-through in rare instances. Reserve Banks could discount paper endorsed by nonmember banks if the member bank had purchased it on the open market from a party other than the nonmember bank.

Examinations and Monitoring of Banks

Given the importance that the Reserve Banks attached to the condition of the banks they were assisting in stress situations, the examination and monitoring of the banks was crucial. As noted in chapter 2, the examination process in the 1920s provided considerable insights into many aspects of the workings of the banks. All six Reserve Banks that completed TBSRs included some discussion of their interactions with examiners when deciding whether and how much discount window credit might safely be provided. When a bank known to be troubled approached the Federal Reserve for credit, it appears that Federal Reserve officials would conduct a special examination. Sometimes the Reserve Banks sent their own examiners for special examinations. In other cases, they would work with the OCC to set up the special examination, and Federal Reserve officials might accompany the OCC examiner; in its TBSR, FRB San Francisco specifically notes one instance in which the managing director of a Reserve Bank branch accompanied the OCC examiners to visit a troubled bank.[16] Moreover, examiners and related officials appear to have been valuable in heading off instances of stress; FRB Dallas reported that in at least one instance a member bank requested that a Reserve Bank official be sent to help the bank analyze its liquidity-management issues to reduce its need to borrow (TBSR).

The TBSR for San Francisco provides considerable detail about the information the Reserve Bank used to assess the condition and prospects of borrowing institutions. While much of this information likely came from the examiner reports, it is possible that FRB San Francisco was maintaining additional internal records for some of the more troubled institutions. For instance, FRB San Francisco monitored the ability of the board of directors to personally support the bank; in some of the case studies listed in the TBSR, there are anonymized lists of the directors, the numbers of shares they owned, and estimates of their net worth. That information would enable the Reserve Bank to judge the directors' ability to support the bank. The TBSR also notes that the Reserve Bank tracked the character of the bank managers, observing whether they were perhaps too optimistic or whether they were conservative.

Beyond assessing the condition of the borrowing bank, the examination process also reportedly provided the Reserve Banks with insights into the quality of the collateral being used at the discount window (Senate Hearings 1931, 704). Such information would have aided the Reserve Banks in determining whether excess collateral would be required and, if so, how much would be needed. According to Blair (1928), FRB Chicago used the examiner reports when determining excess collateral requirements. Indeed, on the basis of the examinations that FRB Chicago conducted, or its analysis of the examinations done by others, the Reserve Bank stated that it divided banks into various grades, which then affected whether the bank's endorsement would be considered sufficient collateral or whether excess collateral might be required (Heath 1929).[17] These grades were articulated in the following way:

- Good Banks. "G" indicates that generally the condition is satisfactory, that management is good, and that prudent banking methods are practiced. The endorsement of such banks on rediscounts is considered a good credit risk.
- Second Grade Banks. "R" indicates that while not in a serious condition, the bank evidences wrong tendencies, with unsatisfactory assets—tendencies which with proper effort may be corrected but if permitted to continue may become serious. As the rating indicates, these banks are second-class credit risks.
- Third Grade Banks. "A" indicates banks in a very unsatisfactory condition—unsound tendencies or assets. The endorsements of such banks may offer little in the way of security.

- Fourth Grade Banks. "D" indicates that the condition is decided bad—possible impairment of capital or the solvency of the bank or integrity of the management even may be questioned. Endorsement cannot be considered as security. (Heath 1929)

The Reserve Banks could also monitor the banks and base lending decisions on the past history of discount window use. This information showed the Reserve Banks which banks were frequent borrowers, which were seasonal borrowers, and which repaid their discount window loans promptly. FRB Dallas reported, "A careful record of its [a bank's] annual borrowing is kept in our files" (TBSR). In cases where the bank was borrowing progressively more credit, FRB Dallas would communicate with the borrowing bank and try to convince them to change their behavior and limit their use of the discount window.

Stigma

Stigma refers to the idea that banks experiencing liquidity issues are reluctant to borrow from the discount window because they are concerned that this borrowing might be discovered and interpreted as a sign of trouble, leading to deposit withdrawals or other creditor exits. Those withdrawals would intensify the liquidity issues. Consequently, stigma makes it more difficult for the discount window to be used to respond to liquidity issues and impairs its effectiveness as a crisis response tool.

It is difficult to know how problematic stigma was in the 1920s. The discount window was widely used in this decade, especially to address seasonal funding needs. That use suggests that stigma was not a substantial problem.

However, contemporary policymakers do suggest that stigma influenced how banks approached using the discount window. For example, Rich (1924) reports that in 1924 stigma was a relevant concern in parts of the FRB Minneapolis District, where economic concerns had triggered serious concerns about the health of the banking system: "Member banks hesitate to rediscount with us for fear that the knowledge that they are increasing their borrowings may cause them serious trouble. This is illustrative of the sensitiveness of the situation. Where the condition of the public mind is as bad as that, there is some question as to whether outside assistance, if the [Reserve] bank is at all involved, would save the situation." Consequently, when using the discount window to respond to episodes of financial stress, Federal Reserve officials were likely sensitive to the possible perception of discount window use as a sign of weakness and the likelihood that the public would be aware of its use.

Currency Funds

Currency funds (also referred to as currency depots) were substantial pools of Federal Reserve notes (i.e., cash) that the Federal Reserve maintained in cities where there was not a Federal Reserve Bank, branch, or agency. The notes were held in the custody of one or more member banks in that city. The member bank holding the notes needed to provide securities to the Federal Reserve as collateral.[18] However, this was not a loan to the bank holding the notes; the notes were still the property of the Federal Reserve. Instead, banks in the area could borrow the notes from the Federal Reserve by requesting a discount window loan, pledging collateral in the typical way, and then withdrawing notes from the pool rather than having funds shipped to them from a Reserve Bank or branch. The bank with custody of the notes would record the withdrawal and the replenishment of the pool when the notes were returned.

Some currency funds were set up to supply member banks when there were to be periodic spikes in the need for currency. Having currency on hand reduced the need for shipments between the member banks and the Reserve Banks. Some of these needs pertained to regular, fairly mundane needs. For instance, a currency fund was maintained for a long time in the mining town of Scranton, Pennsylvania, where monthly paydays involved significant movements of cash among individuals in the town and poor rail facilities sometimes delayed the arrival of currency from FRB Philadelphia (Board of Governors 1938, 45). In this instance, currency could be drawn from the currency fund when rail shipments were delayed, and the currency fund was replenished when the shipment arrived. Maintaining a currency fund in this or similar locations also helped minimize the requests for Federal Reserve branches or agencies. In addition to the one in Scranton, currency funds for similar purposes were established in Johnstown, Pennsylvania, in 1924 and Miami, Florida, in 1925 (Board of Governors 1938).

In other cases, currency funds were set up to deal with potential spikes in demand for Federal Reserve notes associated with stress events when runs, or the potential for runs, might drain precipitous amounts of cash from the nearby banks. For these temporary funds, the general practice was to have officers or employees of the relevant Federal Reserve Banks stationed at the places where the funds were located. Currency funds for this purpose were established in Boise, Idaho, in 1921 and in Tampa, Florida, in 1929. These two episodes are discussed in the case studies presented in chapter 5.

Communication and Persuasion

The final tools available to the Federal Reserve officials were their status, which could persuade others to address the stress, and publicity, which could showcase their support and promote confidence. In some cases, the use of persuasion was intentionally public, with Federal Reserve officials making it known that they were taking strong actions to address a problem. To the extent that the problems were caused by the public's loss of confidence in the liquidity of banks and by the resulting bank runs, the publicity associated with the responses likely played an important part in restoring calm. In other cases, the persuasion took place behind closed doors, with Federal Reserve officials using their position to work with bankers to find a cooperative solution or, in a few cases, to pressure the bankers to come to a solution.

The case studies also provide examples of situations in which the stress required capital injections or other support from bankers or investors. Federal Reserve officials appear to have, at times, been helpful in encouraging the relevant parties to work together to resolve the situation. In some cases, the promise that the Federal Reserve would ensure the availability of support from the discount window was vital in enabling the interested counterparties to reach this compromise. In other cases, Federal Reserve officials appear to have pushed bankers and investors to do more to ensure that the response was large enough to reassure the public that the problems were being addressed.

When used generally, publicity could take a variety of forms. In some cases, Federal Reserve officials made public statements or issued press releases. In other cases, they simply carried out their support actions in a high-profile manner that received attention from the press. (It is not always clear whether Federal Reserve officials intentionally provided the information to the press). As will be described in the case studies, there appears to have been a fair bit of publicity surrounding the use of currency funds. This suggests that, in addition to providing cash to a locality, making sure the public knew that ample cash was available on-site was likely a key part of ensuring that the response successfully promoted confidence.

CHAPTER FOUR

Philosophy Regarding Emergency Liquidity Support

Policymakers at the Federal Reserve understood that the Federal Re- serve System was intended to provide support and liquidity to banks during periods of stress. Policymakers also recognized that providing li- quidity at such times was fraught with risk. Liquidity and solvency issues at many banks were often intertwined, especially when a significant portion of the banks' assets consisted of illiquid agricultural loans that would only mature several months in the future, and it was difficult to tell whether additional credit would save the bank or just allow it to take more risk and deepen its potential losses. This chapter explores the general thinking of policymakers in the 1920s regarding how the Federal Reserve should weigh a variety of considerations when making decisions about lending to banks experiencing stress. The chapter is organized around different is- sues that mattered to policymakers and explores how each of the different Reserve Banks thought about the issues. Generally, the Reserve Banks had similar opinions, but there are variations in the framing. Quotations from correspondence, speeches, and similar sources are used fairly exten- sively so that the reader may understand the thinking of policymakers in their own words. (Some prior episodes of emergency liquidity provision in the United States that may have shaped the thinking of Federal Reserve policymakers are discussed in appendix 1.)

Dealing with Individual Weak or Overextended Banks

One of the most important considerations in lending in a stress situation is the condition of the borrowing bank itself. When considering lending to an individual bank, the Reserve Banks emphasized the importance of making sure the bank was solvent.[1] Sometimes the focus was on the bank's current solvency, while at other times the focus was on long-run solvency. Lending to solvent banks was important to the Reserve Banks as a way of protecting themselves from credit risk. If they were convinced that the borrowing bank was fundamentally solvent, the Reserve Banks generally reported that they would provide robust support to help it sustain its operations.

The risk-taking behavior and practices of the banks' managers significantly influenced their banks' solvency and prospects. From the Troubled Bank Survey, it is clear that the Reserve Banks were quite averse to lending to banks that were in trouble as a result of what Reserve Bank officials considered to be bad banking practices. Precisely what practices were considered problematic varied somewhat across Reserve Banks, but many of them were concerned when the commercial bank was perceived as giving preference to loan customers—through excessively sized loans or continued lending even after the loan customer was no longer creditworthy—over deposit customers or equity holders. In some cases, the Reserve Bank reported that they refused to lend to banks that they believed intentionally made very risky choices. Where possible, the Reserve Banks generally supported the idea of identifying risky behavior and intervening earlier to urge improvements to prevent the banks from getting into trouble.

FRB Dallas

FRB Dallas officials noted in their TBSR that they were reluctant to lend to banks that were in an "extended" condition. An extended condition was one in which the loans made by the commercial bank far exceeded the bank's ability to fund them using deposits. Allowances were made for seasonal variations in loan demand and deposit flows so that seasonal lows in loans could be compared with seasonal peaks in deposits; banks whose loans always exceeded deposits were viewed with a wary eye. This concept was similar to the leverage of the bank, but with more emphasis on the depth of the deposit base.

Policymakers at the Reserve Bank were concerned that overextended banks might be providing more credit than the community could use in a responsible fashion: "It became apparent that the [overextended] banks had been saturating their communities with credit, causing a serious inflation of local values, and had been making loans largely against expectations and prospects of an uncertain and hazardous nature [e.g., future crops] rather than against existing values and a present ability to pay" (FRB Dallas, TBSR).

FRB Dallas officials viewed these banks as prioritizing growth rather than what they regarded as the sounder banking policy of operating so as to protect the depositors: "[An overextended bank was] operating with the idea that its first duty was to help its borrowing customers make a crop by extending to them additional advances on the theory that that was the only way it could protect the loans already made. Thus the bank's policies and practices were dictated by a concern for the interests of its borrowers rather than by a concern for the interests of its depositors" (FRB Dallas, TBSR).

The officials argued that becoming overextended tended to reflect poor choices on the part of the bank's management. They further noted that the District contained many examples of prudent banks that had operated successfully amid droughts and challenging agricultural conditions. These banks had been able to accommodate their customers by expanding lending considerably during the harvest season and then reducing lending thereafter so that, on average, lending was in line with deposits. FRB Dallas officials argued that providing large amounts, or a continuous supply, of discount window credit to banks that became overextended, especially through poor management or bad policies, tended to result in additional losses that harmed the depositors and the community. FRB Dallas's TBSR stated that a wiser course of action was to close such banks promptly.

FRB Minneapolis

The TBSR submitted by FRB Minneapolis emphasized the importance of the long-term prospects of the commercial bank. Banks that were expected to be able to return to a sound condition were supported: "The general policy of this bank in extending credit to its weakened or overextended member banks has been to afford support in every case where there seemed to be a reasonable assurance that assistance would permit a member to regain a sound footing" (FRB Minneapolis, TBSR). By contrast, Reserve Bank officials considered it "hazardous" to support banks that were in an "unsatisfactory condition." Doing so was viewed as likely to simply enable the banks to make further bad decisions and exacerbate losses.

FRB Chicago

FRB Chicago expressed similar sentiments, indicating that the proper policy of a commercial bank was to protect the depositors first and the bank's loan customers last: "We are firmly of the opinion that the prime obligations of any bank are—first, to its depositors; second to its stockholders; and third, to its borrowers. To bring about proper recognition and observance of these obligations, we are at all times willing to co-operate so far as we can consistently with the management, the directorate, and the supervising authorities" (TBSR). Banks that had been overextended for some time were viewed as having these priorities reversed, and FRB Chicago officials sought signs of policy changes before providing extensive discount window support.

FRB San Francisco

Policymakers at FRB San Francisco also expressed the view that there should be caution about lending to overextended banks. This thought was articulated in a letter from the Federal Reserve agent:[2]

> A Bank's first obligation is to its depositors. No course should be followed which jeopardizes a bank's ability to pay depositors according to the agreed terms. A bank's second obligation is to its shareholders, to those who have placed their investment funds in charge of the directors and officers, with the purpose of deriving earnings from such investment. . . . [A bank prioritizing lending] is probably rarely actuated by a purely patriotic purpose of serving the community, but is more apt to be actuated by a desire for greater importance through rapid extension of business beyond its own means, and often, under the guise of helping the community, makes advances for the promotion of the private enterprise of directors and officers. (Perrin 1926)

FRB Kansas City

Statements by FRB Kansas City illustrate that, at times, Reserve Banks might take a more flexible approach and that solvency rather than overextension was the key concern. In his testimony before the Joint Commission of Agricultural Inquiry, Kansas City Governor Jo Miller stated that he considered it important for the Reserve Bank to go to great lengths to save individual banks, even ones in a precarious position, as long as they were solvent and doing so posed no risk to the Federal Reserve Bank. Governor Miller did feel strongly that it was not appropriate for the Reserve Bank to take risks to save insolvent banks:

> In dozens of cases we have saved them [member banks] from bankruptcy, or from the hands of a receiver, because when we feel that a bank is solvent, although overextended, if there is any chance at all to save that bank and its clientele from disaster we give it every aid that it is possible to give up to the very point of taking the risk ourselves. We feel, however, Mr. Chairman, that we are not called upon to assume the risk and losses of an insolvent institution which has been brought to that State by unsound management. (Joint Commission of Agricultural Inquiry 1921–1922, 3:771)

A rather similar position is articulated by FRB Kansas City in its TBSR, where the Reserve Bank again indicates that considerable effort should be made to save solvent institutions. There is an additional subtlety, though, in that, in the TBSR, FRB Kansas City notes that it may be appropriate to provide support to a bank in questionable condition to enable the owners to restore it to solvency:

> The results of the policy of continuing to rediscount paper where the bank's statement showed it to be in a hazardous condition have not always been successful in saving the bank, but in a great many cases it has certainly proven worth while and no member bank in this District can honestly say that it was compelled to close for the reason that the Federal Reserve Bank of Kansas City withheld from it credit when it had eligible paper to offer and the management of the bank was honest. Many banks that were saved by this policy are now in good condition and are serving their communities well. In many cases good crops and a return of good prices have assisted us in our efforts to re-establish a number of banks. In other cases, it has afforded an opportunity for a consolidation or for the stockholders to get themselves in position for an assessment and thereby re-establish the solvency of the bank. (FRB Kansas City, TBSR)

Lending in Situations Where There Were Concerns about Systemic Risks

In situations where the Reserve Banks were concerned about systemic financial instability, they indicated a willingness to be more expansive in their lending, even to the point that they might take meaningful credit risk. Provision of liquidity support in these cases was viewed as necessary to prevent significant financial turbulence that would have serious economic consequences. Sometimes the focus of concern regarding systemic instability was the bank's connections, or interconnections within the banking system generally; the Reserve Banks were clearly attentive to the relationships that a bank seeking support had with other banks and with the community. In several cases, the Reserve Banks indicated that decisions about the extent of discount window lending were influenced by the connections between the bank and correspondents or within a chain or group of banks.[3] In other cases, the systemic risks were viewed as originating outside the banking system but where lending by the banking system, supported by the Federal Reserve, would be necessary for preserving stability. In these situations, the Reserve Banks appear to have been more inclined to find ways to assist banks that played critical roles in the community.

There is an obvious tension between the approach to considering lending to individual banks, where there was an emphasis on solvency, and the approach when lending in systemic situations, where the Reserve Banks expressed a willingness to lend to questionably solvent institutions. It is not clear how they reconciled these approaches. It appears that the circumstances of individual situations guided the Reserve Bank responses.

FRB San Francisco

The most detailed discussion of the role of economic and financial conditions in shaping how a Reserve Bank should respond in emergencies was provided by officials at FRB San Francisco. In particular, the TBSR from FRB San Francisco described three types of crises and the ways the approach to lending should differ across them.

The first type of crisis was a widespread or "national crisis," such as a collapse in crop prices affecting a large portion of the district or country. FRB San Francisco argued that such a crisis called for "the greatest degree of support from Federal Reserve Banks because those banks remain the only agency from which credit can be obtained" (TBSR). Strong action in these situations would be important as "public confidence in banks, as distinguished from the bank [requesting the discount window loan], will easily be so shaken as to involve a widespread area." In other words, a national crisis called for the strongest response by the Federal Reserve, as there would be no one else to provide credit.

While generally supporting lending during a national crisis, FRB San Francisco did not say that this was always the best solution, and, in fact, the Reserve Bank argued that there could not be a predetermined rule for how to respond as it would depend on the facts and circumstances of the crisis. In some cases, FRB San Francisco argued that the Federal Reserve ought to lend to prevent serious losses to the economy and the member commercial banks even if it meant possible losses to the Reserve Bank; at other times, encouraging banks to lend would only result in those banks taking more losses and impair their ability to provide credit once the emergency had passed:[4]

> Any pre-determined rule for Federal Reserve Bank guidance in supporting member banks in weakened condition during a national crisis would be of no value, because it would be impossible to determine in advance the nature of conditions arising out of the crisis. Withholding of credit under one set of circumstances might lead to disaster and much greater loss to banking, trade, and commerce than if credit were extended as the situation would warrant, even if granted by Federal Reserve Banks at the risk of loss. On the other hand, a free granting of credit might subject banks, trade and commerce generally, to unjustifiable loss, in which the Federal Reserve Banks would share. (FRB San Francisco, TBSR)

The second type of crisis was a "community crisis" that affected many banks in a limited area. In such a crisis, FRB San Francisco argued, there should be a strong private-sector response that might be aided by the Federal Reserve. Reserve Bank officials stated that addressing such a crisis should involve injections of new capital and a shift by borrowers toward the strongest banks: "[Such a crisis] distributes through every conceivable agency the burden of necessary financing by stockholders for the purpose of restoring strength to their banks and enabling borrowers with good credit or securities to replace their loans with those better able to carry them under existing circumstances." FRB San Francisco argued that Federal Reserve involvement to aid troubled banks during such an event should depend on the extent to which the banks seeking discount window loans were able to access other sources of support.

The final type of crisis was an "isolated crisis" in which only one bank was in trouble. FRB San Francisco argued that in this case if the bank was solvent and under dependable management, then the Reserve Bank should lend as long as the bank had eligible collateral. If the solvency of the bank was questionable, then the extent of Federal Reserve Bank assistance would be determined "by the ability and willingness of stockholders to provide the means of restoring the bank to solvency." This answer implies that if the management of the bank was unsound, then the Reserve Bank ought to provide minimal, if any, assistance.

FRB Chicago

When commenting on the impact of economic conditions, FRB Chicago focused mostly on Iowa, which, like many other agricultural parts of the country, had experienced an "inflationary period" and then a "reversal" in 1920 and 1921. FRB Chicago officials argued that responding robustly to such situations was important for the communities in question and, as noted in an extended version of the quote from the introduction, that the Reserve Bank had indeed responded in an appropriate manner:

> Our board of directors believed at the time that the very critical situation should be met as far as possible through a broad liberal policy on our own part, even though in pursuing any such policy, we were faced with a possibility of considerable loss. Any other policy at the time would undoubtedly have resulted in an almost complete business collapse in the state of Iowa. We believed then and we still believe that the general policy pursued was the proper one. We had in view as well, the community situation. We extended very large lines of credit to many individual banks. No doubt in some cases we make mistakes; that was inevitable. We feel, however, that our record is evidence that we were willing to go to the limit to help the general situation as well as the individual member banks, and the communities in which they were located. The very small percentage of loss sustained, and the still small indicated loss yet possibly to be taken, indicates also that we were at all times mindful of the safety and integrity of the Federal Reserve Bank of Chicago. (FRB Chicago, TBSR)

In addition, the FRB Chicago TBSR stated that considerable accommodation was provided to one bank because the liquidity demands on the bank were the result of demands by a "large number of smaller correspondent banks." Later comments indicate that the bank in question had approximately a hundred small bank correspondents. These statements highlight that the position of the bank within the interbank network was an important consideration for the Reserve Banks. Indeed, FRB Chicago reported that the discount window loan that it provided in this instance was large and equal to at least double the bank's equity (capital and surplus).[5]

FRB Atlanta

The boom and subsequent collapse in cotton prices had a dramatic impact on the economies of the southern states and the banks that supported the agricultural economy. Consequently, they had a strong influence on the thinking of FRB Atlanta. The Reserve Bank made a concerted effort to support the banks in the affected areas. For instance, as reported by White (2015), the Reserve Bank adopted a more liberal lending policy in North Georgia, which had been hit by a succession of poor crops and was particularly economically depressed.

Perhaps because of these experiences, Governor Maximillian Wellborn noted that if the failure of a bank would cause significant harm to the community, the Federal Reserve might consider providing support even if it meant the risk of loss.

> In order to be of real value, there are times when a reserve bank simply has to risk a loss. The regional banks were not created as profit making institutions; and when, in the calm and deliberate judgement of reserve bank officials, a member's failure would have a serious effect upon its community, when we are convinced that its officers and directors are capable and honest and willing to cooperate with us to save the bank from a situation that arises through adverse conditions, and when there is a reasonable chance that a further advance from the reserve bank will pull the member through, in such circumstances I think we are only fulfilling our duty and justifying our existence when we make the advance the member bank requires. (Wellborn in Conference of Governors 1926, 46)

This willingness to extend credit appears to have depended on the level of stress in the banking system. Governor Wellborn noted that policies ought to differ between periods of emergency and periods of calm. Emergencies called for bold action by the Reserve Banks, while during calm periods, the member banks should be expected to stand on their own: "We have been uniformly considerate and liberal with those country banks which were caught in the cyclone of 1920, but now that they have been given every opportunity to work out of their difficulties, we believe that they should conduct their business with reasonable prudence and conservatism" (Wellborn 1923).

FRB Dallas

In contrast to the cautious approach to lending to individual banks that were overextended, officials at FRB Dallas appear to have been considerably more proactive in responding to situations that were more systemic in nature and that were not the result of poor choices by individual managers. That more aggressive approach was evident when FRB Dallas sought to support member banks even as numerous banks failed amid the boom and bust in cotton prices and the drought that affected agricultural conditions. As Kilman (1961) describes in his history of FRB Dallas, in 1922 as farmers, ranchers, and their banks were struggling to cope with the drought, the Board of Directors of FRB Dallas "approved a policy of making advances to banks, even those in an extended condition within reasonable limits of safety" (104). He reports that the directors sought to balance the danger that further suspensions might spill over and negatively affect well-managed banks against the possibility that banks that suspended with loans outstanding to the Federal Reserve might generate losses to the Reserve Bank.

There was another challenging period for cotton production in 1925 because of a drought. FRB Dallas noted in its TBSR that during this episode it again provided a considerable amount of credit through the discount window, but on a more conservative basis. FRB Dallas officials argued that this approach resulted in a better outcome for both the Reserve Banks and the member banks in those communities:

> Illustrative of the effects of a conservative credit policy in times of agricultural depression is the situation at this time in the 65 Texas counties in the "drought zone" of 1925. While we met the credit demands of banks in that section in such a manner as to bring us no complaints, we made it clear to them, through our loan policy, that the year 1926 would be no time for a general expansion of credit in their section. Had we made loans in large amounts to these 65 counties following the drought of 1925, their member banks would now be caught by the price situation in a seriously overextended condition. As it is, these banks . . . have their situation well in hand. (FRB Dallas, TBSR)

Kilman (1961, esp. 114–115) describes FRB Dallas's proactive approach to handling the drought of 1925–1926. He reported that FRB Dallas sent a special representative to the area to survey the situation: "In anticipation of the heavy volume of rediscount accommodations, the management of the bank [FRB Dallas] made an extensive study of past records of all member banks in the area and analyzed each case to determine which banks would probably find it necessary to borrow during the succeeding year. Some of the banks were visited in order to familiarize them with rediscount requirements, and officers of other banks were invited to come to Dallas for a discussion of their affairs."

Importance of Management and Shareholder Engagement

One common theme across all the Reserve Banks was the importance of high-quality management and strong engagement by equity shareholders in support of the bank. If those were in place, then the Reserve Banks indicated that they were more willing to extend credit. If those were not in place, the Reserve Banks highlighted that it was important to be cautious about extending credit. FRB Atlanta put it simply:

> These fundamental principles are followed by this bank in granting assistance to member banks in a weakened condition:
>
> 1. When the officers and directors of the applying bank are honest and trustworthy, and manifest an interest in restoring the bank to a sound condition.
> 2. When the officers and directors are not using the funds of the bank for their own individual needs or for the needs of the corporations which they control. (FRB Atlanta, TBSR)

FRB Atlanta also described how it implemented these principles when making lending decisions. Officials reported in the Reserve Bank's TBSR that in one case they stopped lending to a member bank once they learned that the president of that bank was personally indebted to the bank and was using funds from the bank to support his other businesses. In another case, FRB Atlanta reported curtailing lending over concerns that the president of the bank was so heavily concerned with outside business interests that he was severely neglecting the bank.[6]

FRB Dallas officials felt strongly that having sound management was important and that propping up incompetent management was likely only to cause more problems and create additional losses. That is expressed in the quote from the introduction (repeated here to facilitate comparisons):

The whole situation simply resolves itself into the proposition that errors of judgement and unsound policies on the part of the management of a member bank cannot be corrected by continuous extensions of credit by a Federal Reserve Bank or any other creditor. Those extensions of credit simply serve to create further opportunities to make the same mistakes of judgement and to further prosecute the same unsound policies with consequences usually vicious for the bank receiving the credit, for the community which it serves, and for the bank extending the credit. (FRB Dallas, TBSR)

Correspondingly, FRB Dallas was cautious about lending in situations in which the management was perceived as poor.[7] Kilman (1961, 124) also states that "[FRB Dallas] recognized, however, that in those cases where a bank's unhappy situation was due to capital impairment on account of losses, or was due to bad management, the continuation of credit extension was not the answer, as it was felt that under such circumstances it was necessary for the bank to be saved 'from within' through the efforts of the banks own directors and stockholders."

FRB Dallas further noted that continued lending by the Reserve Bank might undermine the incentives of the commercial bank's management to run the bank in a conservative fashion. "If the line applied for is considerably in excess of the bank's capital and surplus, and is granted, the stockholders' investment becomes a minority interest, which is likely to reflect itself in the interest which they subsequently take in the bank's ultimate fate" (FRB Dallas, TBSR). This incentive issue further highlights the importance put on responsible management.

Officials at FRB Chicago reported, "The financial responsibility and the determination of the directorate to put the bank in good condition justified our continuing our liberal support," and added that lending depended on the ability of the "stockholders and directors to themselves help the institution, and to clean it up. If there is willingness and ability to do this, we are disposed to assist during the process. If, on the contrary, there is no disposition to do this, we cannot continue to support a hopeless situation" (TBSR). Griswold (1936) corroborates the idea that FRB Chicago considered the character of bank management when they made lending decisions.

One important action that shareholders could take to convince FRB officials to lend was to inject capital into the bank. Several Reserve Banks, including FRB San Francisco and FRB Chicago, indicated in their TBSRs that if the shareholders had recently injected equity or were credibly making arrangements to provide additional equity, the Reserve Banks were more willing to continue to extend credit. While injecting additional equity clearly bolstered the condition of the bank, Federal Reserve policymakers indicated that it also provided a signal about the shareholders' engagement and determination to improve their bank.

Relatedly, Reserve Banks reported being more willing to extend credit to a member bank if the bank's directors (or managers or other shareholders) purchased questionable assets from the bank. As with equity injections, this action improved the condition of the bank and showed the owners' or managers' commitment to making it successful.

Understanding That Lending to Troubled Banks Can Disadvantage Depositors or Investors

Reserve Banks officials were aware that lending to support a troubled bank could end up allowing some depositors to withdraw funds while leaving the remaining depositors in a worse position. Normally, if the bank was insolvent and closed, the depositors would be paid by liquidating the assets of the bank in a roughly pro rata manner. If the bank was really insolvent, the depositors would receive less than 100 percent of their deposits back, but those losses would be shared proportionately (e.g., everyone would receive only ninety cents for each dollar of deposits). If funds from a Reserve Bank loan were used to pay withdrawing depositors, then those withdrawing depositors would receive all of their funds. As a secured lender, the Federal Reserve would have first claim on the assets used as collateral for the discount window loan, and only once the Federal Reserve had been paid in full would any proceeds from those assets be used to pay the remaining depositors. If the assets received by the Federal Reserve as collateral were among the better-quality assets, then the depositors that did not withdraw would only be repaid from the poorer assets of the bank; that would likely mean that their losses would be worse than if the Federal Reserve had not provided a loan. If a Reserve Bank took extra collateral out of concern about the condition of the bank, that could have exacerbated the problem.[8]

FRB San Francisco noted in its TBSR, "Ethics and public policy limit it [discount window] to such action as will not invade the rights of depositors by inequitable preferences to Federal Reserve Banks or among depositors." In addition, "the temporary continuance made possible by

the Federal Reserve Bank's assistance would only result in creating preferences of depositors then existing over depositors at the time of failure
after the Federal Reserve Bank assistance had been given and proven
ineffective."[9]

An Understanding of Moral Hazard and Precedents That Would Be Set through Interventions

Reserve Bank policymakers also understood that their actions might lead
to increased risk-taking or otherwise create poor incentives for banks. The
minutes of the Board of Directors of FRB Dallas for September 13, 1923,
report that the "Board is well aware that actions to support a troubled
bank would set precedent and that other banks would make similar requests for support." Indeed, the directors indicated that the first such request occurred within days of their original action. The directors of FRB
Dallas noted that they needed to carry out a balancing act. To prevent the
moral hazard concerns, the Board of Directors of FRB Dallas considered
it best to avoid providing preferential support to the greatest extent possible while at the same time acknowledging that there would inevitably be
times when they would need to provide extraordinary support to prevent
a substantial crisis.

The Importance of Public and Depositor Confidence

Public confidence in local banks was viewed as critically important, and
the Reserve Banks were attentive to whether the closure of a bank might
cause a loss of confidence in other banks in the community even if there
were no formal connections among the banks. For example, in its TBSR,
FRB Minneapolis described several instances in which public confidence
was "unsettled" because of the failure of other banks and mentioned its
concern that the failure of yet another bank would lead to additional failures. In these situations, the Reserve Bank was more willing to extend
discount window loans to support market confidence. Moreover, FRB
Minneapolis officials considered there to be a collective aspect to public
confidence and mentioned that the Reserve Bank ought to take steps to
promote general confidence in the banking industry. Faced with the challenging economic conditions of the early 1920s, the Board of Directors

of FRB Minneapolis indicated that, "in view of the widespread and severe strain upon credit, it is highly essential that the general situation be protected by affording all possible support to members requiring special attention at this time. The Federal Reserve Bank must guard against any weakening of public confidence, and the burden of maintaining financial stability in this district falls upon it at this time" (FRB Minneapolis 1920–1924, June 14, 1920).

FRB San Francisco noted, "Unwarranted loss of public confidence in a particular bank, resulting in a run, may be a sign of weakness. . . . There will be the question as to whether the supply of eligible paper will be sufficient to stop the run and restore public confidence. The Federal Reserve Bank is serving the public interest in freely lending every legal assistance, even though doubtful as to the sufficiency of eligible paper to stop the run."

Governor Wellborn of FRB Atlanta suggested that there was an expectation that the Federal Reserve would stand behind the member banks and that this support provided confidence during stress periods. Correspondingly, he argued that not demonstrating that expected support could be disastrous: "As so many non-member state banks have failed, we feel that, if a national bank or a state bank which is a member, should fail in an important section, it might bring on very serious results for our agricultural member banks and their communities" (Wellborn 1921).

The concern that confidence in a bank might be undermined by nearby failures was mentioned by FRB Dallas officials in their statements as well. They indicated in the TBSR that the Reserve Bank had a policy of reaching out to "well-managed" member banks to volunteer the use of the discount window to provide assistance during local emergencies arising from suspensions of banks in the community or immediate vicinity. While FRB Dallas reported that there was little take-up of such offers, the proactive approach indicates that this issue mattered to Reserve Bank officials.

The Reserve Banks were also aware that the provision of discount window loans could affect local confidence and, if the support was seen as a signal that the bank was in trouble, worsen an already tenuous situation. Garrett (1968) reports that FRB Atlanta officials would meet with the management of banks that were experiencing deposit withdrawals and that "rumors of the nature of these conferences almost invariably leaked out. This was generally followed by increased deposit withdrawals, which, together with the banks' inability to obtain further funds from us on the paper offered, resulted ultimately in their closing" (308).[10]

Appropriate Use of the Discount Window and Discouragement of Speculative Activity

One issue that strongly concerned the Reserve Banks, especially with respect to the discount window, was the "appropriate use" of the funds and the possibility that they would be used for speculative activity. While the use of funds for speculation seems unlikely during an emergency situation, it was potentially a concern in the period leading up to the emergency, especially if it was associated with an increased use of leverage and an increase in the likelihood that a bank was overextended.

Detailed statements regarding the appropriate use of discount window credit were provided in the *Annual Report* of the Federal Reserve Board in 1923 and 1926. For instance, in the 1923 report, the Board stated that "credit for short-term operations in agriculture, industry, and trade . . . for the purpose of financing the movement of goods through any one of the successive stages of production and distribution into consumption is a productive use of credit" (34). Use of the discount window to facilitate such activity was viewed as perfectly appropriate. The 1926 report echoed similar thoughts but also highlighted the idea that the use of the discount window was intended to be temporary: "The funds of the Federal reserve banks are primarily intended to be used in meeting the seasonal and temporary requirements of members" (4).

The use of funds for speculative purposes was viewed as inappropriate. The 1923 *Annual Report* noted that discount window credit was not allowed to be used to finance the carrying of securities or investments other than US government securities. Further, it was noted that discount window credit should not be used to store goods in the hope that the prices of those goods would rise; that was viewed as another form of speculative activity.

There were a few periods when concern about speculative activity came to the forefront. One such period was amid the post–World War I boom in agricultural and farmland prices. For instance, FRB Chicago warned regularly in its monthly *Report of Business Conditions* that conditions in farmland were dangerously speculative and that a concerning share of land sales were occurring on the basis of the expectations of rising prices. In one particularly colorful warning about the dangers of such speculation, FRB Chicago described the history of land prices in England after the end of the Napoleonic Wars, when prices fell by 50 percent (FRB Chicago 1919; Griswold 1936). Another period of concern about speculative activities was related to the stock market run-up in the late 1920s. Federal Reserve officials were quite concerned that the rise in equity prices was being financed by a rise in margin credit that was siphoning funds away from productive uses.

One response to concerns about speculation was the use of "direct pressure." Under direct pressure, the Reserve Banks asked borrowing member banks about the use to which they put funds obtained from the discount window and about their lending activities. Discount window credit was limited or denied to banks that were heavily involved in lending to finance speculative activities or providing margin credit to finance stock purchases. However, some policymakers were concerned about the use of direct pressure as it was often difficult to distinguish between productive and speculative uses of credit. In addition, direct pressure might not limit the funds used overall for speculative purposes; funds borrowed by banks using them for productive purposes might still flow to banks engaging in speculative behaviors, and the direct pressure might influence the behavior of member banks but not that of nonmember banks (see Anderson 1971, 145–48; Friedman and Schwarz 1963, 253–66).

The other response to concerns about speculative uses of credit was to raise discount rates. The idea that higher rates might discourage lending supporting speculative activities was one reason for the experiment with progressive discount rates discussed in chapter 3. It was thought that banks would be more cautious and focus on productive credits if the structure of interest rates disincentivized significant use of the discount window (see Rieder 2020). However, this experiment was viewed as unsuccessful and was abandoned. In other cases, the Reserve Banks simply increased the discount rate to put upward pressure on all interest rates. Such policies did eventually reduce speculative activities but had a significant impact on overall economic activity (see Friedman and Schwarz 1963).

Once asset price booms start to collapse, the concerns that central bank credit might boost a speculative bubble diminish rapidly. However, decisions about central bank liquidity provision are still fraught. On the one hand, providing credit could enable banks to avoid selling assets in a fire sale or in ways that would exacerbate the downward pressure on prices; if prices recover, that would in turn promote a recovery in the banking sector. On the other hand, if prices continue to trend down, additional credit might only increase the losses incurred or result in banks that are "frozen"—forced to keep rolling over loans to existing borrowers to prevent defaults while lacking the resources to extend new loans to growing businesses.

In response to the collapse of agricultural prices in the early 1920s, different Reserve Banks tried somewhat different approaches. Some, such as FRB Atlanta and FRB Dallas, provided substantial amounts of credit to their banks for extended periods. Many banks survived because of these efforts, but quite a number of banks failed with discount window credit outstanding. Other Reserve Banks provided credit during the period of most intense stress but more rapidly pivoted to tighten policies to promote a faster but more painful resolution of the challenges. Notwithstanding the efforts described in chapter 5 to support individual banks, Griswold (1936) reports that FRB Chicago was reluctant to rediscount substantial amounts of agricultural paper for its member banks after the immediacy of the emergency had passed. That, in turn, reduced the willingness of the member banks to roll over their existing loans. Griswold (1936) suggests that these pressures occurred in part as FRB Chicago approached its legal reserve requirement. Nevertheless, the political outcry about the pressures placed on banks by some of the Reserve Banks resulted in a congressional investigation under the title of the Commission of Agricultural Inquiry. As a result of this inquiry, Griswold reports, FRB Chicago reduced the pressure on banks to liquidate their loans.

The challenges faced by the Reserve Banks amid the collapse of the agricultural boom are in many ways similar to those that appeared in the savings and loan (S&L) crisis of the 1980s and early 1990s. In that episode, many thrifts suffered devastating solvency challenges. Regulators were pressed to find solutions that would support the local communities. However, some of the regulators' actions, such as providing discount window loans to keep the S&Ls operating while regulators sought to arrange mergers or acquisitions, were blamed for increasing the costs to the deposit insurance fund. As a consequence, Congress passed the Federal Deposit Insurance Corporation Improvement Act (FDICIA). That act imposed various triggers for "prompt correction action" that would close banks as their capital became depleted and placed restrictions on the ability of the Federal Reserve to lend to undercapitalized banks. Congress also set up the Resolution Trust Corporation as a special way to handle the assets of failing S&Ls (see Federal Deposit Insurance Corporation 1997, 1998).

Case Studies of Federal Reserve Interventions

The Reserve Banks provided emergency liquidity support in quite a range of situations. In some cases, their responses were focused on getting ahead of events and ensuring that sufficient cash was on hand to deal with potential crises. Reserve Banks also responded to runs that were already underway, in which decisions needed to be made quickly about whether to provide liquidity support to keep the banks open or have the banks close. A third situation involved lending to help banks respond to longer-term liquidity strains; such lending was particularly challenging, as the solvency of the bank in question would likely only be known at a much later date (such as at the end of harvest season). Finally, there were instances in which the Federal Reserve Banks stepped in to prevent a disruptive failure by a commercial bank and facilitate a more orderly resolution. This ordering is used to present the case studies; over the course of the chapter, the episodes involve situations where the liquidity needs become progressively longer lasting and more intertwined with the solvency challenges.

The case studies involve the two liquidity tools described earlier: currency funds and the discount window. Currency funds were only used in a few instances to respond to stress, at least during the 1920s; there were more instances of their use in the early 1930s, a number of which are described briefly in appendix 2. The discount window was used far more frequently to respond to stress. As demonstrated in these case studies, it

proved to be a very versatile tool. The extent to which either public com-
munications or moral suasion were employed is also discussed.

The situations reviewed here draw heavily, but not exclusively, from the
episodes that were described in the TBSRs. As such, they are not a random sample but instead represent episodes in which the Reserve Banks
viewed themselves as having acted appropriately and successfully. Thus,
these episodes shed light on the factors that the Reserve Banks considered when determining whether to provide emergency liquidity support
and that contributed to successful interventions. They do not shed light
on unsuccessful interventions or on situations where the Federal Reserve
perhaps should have acted but did not. The episodes were also selected
to highlight the range of situations in which support was provided and to
be at least somewhat balanced across Reserve Banks to offer some sense
of the similarities and differences across the system. A large number of
officials were involved in the interventions. For ease of reference, a list of
high-ranking Federal Reserve and OCC officials is included in appendix 3.

Interventions Involving Use of
Currency Funds

Currency funds allowed the Federal Reserve to place large amounts of
currency in locations where the cash could be needed. If there were concerns about the health of the banks, depositors may have preferred to
have more cash available—which was riskless and which could be used
for transactions if the banks closed. Having more currency on-site likely
would have supported depositor confidence and reduced concerns about
the need to hurry to the bank to withdraw ahead of others and thus reduced the incentive to run. Moreover, in the two case studies described
here, the establishment of the currency fund and the shipment of currency
were well publicized. The public knowledge that the authorities were providing support and ensuring the ready availability of cash may have importantly promoted public confidence.

Having the currency available while it was still the property of the
Federal Reserve may have facilitated its distribution. With the currency
fund, any nearby member bank could obtain cash from the fund, and the
transaction was a bilateral borrowing action in which the Federal Reserve
itself would judge the quality of the borrowing bank and the collateral.
Providing the money to the first bank through a loan would have required

the Federal Reserve to rely on that bank's willingness to extend credit to other banks to further distribute the money.

Boise, Idaho — December 1921 — FRB San Francisco

The first use of a currency fund to respond to an episode of financial instability appears to have occurred in Idaho in December 1921. As in many other episodes discussed in this chapter, the financial instability was rooted in the postwar bust in agricultural conditions. In Idaho this took the form of a drop in the price of livestock, which forced many ranchers into bankruptcy. Declines in the prices of metals and other mined commodities only added to the challenging environment. Pressure on the banking industry is evident in the deposit totals for the state, which dropped more than 25 percent, from $108 million to $78 million, between June 1920 and June 1921 (Board of Governors 1959).

These economic challenges resulted in a number of bank closures over the course of 1921. The pace of closings accelerated around year-end. The first banks were closed because of their own fundamental issues; however, as more banks closed, the reasons for closure appear to have shifted and more banks were closed amid runs and increasing concerns about a contagious deterioration in confidence. The first bank to close its doors was the First National Bank of Burley, which national bank regulators indicated was "unable to realize on loans," implying that many of its borrowers could not repay their loans and that the bank was insolvent. A receiver was appointed on November 30, 1921 (OCC 1921). This closure was followed in fairly rapid succession by others. The Citizens State Bank of Buhl suspended on December 2, 1921, amid reports in the local newspaper of rising concerns about delinquent loans; the newspaper expressed the hope that the suspension would be temporary and declared that other local banks were in excellent condition (*Filer Record*, December 8, 1921, 1). The First National Bank of Mountain Home suspended on December 7, 1921. The local newspaper reported that bad loans had been accumulating at the bank amid the slump in livestock values and that a run the day before had depleted the cash "almost to the vanishing point" (*Mountain Home Republican*, December 10, 1921, 1).[1] Perhaps signaling a deterioration in confidence and potential contagion, the Commercial State Bank of Burley experienced heavy withdrawals and was forced to suspend on December 9 (*Burley Bulletin*, December 15, 1921). The First National Bank of Wendell closed the next day (*Rand McNally* 1922).

Amid a growing emergency situation, officials at FRB San Francisco decided to establish a currency fund in Boise (Board of Governors 1938).[2] One motivating factor for this decision was the distance of the region from the nearest Federal Reserve Bank branch in Salt Lake City and the challenges of making the trip amid winter conditions; if a sudden demand for currency were to materialize, it would take some time to ship the funds to Idaho (Vest 1925). One million dollars was sent to Boise and held at the First National Bank and the Boise City National Bank (FRB San Francisco 1921–1934, December 20, 1921); these were two of the largest member banks in the city. Two officials from the Salt Lake City branch of the Federal Reserve remained on-site to oversee the funds and make sure that all disbursements were correctly accounted for. Standard credit controls for the use of currency from the fund were in place which meant that officials on-site would not allow cash to be drawn from the currency fund without the approval of the manager of the Salt Lake City branch or of officers of FRB San Francisco (Perrin 1921).

The $1 million sent to Boise provided a fair amount of liquidity. At this time, there were three national banks in Boise and one very small state title company. In September 1921, the three national banks cumulatively had on hand about $1.7 million in cash and exchange (OCC 1921). So the addition of $1 million in currency would have provided a sizable boost to the liquid resources available in the city. While the interbank balances held in Boise were not very large — "due to banks" was reported at only about $1 million for the three national banks in September — the *Rand McNally Bankers Directory* (1922) indicates that a significant portion of the banks in Idaho listed one of the Boise banks as a principal correspondent. Those correspondent relationships could have put significant pressure on the banks in Boise if runs became widespread in the state. However, these relationships would also have greatly facilitated the distribution of liquidity around the state should that have become necessary.

This currency fund and the availability of cash were well publicized. Newspapers in Moscow and Burley carried news stories regarding the $1 million in currency that had been delivered to the Boise banks almost as soon as the cash arrived (see, for instance, the *Daily Star-Mirror* of Moscow, Idaho, December 15, 1921, 1). The speed and coincident timing of the newspaper stories suggests that either the bankers or the Federal Reserve officials alerted the press to the arrival of the cash. The newspapers reported that these funds were for the use of the representatives of the Federal Reserve Bank (as opposed to being loans to the banks) and that representatives of the Federal Reserve would remain on-site to oversee their use.

This response appears to have been successful. There do not appear to have been any additional bank closures in Idaho for the next several months. (The next closure listed in the *Rand McNally Bankers Directory* occurred in June 1922.) The currency fund was closed in March 1922, once officials on-site felt comfortable that "the emergency under which currency was placed in Boise no longer exists" (FRB San Francisco 1921–1934, March 21, 1922).

Tampa, Florida—July 1929—FRB Atlanta

A currency fund was also used to address financial instability in Tampa, Florida, amid a panic in the summer of 1929.[3] This episode was considerably more severe than the one in Boise, and the currency fund was only one component of the overall response of the Federal Reserve.

As described in Carlson, Mitchener, and Richardson (2011—hereafter cited as CMR 2011), the panic resulted from an infestation of the Mediterranean fruit fly among the Florida citrus crop. This particular fruit fly had a life cycle that allowed it to spread quickly, and, while it preferred citrus, it was capable of consuming a variety of other crops and was known to have devasted agriculture in other countries. Hence, when the infestation was discovered in early April, efforts to eradicate it started immediately. These efforts involved the destruction of a significant portion of the current citrus crop as well as a significant number of citrus groves, particularly in the area around Orlando, where the fruit fly was concentrated. Other states, and a number of other countries, banned the importation of fruits and vegetables from Florida. The eradication efforts proved effective in eliminating the fruit fly, but these efforts and the embargoes caused considerable losses to the farmers. The losses in turn created uncertainty about the ability of the farmers to repay any loans they owed to their banks.

Ultimately, concerns arose about the condition of the banking sector and its ability to absorb likely losses. CMR (2011) report that the first bank failures in the citrus-growing regions occurred in May even as the stress on the banking system continued to build. There were heavy deposit withdrawals from the banks, especially in the citrus-producing regions of the state. The stress spread from the banks in the citrus-growing regions to the banks that were their correspondents or that did business with them.

Citizens Bank and Trust Company of Tampa (Citizens Bank) was a particularly important correspondent and was called on to support its respondents. Citizens Bank provided a significant amount of liquidity support and borrowed a considerable amount from the Federal Reserve to do so.[4]

Deposit withdrawals at local banks accelerated at the end of June, and on July 17, 1929, the pressures on Citizens Bank became too much, and the bank was forced to close. Its closure resulted in a further deterioration of the situation, with runs occurring in St. Augustine, St. Petersburg, and Orlando and bank closures surging across the state (CMR 2011). While the roots of the crisis were concerns about the solvency of banks providing loans to citrus farmers, at this point the episode was a full-blown panic, with deposit withdrawals being driven by concerns about bank liquidity and depositors' concerns about their ability to immediately access their deposits. Other banks in Tampa experienced withdrawal pressures and were faced with a critical situation. FRB Atlanta believed that the runs were affecting banks that were fundamentally sound: "That the loss of confidence is not confined to depositors of the weak banks in Florida is evidenced by the runs upon the St. Augustine National Bank and the First Bank of Gainesville. In the case of both of these banks we offered the services of this bank" (FRB Atlanta, 1929, 1621).

FRB Atlanta stepped in to stop the panic and stabilize the situation. Part of this response consisted of establishing a currency fund in Tampa and sending $1 million to the city. The currency fund was intended to "relieve such emergency situations as may occur" and to ensure that an ample supply of cash would be available to meet withdrawals (Board of Governors 1929, July 16, 1929).[5] Federal Reserve officials viewed the closure of another major bank in the city as likely to be devastating to confidence in the banking system.[6]

The currency fund was placed at the First National Bank of Tampa and the Exchange National Bank of Tampa, both of which also had substantial correspondent banking relationships and were experiencing liquidity pressures as the correspondent banks drew down deposits held in Tampa or requested loans.[7] Keeping these two Tampa banks open was thus vital to stabilizing the situation, and it was hoped that ensuring their access to currency would help prevent the liquidity crisis from cascading. In this case, the two banks were given more control over the currency and the ability to either draw funds themselves or allow other banks to draw currency. The Federal Reserve was fully secured; the commercial banks controlling the currency fund placed in the custody of the Federal Reserve government securities equal in face value to 110 percent of the cash they received.[8] FRB Atlanta officials expected that the establishment of the currency fund "would have a good psychological effect" (Board of Governors 1929, July 16, 1929). In January 1929, banks in Tampa reported having about $10 million in cash on hand (as reported in *Rand McNally 1929*), so the $1 million provided through the currency fund represented a sizable boost to the city's liquid resources.

Unfortunately, it was not enough. Serious runs occurred at both the First National Bank of Tampa and the Exchange National Bank, with over $1 million withdrawn from each bank in a single day. As described by CMR (2011), FRB Atlanta conducted further efforts, including very public displays of support, to stabilize the situation. Cash was flown into the city. The deputy governor of FRB Atlanta appeared on-site along with an additional $5 million in currency. The deputy governor announced that FRB Atlanta was "prepared to send enough money to pay every depositor of the First National and the Exchange National if necessary" (*New York Times*, July 18, 1929, 1). Moreover, the cash received was prominently displayed at the banks. "The arrival of $5,000,000 here today and yesterday from the Atlanta Federal Reserve Bank and the sight of the money in huge stacks in the cages of the bank tellers had a reassuring effect." (*Commercial and Financial Chronicle*, July 20, 1929, 422). CMR (2011) report that more cash arrived subsequently and that, in total, more than $25 million of currency was shipped to Florida to deal with the crisis.

The overall response by FRB Atlanta appears to have eventually calmed the situation in Tampa. Critically, the depositor runs on the First National and the Exchange National subsided. The displays of currency reportedly calmed the depositors. Crowds about the banks were much smaller than yesterday and were there out of curiosity" (*Commercial and Financial Chronicle*, July 20, 1929, 422).

Even after the situation in Tampa was stabilized, the situation in Florida remained precarious. The resources and ongoing support from the Tampa currency fund appear to have been vital in preserving stability. FRB Atlanta officials reported that resources from the currency fund were of great help in supporting banks in St. Petersburg amid difficulties there and were needed again to aid banks in Tampa when pressures there briefly reemerged a few months later (Newton 1930).

The actions of the Federal Reserve were key to stabilizing conditions all across Florida. Using counterfactual analysis, CMR (2011) estimate that had the Tampa banks that served as custodians of the currency fund been forced to close, bank closures would have been twice as high as they actually were. Further, CMR document how close many banks were to exhausting their cash supplies. Amid further runs, loss of confidence, and shortage of currency, many more banks would have been forced to suspend. That quantitative analysis corroborates the anecdotal evidence of contemporary observers.

Interventions Involving Large Cash Shipments

One intervention involved a large shipment of cash outside the borders of the United States. This intervention was unique, but it highlights operational challenges in responses to emergencies.

Havana, Cuba—April 1926—FRB Atlanta

The US dollar began to play an important part in the Cuban economy during the military occupation of Cuba that followed the Spanish-American War. Active trade between the two countries involving sugar, tobacco, coffee, and other commodities as well as increased activity by US banking interests resulted in a further expansion of the role of the US dollar, and it came to be the chief circulating medium of exchange. Much of the physical currency was old, and counterfeit notes plagued the system. So, in 1920, at the request of the Cuban government, an arrangement was made whereby old currency could be collected by the Cuban Treasury or Cuban banks and shipped to the Jacksonville branch of FRB Atlanta for replacement.

The treaties in place at the time, particularly the Platt Amendment to the Treaty of 1903, allowed considerable scope for the US government to be involved in Cuban affairs. There were already solid banking and trade relationships with Cuba, but pressure built on the Federal Reserve to establish an agency in Havana to further develop these connections. Encouragement for some sort of agency came from US President Warren G. Harding as well as from the Federal Reserve's Federal Advisory Council and the American ambassador to Cuba, who urged action "in order to forestall the establishment of a Cuban bank of issue, which was considered highly undesirable, and to check, if possible, the absorption of the Island's private banks by Canadian interests" (Board of Governors 1938, 39).

Consequently, an agency was established in Havana in 1923 and was split between FRB Boston and FRB Atlanta. FRB Boston, which was more connected to the US banks operating in Cuba, received the authority to buy and sell "cable transfers," which were money market contracts used for moving funds, especially internationally, the settlement of which usually involved an agreement to deliver a specified amount of a particular currency at a specified place and time. FRB Atlanta was responsible for supplying currency to meet the needs of the country, including those arising from transactions arranged by FRB Boston, as well as for buying and selling money market instruments with banks that operated out of the Sixth (Atlanta) Federal Reserve District. This arrangement reportedly led to some tension between the Federal Reserve Banks, especially as FRB Atlanta ended up having to shoulder most of the operational costs of the agency (see Board of Governors 1938, 40–41).

A panic struck Havana in April 1926. In Cuba, rumors circulated about the condition of the Royal Bank of Canada and the possibility that it might be forced to suspend payments. These (inaccurate) rumors appear to have originated with a local Cuban newspaper. The public apparently gave credence to the rumors because of the depressed state of the Cuban economy amid low prices for sugar *(New York Times*, April 11, 1926; Garrett 1968, 297). Newspapers also reported that the sugarcane growers had requested that the Cuban legislature place a moratorium on their debt payments; that would have helped the growers but caused significant problems for the banks (*Commercial and Financial Chronicle*, April 17, 1926, 2129).[9]

By the middle of the week of April 6, these rumors of impending bank closures had reached a critical stage and spread to encompass the National City Bank of New York, which had offices in Havana and a number of other cities in Cuba (Board of Governors 1926b, April 30, 1926). Runs on the banks in Havana and a heavy demand for US dollars rapidly depleted the roughly $10 million in cash that was held on the island at the Federal Reserve's Havana Agency. Nevertheless, requests for dollar currency continued to surge upward. As of Friday, April 9, banks with operations in Havana had purchased from FRB Boston cable transfers that provided for the payment of $39 million. Many of these were purchased by New York banks, or through a New York correspondent bank in the case of the Royal Bank of Canada, to ensure that funds were delivered to their Cuban operations (*Commercial and Financial Chronicle*, April 17, 1926, 2129).[10] It was feared that, without sufficient currency to enable the banks to meet the withdrawal demands they expected to face on Monday morning, there would be a large-scale collapse of the banking system in Cuba.

To meet this demand for US currency, FRB Atlanta scrambled to assemble the cash and ship it to Cuba. It was expected that there would be a demand for both smaller and larger bills to meet the needs of depositors. While airplanes could have quickly moved currency to Havana, they could not carry the physical weight of the $26 million of currency that was assembled. Consequently, FRB Atlanta chartered a special three-car train with right-of-way privileges to rapidly make the journey from Atlanta through Florida all the way to Key West. That train left from Atlanta late Saturday afternoon bearing the currency in forty-two pouches of registered mail, as well as a small contingent of FRB Atlanta staff and guards (as described in Garrett 1968; Gamble 1989).

Once the train reached Key West, the money was transferred to the gunboat *Cuba*, which was under the command of the Cuban postal authorities (Gamble 1989). The boat set sail soon thereafter, with the authorities using the time to plan for the distribution of money once the boat had docked.[11] The gunboat reached the Havana harbor at 2:00 a.m. on Monday, whereupon a military guard immediately escorted the currency to the Federal Reserve agency, where it was ready for the agency's 7:00 a.m. opening, which would allow for delivery to the banks before their 9:00 a.m. opening. (Federal Reserve staff arriving in Havana are shown in fig. 5.1.) News of the cash shipment appeared in newspapers even as it was still en route. While this caused some concern among officials about security, it also likely reassured depositors.

The currency that reached Havana on Monday morning was only an initial installment. As reported by Garrett (1968), altogether over $42 million was sent through a variety of transportation methods, all arriving within a matter of days of the start of the panic. It is important to note that this cash did not represent loans on the part of FRB Atlanta but cash that would be used to settle the cable transfers sold by FRB Boston.[12]

In addition, the government of Cuba took its own dramatic steps to stem the panic. On Saturday, as the shipment of cash was being assembled, President Gerardo Machado of Cuba and two of his cabinet secretaries arrived at the main branch of the Royal Bank of Canada to deposit some of their personal funds. The president then announced that he would put his personal fortune and, if necessary, funds from the National Treasury at the disposal of the bank (*New York Times*, April 11, 1926, 1). More quietly, the government deposited $12 million in currency with Havana banks. Those funds, in combination with the funds provided by the Federal Reserve, enabled the banks to meet the demands placed on them on Monday, and the panic subsided.

FIGURE 5.1. Federal Reserve staff arriving in Havana

Source: National Archives, records of the Federal Reserve, "Foreign Agencies."

The actions of the Cuban government and Federal Reserve officials appear to have been successful in stemming the run. Actual withdrawals on April 12 were sizable but were fully covered by the cash the banks had requested, and within a few weeks, conditions were described as normal. Federal Reserve officials received significant praise from the Cuban government and the Havana press for the expeditious manner in which they acted.

While this operation successfully restored order, the experience also pointed out some difficulties in having multiple Federal Reserve Banks oversee the operations in Havana. Soon thereafter, management of the agency in Cuba was consolidated so that it resided just with FRB Atlanta. However, the value of the agency diminished in subsequent years as trade declined more rapidly after a change in the Cuban government and a decision to issue a Cuban currency. The Havana agency was closed in 1938.

Interventions Involving Discount Window Lending

While the use of currency funds was an innovative part of the emergency response in a few situations, a much more typical response was lending through the discount window. As the following examples illustrate, the discount window was a versatile tool that the Reserve Banks could use to respond to a variety of circumstances. The first episodes involved sudden liquidity needs and depositor runs, the next episodes required longer-term support, and the final episodes involved failing banks.

Park National Bank (Charter 9383), Kansas City, Missouri —
November 1926 — FRB Kansas City

The Park National Bank was a small bank located in a suburb of Kansas City. This area had boomed in the early 1920s, and the bank had supported local growth with loans to a variety of real estate developers, housebuilders, and local contractors. However, a subsequent economic slowdown caused many of these loans to sour and resulted in financial difficulties for the bank.

Management and ownership of the bank was dominated by Mr. H. Paynter, the president. The bank's examiner described Mr. Paynter's management as "not only incompetent but it has persistently burdened the institution with a large number and aggregate of various kinds of loans of extremely substandard and doubtful character apparently in order to obtain higher rates of interest and to show larger earnings than be content with more desirable investments at somewhat less interest rates and keep the institution in acceptable condition" (Roberts 1926b).

Concerns about loan losses and the solvency of the bank mounted. In January, the bank had negligible undivided profits and a surplus that was overwhelmed by the estimated losses. Consequently, the comptroller issued a formal notice of capital impairment (Roberts 1926a). The bank raised new equity, and the impairment was corrected in February, but the amount of additional equity provided was just enough to correct the issue and was not enough to deal with all the bank's troubled assets.[13]

At the examination that took place just a few months later, in September 1926, the examiner once again complained that the bank's capital was impaired. The chief examiner noted some trade-offs in attempting another assessment. On the one hand, forcing another assessment might be difficult, as the previous assessment was so recent and shareholders might be resistant to providing additional resources. A failure to raise the funds might result in the bank closing in a disorderly manner. On the other hand, the examiner noted that another assessment might prompt a change in the management, which was viewed as necessary for the bank's survival. Ultimately, the comptroller decided to formally declare the impairment of capital and require another assessment.

The formal notice of capital impairment appears to have had the effect that the OCC authorities had hoped for, as other parties started investigating the possibility of acquiring the Park National Bank. Nevertheless, the notice also intensified the uncertainty regarding prospects for the bank.

Another bank apparently took this opportunity to ratchet up pressure on the Park National Bank even further. In a letter describing the situation, Chief Examiner L. K. Roberts reported: "A small competitive state bank has been trying for some time to acquire the Park National Bank or merge with it.... Since the recent examination and while a re-organization and recapitalization was being attempted, the competitive state bank moved its location to a point immediately across the street from the Park National Bank and it is alleged that officers of the state bank began and continued to spread adverse reports regarding the Park National Bank" (Roberts 1926c).

The situation reached a crisis in mid-November. A nearby banking and trust company, the Federal Trust Company, closed. A number of other banks had held their cash reserves at the company. Rumors circulated about connections between other financial institutions and the company. The inability of the Terminal Trust Company and the Waldo State Bank of Kansas City to access the reserves they held at the Federal Trust Company amid increased depositor withdrawals forced the closure of these two institutions (*Kansas City Star*, November 13, 1926, 3; November 15, 1926, 1). Governor Willis Bailey (1927), head of FRB Kansas City, reported that these bank closings created a feeling of unease in the area and that, during this precarious situation, a bank run that resulted in the closure of yet another bank might cause the situation to spiral out of control. There were rumors linking the Park National Bank to the Federal Trust Company (*Sedalia Democrat*, November 15, 1926). The actual linkages were connections not on the part of the bank itself but rather on the part of the bank's officers who had borrowed extensively from the Federal Trust Company and used their stock holdings of the Park National Bank as collateral. The extent to which these details were known to the public is uncertain, but the rumors certainly resulted in a deterioration in confidence regarding the Park National Bank. Sizable withdrawals from the Park National Bank took place on Saturday, November 13, and all signs indicated that a severe run on the bank would occur the following Monday (Roberts 1926c).

These developments occurred just as a set of investors, led by a Mr. Randall, were poised to purchase and take over the bank. There was an active proposal for Mr. Randall and his associates to purchase 335 of the existing 500 shares of the bank and thereby acquire a controlling interest. The main item in the agreement that still needed to be worked out was determining exactly how many of the bad and questionable assets would be absorbed by the existing shareholders and how many by the new shareholders (Roberts 1926c). Regulators believed that the offer by Mr. Randall and his associates was financially solid, but whether it would be accepted by existing shareholders was unknown as of the morning of Sunday, November 14. Moreover, it was also unclear whether any agreed-to distribution of losses would put the bank on a solid enough footing to allow the new management to make a go of it. (Indeed, bank regulators may well have wondered about the quality of the new management team itself and its ability to face the challenge before it.)

Amid this extreme level of uncertainty about the prospects of the bank, Federal Reserve officials (Mr. Worthington, deputy governor, and Mr. Barley, head of the Discount Department); officials from the examiner's office at the comptroller of the currency (Mr. Roberts, chief national bank examiner of the district); the existing bank management and board of directors; and the prospective bank management met at the offices of the chief examiner on Sunday. It was apparent to all that an agreement needed to be reached and arrangements made to meet the expected exodus of depositors when the Park National Bank opened at 9:00 a.m. the next day. Negotiations lasted all day and well into the night. Nevertheless, at the end of it, an agreement was made to sell the bank, and Federal Reserve officials decided that the prospects for the bank were satisfactorily bright and that sufficient collateral was available that they felt comfortable providing support. With these agreements and understandings in place, the parties turned to preparing to meet the anticipated depositor run.

Officials and bank officers were right to anticipate a run. Even before the bank opened, an estimated two hundred depositors had queued up outside the bank with their withdrawal slips in hand. Local newspapers described the pageantry that took place on Monday morning as the Federal Reserve and the commercial bank acted to restore confidence:[14]

> Nicely timed at exactly 9 o'clock the sirens of motorcycle patrolmen came screeching from the north. They swooped down in front of the bank, came to a quick stop and formed a circle around a vehicle they were escorting. It was an

armored truck from the Federal Reserve Bank. (*La Plata Home Press*, November 18, 1926, 1)

A lane was formed to the bank door and a stream of money poured out of the armored truck and into the bank. There were sacks of bills, big sacks in which a large man could have been tied up. There were little sacks of clinking gold, middle sized sacks of silver dollars, halves, and quarters. (*Kansas City Star*, November 15, 1926, 1)

When the institution opened its doors this morning there were several hundred depositors waiting in line, most of them with checks in their hands ready to withdraw deposits. But when the doors were opened, just inside the bank stood two little girls with arm loads of flowers to be presented to customers. While in plain view was a huge stack of bills, silver and gold, which had been rushed to the bank from the Federal Reserve. (*Warrensburg Star-Journal*, November 16, 1926, 6)

When the doors to the bank opened, depositors still lined up to withdraw their funds, though perhaps with less urgency than before the arrival of the armored car. Governor Bailey reports, "It was then that I mounted a chair in the rear of the room and called the attention of the crowd to the information we had regarding the soundness of the bank, stating who I was, and telling them that the three men heretofore mentioned [Mr. Worthington, Mr. Barley, and Mr. L. K. Roberts] had spent most of Sunday and Sunday night examining the bills receivable and the general condition of the bank" (W. Bailey 1927). Governor Bailey went on to state that, because of these examinations, he was confident in the soundness of the bank and was convinced that no depositor who kept their money in the bank would lose a penny. He also stated that the bank was a member of the Federal Reserve System and that FRB Kansas City, with its full resources, was working to keep the bank open.[15]

Early withdrawals were reportedly heavy. Regulators estimated that total withdrawals that day, combined with those on Saturday, totaled more than $100,000 (Roberts 1926c). Total individual deposits in the bank at the time amounted to only around $650,000, so the size of this two-day withdrawal would certainly have severely strained, and likely would have forced a closure of, the bank had support not been provided.

But support was provided, and these efforts did successfully stop the run. Federal Reserve officials reportedly stayed at the bank until midday when the situation had calmed down. Once it was clear that the run had ended and that the bank would remain open, depositors returned, and money began to flow back in. The bank reportedly ended the day with more deposits than it started with.

The bank was saved. Moreover, Federal Reserve officials believed that they had contributed importantly to a broader restoration of confidence in the local banking sector and reversed the deterioration that had followed from the closure of several institutions during the previous week. Governor Bailey reported, "I felt then, and feel now, that we did the very best that could be done, not only for that particular member bank but for the entire banking structure of this section. . . . We re-established the confidence of the outlying communities in the solvency of the Kansas City banks. In the afternoon of that day, I was called up over the telephone by Mr. Swinney and other heads of the large banks here, congratulating us on the manner in which we had handled the situation" (W. Bailey 1927). The *Kansas City Star* reported the next day that although the Park National Bank maintained a considerable cash reserve as a precautionary measure and many curious depositors came to visit the bank, there were more deposits made than withdrawals.

Soon thereafter, additional scrutiny of the new owners uncovered an "unsatisfactory past record of certain of these individual purchasers" (Roberts 1926c). Consequently, the regulators facilitated a further reorganization of the bank, which resulted in a Mr. Davis and some investors with whom he was aligned buying the bank on November 22, 1926, less than two weeks after the run. These new owners were viewed as safer and more likely to put the bank on a solid footing. While it is impossible to know how Mr. Randall and his associates would have fared, Mr. Davis and his team proved successful. The bank was still operating at the end of 1928, with Mr. Davis still in charge and deposits having held steady or increased slightly.

Polk County National Bank (Charter 4627), Bartow, Florida—
August 1926—FRB Atlanta

In the early 1920s, there was a boom in Florida land prices. That boom ended in a spectacular bust in 1926. A number of banks had been heavily involved in providing loans to land developers during the boom, and the financial position of many of these banks became precarious in the wake of the fall in land prices.[16] One particularly exposed group of banks centered on two individuals: W. D. Manley of Atlanta and J. R. Anthony of Florida (Garrett 1968); these banks were connected through interlocking boards of directors and lending relationships. Acting as a group had enabled them to lend more during the boom but ultimately led to their collective failure during the bust. As word spread about troubles at this banking group, runs occurred on several banks. Jalil (2015) describes a regional banking panic occurring in Georgia and Florida in July 1926 after the shuttering of the Bankers' Trust Company of Atlanta, a central entity in this group. The closure of the banks in the group resulted in more widespread concerns about the condition of the banking sector and the exposure of other banks to real estate. Fears about the possibility that runs might spread led many banks to boost the amount of cash they had on hand, including by drawing down the funds they typically held at correspondent banks; that in turn put pressure on the cash holdings of these correspondent banks.

Against this backdrop, FRB Atlanta officials became particularly concerned about the Polk County National Bank of Bartow, Florida. The bank was considered to be in fairly sound condition overall. It had a net worth of about $360,000 against assets of $3 million, so the associated capital ratio of nearly 12 percent was reasonably high. On the April 1926 examination report, the examiner stated that the bank was solvent and that the management was safe.[17] The bank's loan portfolio was described as including loans to fruit growers, automobile dealers, and real estate developers. Such a portfolio suggests some exposure to the real estate boom and bust, but at that time the examiner did not flag any particular concerns about loan or asset quality.

The bank's liquidity position, though, left something to be desired. The examiner reported, "Over a long period it has been the policy of the bank to indulge in a large loan account in proportion to their deposits, this was eminently true on date of examination. They have refrained from investing in high grade bonds as a means of secondary reserve, their eagerness for large profits, which are always paid out in dividends each year, has, it seems to me, kept them from carrying a secondary reserve" (Examiner Report, April 27, 1926). Examiners were concerned that this lack of a ready source of liquid assets would leave the bank particularly exposed should confidence in it deteriorate and a run occur.

That is exactly what occurred in the late summer, and the situation rapidly deteriorated. Federal Reserve officials were greatly concerned about the potential that troubles at the bank would spread to other banks. The

Polk County National Bank was viewed as a "key bank" whose suspen-sion might cause other closures. Garrett (1968) indicates that Federal Re-serve officials had identified at least three other banks in the area as being likely to close if the Polk County National Bank was forced to suspend operations. Nor were Federal Reserve officials alone in being concerned about contagion. A telegram dated August 3, 1926, from Comptroller J. W. McIntosh to Examiner V. H. Northcutt stated, "It is reported that [Char-ter] 4627 [Polk County National Bank] may be badly in need of funds and in the event that anything should happen to it, it would take down some eight or ten banks with it."

In early August, officials from the Federal Reserve and the OCC were sent to investigate conditions in Bartow to better understand the situa-tion (Garrett 1968). Among other precautionary actions, Federal Reserve officials ascertained the available collateral that could be pledged to the Federal Reserve or to commercial banks if the Polk County National Bank needed to borrow to raise cash. The manager of the Jacksonville branch of FRB Atlanta determined that the Polk County National Bank had $635,000 in paper that could be made eligible for rediscount (though some of it was held by banks in New York or in Tampa, and some adjust-ments might be needed to maximize the ability of the Polk County Na-tional Bank to borrow on a secured basis; see Northcutt 1926).

A national bank examiner who was part of the investigative group re-ported that deposits at the bank had fallen by about $800,000 in the three months since the mid-April examination. That was a precipitous drop that represented nearly one-third of the bank's deposit base. A small portion of these deposit withdrawals were able to be covered by loan paydowns, but the vast majority were covered by borrowings from the Federal Re-serve and from correspondent commercial banks. Garrett (1968, 294) re-ports that early in the stress period the bank needed to borrow $200,000 from the Federal Reserve, up from zero at the time of the April examina-tion, and $500,000 from its correspondents in New York and other cities.

Conditions at the bank continued to deteriorate, and a few days later, a meeting was held for representatives from the Polk County National Bank, an affiliated bank from Avon Park, the Federal Reserve, the OCC, and a large Tampa bank that served as a correspondent for the Polk County Na-tional Bank. The Polk County National Bank had provided some liquidity support to the affiliated bank and its network. The assembled bankers and regulators agreed that funds would be advanced to allow that support to be removed from the balance sheet of the Polk County National Bank. It was also agreed that the Federal Reserve and the commercial correspondent banks would provide liquidity assistance.

These actions and support calmed the situation and enabled the Polk County National Bank to weather the crisis. The exact amount of funding provided by the Federal Reserve at the peak of the run on the bank is unclear. However, when it was examined on November 17, 1926, several months after the run had ended, the Polk County National Bank was still indebted to the Federal Reserve for over $345,000 and to other banks for $280,000. Individual deposits were $540,000 lower than at the time of the previous examination. That suggests that some deposits had returned to the bank relative to what the examiner reported on August 3, but the bank may still have been struggling to adapt to new funding levels.

Over time, the bank was able to pay down its borrowing from FRB Atlanta. Federal Reserve officials deemed their support of the bank to have been a success. However, this success proved unfortunately short-lived, as the bank was forced to close permanently during the 1929 fruit fly episode.

City National Bank (Charter 7514), El Paso, Texas—
January 1924—FRB Dallas

The boom and bust of the early 1920s was particularly pronounced in the area around El Paso.[18] As with many other places, this region was swept up in the agricultural boom, with cattle prices being particularly important. In addition, nearby Fort Bliss served as one of the chief bases for the War Department's operations, and the population of El Paso surged as a result. Economic activity jumped, while real estate values and residential construction soared. Amid an influx of deposits, the banking sector expanded rapidly to support these activities.

The collapse after the end of World War I was equally dramatic. As the War Department scaled down operations at Fort Bliss, people left and business activity declined. Real estate values fell, especially for residential properties, where the stock of housing built for the wartime population was found to have notably exceeded the steady-state demand for accommodations. A drought devastated the livestock industry. A Federal Reserve agent surveying conditions in 1922 characterized them as pitiful as grazing areas dried up and cattle starved in the fields, becoming too unhealthy to be moved to greener pastures (Reordan 1922). The local economic collapse took a toll on the banking industry. The banks worked to sustain local businesses and farmers, but losses accumulated as borrowers struggled to meet their obligations.

The City National Bank was one of the largest banks in El Paso, with assets of about $9 million; it held nearly one-fourth of the deposits in the city. Only the First National Bank, with assets of $15 million, was larger. The City National Bank had a net worth of only about $560,000. That meant that the bank's leverage was high, though not much above the leverage of other banks in the area.

The troubles at this bank resulted from its acquisition of the El Paso Bank and Trust Company near the start of the decade.[19] The El Paso Bank and Trust had been insolvent, and the banking authorities were seeking to deal with the institution without liquidating it. The City National Bank and the Texas commissioner of insurance and banking reached an agreement in which the City National Bank would take over the El Paso Bank and Trust and split the losses with the Texas Guaranty Fund. However, amid ongoing troubles in the agricultural sector, the assets of the El Paso Bank and Trust turned out to be worth even less than had been expected, and the increase in business that the City National Bank had hoped would result from the acquisition never materialized. Moreover, the local economic challenges resulted in a deterioration in the quality of the City National Bank's own asset portfolio.

Although the City National Bank struggled to digest its acquisition, bank examiners generally had positive opinions of the management's ability to handle it. In examination reports from 1922 and early 1923, the management of the City National Bank was characterized as "safe" and the bank directors as being very good and attentive to the bank's affairs. While the asset problems were acknowledged, the bank was considered solvent.[20] These views were summarized in the May 1923 examination report, where the examiner noted, "The bank acquired quite a burden when they took over the El Paso Bank & Trust. However, the management has been working very hard on this stuff and will work all of this out within a reasonable time." Unfortunately, the situation proved unsustainable, and the condition of the bank deteriorated in late 1923 and early 1924.

The City National Bank was not the only bank in the region to experience issues. In February 1924, the examiner reported that rumors were circulating about troubles at several other banks in El Paso. There were a number of bank failures in the vicinity. Local newspapers reported that in December 1923 and January 1924, one bank was closed in Pecos, Texas; three banks in Silver City, New Mexico; one bank in Tyrone, New Mexico;

and one bank in Roswell, New Mexico (see *Pecos Enterprise*, February 1, 1924; *Alamogordo Daily News*, January 10, 1924; January 31, 1924). These bank failures resulted in a further deterioration in confidence in the local banking sector.

The instability of the situation and potential for it to get further out of hand was a serious concern of Federal Reserve officials. The minutes of the Board of Directors of FRB Dallas contain several discussions of the unsettled nature of the situation. The directors in particular noted that the failure of a few specific banks had "added to the general unrest in New Mexico, [and] has accentuated the great concern that we have for that section of the district" (FRB Dallas 1920–1929, February 7, 1924). The fact that several of the banks that closed were not viewed as particularly leveraged or otherwise in poor shape may have supported the belief that efforts would be needed to maintain the confidence of depositors.

In January 1924, rumors that the City National Bank was in trouble became more widespread and withdrawals became persistent (Examiner Report, February 1924; Kilman 1961).[21] A large-scale run occurred on Saturday, January 26, and the bank only survived because it closed early. Attempts by the city's leading bankers to arrange a private solution whereby the First National Bank of El Paso would take over the City National Bank were unsuccessful. The situation was dire, and without emergency support the bank would be unable to open on Monday. Governor Buckner McKinney, head of FRB Dallas, took the train to reach El Paso on Sunday. Bank Examiner Stanley Longmoor, who was on the scene, sent a coded message to the regional head office in Dallas requesting the presence of Chief Examiner Richard Collier, who also hurried to the scene.[22]

It was clear that the City National Bank needed liquidity. It also needed a capital injection; the examiners on hand (Longmoor reported that he was joined by Examiners Henry Brewer and Alexander McCans, to help in assessing the situation) believed that losses totaled around $900,000, well above the net worth of the bank. Wyatt (1924) reported that the managers of the bank reached out to the community to raise capital. In doing so, they reportedly told the citizens of El Paso that the Federal Reserve would be purchasing, without recourse, $500,000 in bad assets from the bank. After being told this, the citizens of El Paso were willing to provide support to help save the bank. These citizens, mostly local businessmen, pledged $300,000 to buy, without recourse, assets from the City National Bank (Wyatt 1924).

Wyatt goes on to state that the idea that the Federal Reserve might make such a purchase came as a complete surprise to Governor McKinney when he arrived in town. That the citizens had contributed with the understanding that the Federal Reserve would be doing the same made Governor McKinney's position even more challenging. However, he immediately and repeatedly refused to purchase any assets, stating that he could not lawfully purchase, without recourse, bad assets from the City National Bank.[23] Nevertheless, Governor McKinney did want to prevent the failure of the bank and entered into discussions about what could be done.

After lengthy negotiations, at around 11:00 p.m. on Sunday, FRB Dallas and the City National Bank reached an agreement about support. The arrangement was highly unusual. As described by Wyatt (1924), to ensure that sufficient cash was available to allow the bank to open, FRB Dallas agreed to make a deposit of $500,000 in the City National Bank. As security, FRB Dallas was to receive "full benefit" of a 100 percent assessment against existing shareholders ($500,000), which would be paid to FRB Dallas as it was received, and that $500,000 of paper that had already been charged off but upon which efforts to collect were continuing would be provided to the Federal Reserve as additional collateral.[24] Further, the directors of the City National Bank also agreed that FRB Dallas would have first and prior lien on the assets of the bank in the event that the bank suspended before all of the assessment was paid in.

The examiners estimated that these injections—$500,000 from the assessment on the shareholders and $300,000 from local citizens—plus various existing loss reserves in the bank would likely be sufficient to remove the bank's remaining bad assets. The liquidity provided by the Federal Reserve would enable the bank to open and provide time for the assessment to be collected.

There was also a change in the management of the bank. The old president and chair of the bank's board of directors were removed and new ones installed. The new president was well known to the Federal Reserve; he stepped down from his role as manager of the El Paso branch of FRB Dallas to take the job (City National Bank of El Paso 1924).

The Federal Reserve Board in Washington, DC, supported the efforts to stabilize the situation in El Paso. In the midst of the intense discussions, Governor Daniel Crissinger sent a telegram strongly supporting the actions being contemplated by FRB Dallas (there were communication issues between El Paso and Washington, DC, that evening. The telegram that made it through was to President James McNary of the First National Bank of El Paso, to be relayed to FRB Dallas officials):[25]

It is not possible to get the Board together tonight. Several do not answer phone. I am of the opinion that Board will offer no objection to anything Mr. McKinney may do in the exercise of his judgement to save the situation. Board will no doubt approve liberality on the part of McKinney that will be helpful. Board has no power to order McKinney to do things requested, but will be highly pleased if by going to the limit dictated by his judgement the situation can be saved. Willing to bring before Board early in morning. (Crissinger 1924)

Governor McKinney subsequently spoke to Governor Crissinger by phone, relaying to him the plan for a deposit and warning him that it had the potential to result in losses to the Federal Reserve. Governor McKinney reported that Governor Crissinger remained supportive of the actions of FRB Dallas even with this warning (McKinney 1924a).

A press release was issued to bolster confidence in the institution. On Monday, a full-page advertisement-style statement appeared in local newspapers expressing the regulator's confidence in the bank. The statement read:

> The national bank examiner has just completed a very careful examination of the City National Bank, El Paso, Texas, and all vital conditions imposed have been met and all assets estimated by the examiner to be of questionable solvency have been eliminated.
>
> As a result of this examination the examiner is wholly satisfied as to the solvency of the bank. It possesses ample cash resources for its current needs.
>
> The examiner expresses gratification of the noble response of the citizenship of El Paso in bringing about an adjustment that insures an institution of value to the community.

> Signed,
> R. H. Collier
> Chief National Bank Examiner
> S. A. Longmoor
> National Bank Examiner
> (*El Paso Times*, January 28, 1924, 7)

Moreover, an article in the newspaper reported that the Federal Reserve System was standing behind the bank and providing it the support "it is properly entitled to as a member of the great Federal Reserve system" (*El Paso Times*, January 28, 1924, 1). As part of that support, the newspaper stated, $1 million in cash was being delivered to the bank from the vaults of the Federal Reserve.[26]

The regulators' actions succeeded in stopping the run on the City National Bank. The bank remained open and does not appear to have faced further significant withdrawal pressures. Indeed, neither newspaper reports nor correspondence among banking regulators indicate unusual strains on the banking system in that city during the next few months. (But conditions in the wider region remained precarious. Just a week later, Federal Reserve officials were in Albuquerque, New Mexico, to respond to another crisis there.)[27]

The decision to intervene was driven importantly by concerns about the stability of the banking system around El Paso. The officials of FRB Dallas were convinced that, had they not intervened, the instability would have spread and caused a serious regional financial shock: "The bank's [City National] deposits were about five and half millions of dollars. It has been a very popular institution in El Paso and a very prominent factor in the development of that section of the country; its failure would have been very disastrous to the community and beyond question swept down other institutions. Just where the effect of its closing would have ended we can only surmise" (FRB Dallas 1920–1929, February 7, 1924). FRB Dallas, along with the citizens of El Paso, who provided needed equity, "responded nobly in an emergency and averted a crisis," in the words of Examiner Longmoor.

While the intervention succeeded in preventing a disorderly collapse and a spreading panic, the final result was an orderly failure of the City National Bank rather than a return to profitability. The bank suspended operations and was placed into receivership in May 1924. The bank's total losses were on the order of $2 million, well in excess of the $800,000 estimated by the examiners just a few months earlier. Still, the suspension in May appears to have involved minimal spillovers and did not cause a widespread regional panic.[28] McNary (1924) stated that the limited spillovers and orderly nature of the closure occurred as the citizens of El Paso had come to expect the closure of City National; had that bank closed in a disorderly manner in January, the officers of the First National Bank believed that the effect would have been disastrous. Thus, it seems that the actions of FRB Dallas accomplished the main goal of Federal Reserve officials.

There turned out to be significant challenges in realizing on the assets of the City National Bank and on the assessments of the shareholders. Efforts by FRB Dallas to smooth the job of the receiver involved a will-

ingness to write off some of its claims. In its TBSR, FRB Dallas noted
that doing so resulted in losses totaling $100,000.[29] Despite the efforts by
Federal Reserve officials, the process of dealing with residual claims and
collateral became bogged down in prolonged litigation and prevented
resources at the bank from being usefully redeployed in the community
(FRB Dallas 1926). Hence, the Reserve Bank viewed this episode as only
a partial success.

Stock Yards National Bank (Charter 6732), South St. Paul,
Minnesota—1920 to 1921—FRB Minneapolis

The Stock Yards National Bank was a notable bank in the financial circles
of the Twin Cities metropolitan area. With assets of nearly $7 million, it
was a midsize institution: not one of the largest—those banks had assets
of as much as $100 million—but certainly not the smallest bank either.

The Stock Yards National Bank stood out in its prominence in the region's livestock industry and the proportion of its activities that involved
connections with other banks. When they reviewed the bank in 1919 and
1920, examiners noted that it maintained its own sizable operations involving the financing of livestock activities—such as the feeding and mar-
keting of horses, sheep, and hogs—and also that it played a role in supporting the operations of smaller town banks involved in these activities.
For some of these banks, the Stock Yards National Bank provided liquidity directly through loans or purchases of certificates of deposit offered
by those banks. In other cases, the exposure was indirect, such as through
rediscounting or purchasing loans made by those banks.[30] The network of
smaller town banks that the Stock Yards National Bank maintained was
quite extensive, spanning most of the Ninth Federal Reserve District. The
examiner estimated that these direct and indirect exposures added up to
nearly $3 million, equal to about three-fourths of the bank's loan book. In
addition, in July 1920 the examiner reported that 425 respondent banks
maintained accounts at the Stock Yards National Bank, with the total balance of these accounts being $1.9 million. (The number of accounts had
been growing rapidly; at the start of 1919, the examiner reported that the
bank had 315 respondent accounts.) Thus, nearly one-third of the bank's
liabilities consisted of interbank deposits. Finally, the Stock Yards National Bank itself maintained correspondent connections with 22 banks,
which would have provided valuable links to the payment system for the
bank's many respondents.

The examiner thought that the bank was well run in 1919, near the peak of the agricultural boom: "Loans are generously and yet judiciously placed and the various lines are being frequently checked and the property inspected by a staff of field examiners and the executive force of the bank. The credit files are complete and exhaustive in information concerning the worth, and personal habits and financial history of borrowers, and there is every evidence of care, and conservatism in the conduct of the bank, and of every precaution being taken to confine the element of risk to the minimum" (Examiner Report, January 1919).

In the early 1920s, through both its direct exposures and the exposures of the banks with which it had connections, the Stock Yards National Bank suffered rising asset-quality issues, which reflected the deteriorating conditions in the agricultural sector. Crop prices for corn and wheat remained low. Drought made for difficult livestock feeding conditions in large sections of Montana and the Dakotas. These asset-quality issues showed up on the bank's balance sheet as a sharp rise in the volume of assets characterized by the examiner as either "slow" or "doubtful," which swelled from just under $50,000 in July 1919 to nearly $1,100,000 in July 1921.

Amid these challenges, the managers of the Stock Yards National Bank believed that it was vital to exert considerable effort to support their loan customers. They believed that many of these borrowers were fundamentally sound and would pull through in another year or so; not supporting those customers would result in defaults and immediate losses to the bank. The managers described the situation in a letter to the examiners of the OCC: "No doubt you are aware of the tremendous losses together with low prices which have affected the livestock business in the Northwest the past two years. The winter of 1919–1920 was the hardest winter which our section of the country has had to contend with for thirty years past, and owing to the severe winter and the high price of feed, to safe-guard our loans it was necessary for us to advance money to farmers and ranchmen to protect and keep the livestock growing" (Stock Yards National 1921a).

A follow-up letter, after an examiner criticized the condition of the bank's loan book, put the necessity of continued support by the bank for its customers even more starkly: "We wish to state further, that to force liquidation of many of the loans under criticism, before the natural liquidating period mentioned, would mean destruction to the borrowers and a bad blow to the cattle industry, which, we must all admit, the country at large is vitally interested in, and which needs encouragement in the way of financial aid, especially as before mentioned, until fall liquidation, and also the probable closing of various banks, both National and State, if you would force us to liquidate the loans which you have under criticism" (Stock Yards National 1921b).

FRB Minneapolis agreed with the Stock Yards National Bank that it was imperative for the bank to support its customers. Moreover, FRB Minneapolis believed that it was crucial for the Reserve Bank to support the commercial bank in doing so. Deposits at the Stock Yards National Bank tumbled during the years it experienced difficulties; between January 1920 and February 1921, deposits of individuals fell from $4 million to $2 million, while deposits of country banks fell from $3.3 million to $1 million. (These two categories constituted nearly all the deposits.) Borrowing from the Federal Reserve was a key part of making up the difference. In its TBSR, FRB Minneapolis reported, "The advances of the Federal Reserve bank of Minneapolis were comparatively small in 1919 but as the crisis of 1920 developed, they advanced rapidly to a high point of $1,876,397 in August of that year." In the examination report for July 1921, borrowing from the Federal Reserve was reported to be $1.5 million at a time when the total balance sheet of the bank had fallen to only about $4.75 million; thus, the Federal Reserve was financing nearly one-third of the bank's balance sheet. FRB Minneapolis reported in its TBSR that the bank continued to borrow very heavily until the early part of 1922.

While the support provided to the Stock Yards National Bank was considerable, FRB Minneapolis was also providing considerable support to many of the major Twin Cities banks. In October 1920, the Reserve Bank collected balance sheet statistics from the sixteen largest banks in Minneapolis and St. Paul, which included the Stock Yards National Bank, to compare the Reserve Bank's support for these banks to the support the sixteen banks were providing to country banks (table 5.1). FRB Minneapolis calculated that it was rediscounting nearly $72 million in loans for these sixteen banks, while they in turn were rediscounting over $78 million in loans for the country banks. (For comparison, total assets of these sixteen banks on the 1920 autumn call report, as reported in the Annual Report of the Comptroller of the Currency for 1920, were about $350 million.)

A meeting was held with these banks in the autumn of 1920 to discuss the situation. After this meeting, FRB Minneapolis officials wrote that they considered the extent to which these banks were borrowing from the Reserve Bank to be of serious concern but also to be absolutely necessary. The structure of credit was clear: the farmers needed credit from their

Table 5.1. **Distribution of lending to banks and borrowing from the Federal Reserve in the Twin Cities**

	Lending to country banks ($)	Borrowing from FRB Minneapolis ($)	Capital and surplus ($)	Ratio lending to equity	Ratio borrowing to equity
Bankers National (Mpls)	405,000	241,879	1,000,000	0.4	0.2
First National (Mpls)	17,888,300	27,865,982	10,000,000	1.8	2.8
Lincoln National (Mpls)	701,010	449,217	600,000	1.2	0.8
Metropolitan National (Mpls)	405,000	838,048	600,000	0.7	1.4
Midland National (Mpls)	6,125,000	5,448,886	1,500,000	4.1	3.6
Northwestern National (Mpls)	16,288,469	16,229,872	6,000,000	2.7	2.7
American National (St. Paul)	1,095,371	370,000	500,000	2.2	0.7
Capital National (St. Paul)	2,569,590	4,205,198	1,200,000	2.1	3.5
First National (St. Paul)	13,410,740	6,200,301	5,000,000	2.7	1.2
Merchants National (St. Paul)	10,290,000	7,524,472	3,500,000	2.9	2.2
National Exchange (St. Paul)	196,400	275,000	400,000	0.5	0.7
People's Bank (St. Paul)	681,329	413,900	600,000	1.1	0.7
Twin Cities National (St. Paul)	209,270	182,500	240,000	0.9	0.8
Central Bank (St. Paul)	838,000	276,560	240,000	3.5	1.2
Stock Yards National (S. St. Paul)	6,944,000	1,393,909	500,000	13.9	2.8
Total	78,047,479	71,915,724	31,880,000		

Source: FRB Minneapolis (1921).
Note: Abbreviations: Minneapolis (Mpls) and South St. Paul (S. St. Paul).

local country banks, the local country banks needed support from the major banks in the Twin Cities area, and Federal Reserve provided the foundation of support for the city banks. Not long thereafter, Agent John Rich articulated this thinking in a letter to Governor Harding:

> There is no liquidation and no prospect of liquidation. There is a better disposition to move some of the accumulated grain on the farms, but the proceeds from these sales will be eaten up by the farmers in taking care of current expenses. The average bank has little or nothing to loan and the amount of accommodation the banks can afford the farmers will be considerably less than in previous years. The farmers and stockmen must have support until they are again

in position to take care of themselves. . . . A considerable part of the borrowings of the Twin Cities banks has gone to the assistance of non-member banks.
During 1920 and so far this year, I have not been able to see how this could be
avoided without serious danger to the whole banking situation. . . . During the
past sixteen months, it has been obvious that someone must take care of the
non-members and that the alternative would have been many bank failures, and
that the ultimate source of credit is the Federal Reserve Bank. (Rich 1921)

This statement provides the reasoning for the considerable support that
FRB Minneapolis provided to the Stock Yards National Bank. Given the
bank's extensive connections to other banks, its continued operation and
ability to provide liquidity constituted a critical part of FRB Minneapolis's support for the region.

When providing support, even in the face of the considerable asset-
quality issues, Federal Reserve officials were reassured by the clear efforts
of the bank's owners to stand behind it. The owners were attentive to the
manager's performance, and they made changes as concerns arose that
the bank officers were not up for the challenges facing the bank. A new
president was brought on in May 1921, and a new cashier was installed
about a year later. Shareholders were also willing to contribute additional
equity; in January 1922, they voted to make a voluntary assessment on
themselves of $346,000, about 100 percent of the capital paid in.[31] The
shareholders' strong support was well noted by the examiners, who wrote,
"The interests back of the bank are so large and their action in its behalf
has been so pronounced in the remote and recent past that there is every
reason to believe they intend to stay with the bank and see it through"
(Examiner Report, February 1921).

FRB Minneapolis saw the Federal Reserve's support of the Stock
Yards National Bank as a success.[32] The bank survived the early 1920s and
thrived during the decade. In its TBSR, written several years later in 1927,
FRB Minneapolis reported, "Its present deposits of more than $7,000,000
compare with deposits in July 1921 of only $2,574,000. The bank is at pres-
ent in excellent shape; but could hardly have regained a sound and solvent
position except for the assistance rendered by the Federal Reserve Bank."

*Live Stock National Bank (Charter 5022), Sioux City, Iowa — 1920 —
FRB Chicago*

FRB Chicago's support of the Live Stock National Bank and the rationale
for that support were similar to those of FRB Minneapolis for the Stock

Yards National Bank. The Live Stock National Bank was a midsize bank with assets of about $6.8 million as of 1920, again similar to the Stock Yards National Bank.

The Live Stock National Bank occupied a more prominent place in its community than the Stock Yards National Bank but had less-extensive network connections. Part of the greater prominence was simply that there were fewer banks in Sioux City, and they were less dispersed in size than was the case in the Twin Cities; the Live Stock National Bank was the third-largest bank in the town, with the largest bank being just over twice its size. More importantly, the Live Stock National Bank's role in facilitating transactions in local cattle markets made it critical to the local economy. The examiner noted that the bank typically had a substantial amount of one-day overdrafts resulting from the late-day timing of payments that livestock commission merchants received from sales to meat packers. The relationships between the bank and local traders and merchants that allowed the extension of these overdrafts were thus central to managing this payment process. Since the overdrafts were only overnight, the examiner did not feel the need to criticize them despite their magnitude.

The Live Stock National Bank also played a valuable role in supporting the local livestock industry and extending loans to cattle farmers. As with the Stock Yards National Bank, there was an affiliated cattle company—the Sioux City Cattle Loan Company. This company was quite closely tied to the bank and was reported by the examiner to have an interlocking board of directors and set of officers. In January 1921, the examiner reviewed both companies with an eye toward ascertaining whether inappropriate transactions were taking place between the two companies but found no evidence of it.[33] While the examiner did have some concerns about the close connection between the institutions, he noted, "From a practical standpoint it appears that it is very desirable for the cattle loan company to continue operation in a co-operative manner with the bank more so in view of the fact that both institutions are putting forth their entire efforts toward the financing of the cattle industry."

In 1920, the Live Stock National Bank faced increasing requests to provide loans to cattle ranchers and country banks, while at the same time experiencing challenges maintaining its own funding base. In a letter to the deputy comptroller, the bank's managers noted that many farmers had been unable to sell much of their livestock in the previous year owing to the poor prices and a breakdown in the transportation system. Those difficulties had in turn affected the country banks that did business with the Live Stock National Bank and resulted in those banks being unable to repay many of the extensions of credit from the Live Stock National Bank. That generated requests for additional support. The country banks' need to provide funds to their rancher customers also resulted in these respondent banks reducing the balances they typically maintained at the Live Stock National Bank, which put a fair bit of pressure on the funding base of the Sioux City bank. As a consequence of the need to support existing customers and the challenges in raising the funds required to do so, the bank found itself unable to extend loans to new customers (Live Stock National 1920a, 1920b).

Amid these circumstances, support from the Federal Reserve was critical.[34] In its TBSR, FRB Chicago reported that in 1920 it extended loans to the bank of as much as $1,534,000 (compared with deposits of $2,900,000). The examiner noted in his January 1921 report that borrowing from the Federal Reserve had increased even further to $1.7 million, while deposits had decreased further to $2.6 million.

FRB Chicago reported that its willingness to extend the credit was "based very largely on our confidence in the stockholders' ability to care for any emergency which might arise with the bank" (TBSR). That confidence was key as troubled assets accumulated at the bank. Slow and doubtful assets mentioned in the examination reports snowballed from $81,000 in April 1919 to $225,000 in June 1920 and $1,300,000 in August 1921. At this last date, possible losses threatened to impair the capital of the bank. There were concerns about the ability to raise additional capital through an assessment of shareholders. Instead, the large stockholders of the affiliated Sioux City Cattle Loan Company provided a joint personal guarantee to the Live Stock National Bank against any loss that might occur on cattle paper that had been endorsed by the loan company. Regulators, both the OCC and the Federal Reserve, had concerns about the form and sufficiency of this guarantee, and the legal document underwent several iterations, but eventually a bonding document was structured that was acceptable to all parties, and the regulators were confident that the bank's solvency would be maintained (Live Stock National 1921).

An additional reason that the Federal Reserve retained its confidence in the bank was an improvement in the management. Shareholders ousted the old management in June 1920, as they thought that the bank's problem assets were the result of the managers' poor choices. The new management was considered more competent and materially improved the quality of the bank's asset portfolio in only a year.

The discount window loans extended by FRB Chicago successfully supported the bank. Several years later, the bank was still in existence and operating under the same (new) management, though it remained somewhat smaller in size than had been the case in 1920. FRB Chicago reported, "The assistance we extended helped it very materially in working out an adequate program of readjustment, which was a benefit not only to the bank, but to the live stock industry in general and its customers engaged in that industry" (TBSR).

First National Bank (Charter 2363), Shenandoah, Iowa—1924 to 1926—FRB Chicago

The episode involving the First National Bank in Shenandoah, Iowa, is one of the few examples provided in the TBSR where "success" involved ceasing lending and triggering the closure of the bank. As such, this example provides some insights into the factors that limited the support a Reserve Bank was willing to provide.

The bank was a modestly sized institution in southwest Iowa with assets of $1.7 million. Like many nearby banks, the First National Bank had gotten caught up in the boom in real estate and crop prices at the start of the decade. While the bank's condition was troubled, the managers and owners were not so overwhelmed that the bank clearly needed to be closed; however, they were also not fully able (or perhaps willing) to invest the time or resources to completely put it right. As a result, the bank muddled along for several years.

The challenging state of affairs was clear in 1924. The examination reports and correspondence to the bank from the OCC in that year contain a litany of concerns:

> The report of an examination of your bank completed February 15 shows a very unsatisfactory and extended condition and that no progress has been made since the previous examination in placing your institution in an improved condition. In fact, the objectionable assets have materially increased; the liability on account of rediscounts, bills payable and bonds borrowed has increased . . . overdrafts amounted to $30,889.48, and included the accounts of officers, directors, and their concerns and families, some being in large amounts . . . while the loans dependent upon real estate security taken for debts previously contracted aggregated $237,493.55, most of which are [secured by] second mortgages . . . and there are numerous large lines of a slow and doubtful

character, all of which indicates beyond question that in the past the directors as well as the active management have utterly disregarded the very principles of conservative and safe banking, the result being that the bank is now at the danger point and calls for prompt and efficient action along constructive lines. (Comptroller 1924)

The examiners viewed the managers of the bank skeptically. They characterized Mr. E. Read, the active manager, as a "rather shrewd person [who] is good on making promises but short on fulfilling them" (Examiner Report, August 12, 1924). And further: "On every doubtful loan the Reads have some indefinite story of how it is going to be finally paid but it is always smothered amid a mess of hazy details. They [the managers] will never admit any loss and would have you believe that all the loans will work out when their county again becomes normal." The deflection of blame and promises that things would get better soon (maybe) is apparent in the correspondence the bank sent to the OCC. For example, in one letter, bank officials wrote, "There has been almost no crop movement because of bad roads and low prices, but we believe that the next sixty days will result in the movement of a good deal of corn and subsequent relief. We are giving our best efforts to get our paper in the best shape possible as to security, even though we may not get the money on it" (First National Bank 1924).

The next examination revealed little improvement. That spurred a meeting between the chief national bank examiner of the district and the directors and management of the bank. Again, promises were made, but, as described in a letter from the chief examiner to the comptroller, managers of the bank again fell short (Sims 1924). At the meeting, the directors of the First National Bank outlined a plan to recapitalize the bank through voluntary contributions from existing shareholders. The contributions would be sizable enough to allow the losses estimated by the examiners to be written off, the capital of the bank to increase, and the surplus fund to be restored.

The shares of the bank were tightly held. Of the five hundred equity shares outstanding, three hundred were owned by the president of the bank, Mr. T. Read, who had established the institution some fifty years earlier; twenty shares were owned by his eldest son, Mr. E. Read, who was a vice president and the active manager; and another ten shares were owned by another son, Mr. H. Read. Given their shareholdings, the Read family's pro rata contribution was fairly large. They did not have sufficient cash on hand to make the requisite injection, so they sought to borrow the money from their main correspondent bank in Chicago. However, that bank declined to offer them a loan.

Unable to make their planned equity contribution, the Read family then turned to questioning the classification of certain loans as doubtful by both the recent and previous examiners and asserted that the estimated losses were far in excess of what was likely to occur. This strategy also did not work. The chief examiner opined that the loss estimates were not excessive and that considerable doubtful paper would have to be removed from the bank.

As a final alternative, the Reads asked if they might substitute personal notes for some of the loans about which the examiner had raised questions. In the opinion of the chief examiner, this would not help the bank: "Knowing the dilatory manner in which they [the Read family] do things, such action would probably result in their notes remaining permanently in the files and under the circumstances your Examiner feels that the estimated losses shown by the Examiner should either be charged to the bank's profits and surplus or unconditionally removed by cash capital being paid in the institution" (Sims 1924).[35]

There remained considerable back-and-forth between the bankers and the regulators about dealing with the problems at the bank. The managers would charge off some minimum level of bad assets after each visit by the examiner, but never enough to completely clean the books. Over the subsequent few months, more loan issues would surface, and during the next examination, the examiners' estimates of losses would be about the same as in the previous examination, despite the charge-offs.

One probable reason that regulators exercised forbearance in dealing with this bank was that the owners maintained controlling interests in four other nearby banks. The activities were centered on the First National Bank of Shenandoah, and regulators were concerned that if that bank failed, the other four banks would also be forced to close. The closure of several banks in short succession could trigger a larger loss of confidence in the area and put strains on other banks.

This was the situation into which FRB Chicago was lending. The lending had started in 1919, when the bank was in high standing and the prospects of the community were strong with fertile land and high agricultural prices. Lending by FRB Chicago had peaked in 1920, but the First National Bank had been a perpetual borrower ever since.

An effort to wrest control of the bank from the existing management made some headway in December 1925. Several directors forced the organization of an operating committee that would handle the collection of existing loans to try to liquidate as many as possible and to take an active role in making decisions on loan renewal. However, there is no evidence that they were able to inject any equity into the bank or generate any additional write-offs of the bad debts.

After lending to the bank for years and being attentive to the OCC's efforts to rehabilitate it, FRB Chicago eventually became unwilling to extend discount window loans. In the TBSR, it described its decision:

> The bank at the beginning of the period [since 1919, when it began to borrow] was considered to be in strong condition, its owners having very substantial financial responsibility. Loss in values not only impaired the bank's resources, but also those of the owners. Finally, the bank became land-locked and frozen and further assistance could not be given for two reasons: first, additional eligible paper was not available, and, second, no feasible plan to put the bank in sound condition could be carried through because the entire community lacked the required capital.
>
> In carrying the bank on as we did, we gave it every opportunity to absorb the losses as they were determined, and, while during this period $300,000 of losses were charged out, the bank reached the limit of its own resources and those of its owners. The community during this period was given an opportunity to readjust itself to a large extent. (FRB Chicago, TBSR)

Once FRB Chicago stopped extending discount window loans, the bank was forced to close. A receiver was appointed on May 13, 1926.

First National Bank (Charter 5567), Williston, North Dakota —
October 1923 — FRB Minneapolis

The First National Bank of Williston was located in the northwest part of North Dakota. A number of banks in this area closed in late 1922 and early 1923 after several years of challenging harvests and general economic uncertainty. In the May 1923 examination report for the First National Bank that was written up following the on-site visit, the examiner reported, "One bank in Williston has closed prior to the start of this examination and the Williams County State Bank was on the verge of closing during the examination, and has closed since examination was completed." The closings of the other banks in Williston had left the First National Bank as the only bank in town. While the population of Williston was only about four thousand, it was one of the largest communities in the region. Federal Reserve officials were concerned about a loss of access to banking services in such a town. Moreover, according to the May 1923 examination report, the First National Bank was an important liquidity provider to other banks in the region and played a role in lending to local businesses, farmers, and ranchers. The possible loss of a key liquidity provider was seen as likely to have serious negative effects on the region's banking sector.

The bank was a perpetual borrower from the discount window. FRB Minneapolis noted in its TBSR that the average discount window borrowing was positive in every month between January 1920 and August 1923 (see fig. 5.2). In the second half of 1921, the bank was borrowing amounts of over $300,000. That far exceeded the bank's paid-in capital of $75,000 and funded a significant portion of the bank's $1.7 million in assets.[36]

In the summer of 1923, the bank was in serious trouble. About half of its assets were characterized as slow, doubtful, or otherwise undesirable. The examiner anticipated that the losses the bank would likely incur would completely wipe out its loan loss reserves and seriously impair its capital. OCC officials wrote to the bank on July 13, 1923, stating that unless it took drastic action to improve the situation, a formal notice of a

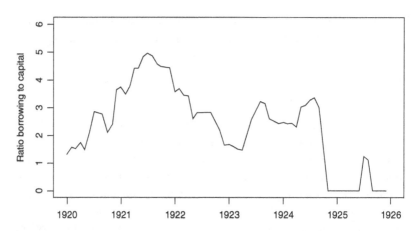

FIGURE 5.2. Borrowing from the Federal Reserve by the First National Bank of Williston relative to capital

Source: FRB Minneapolis, TBSR (1927), for borrowing and Office of the Comptroller of the Currency, *Annual Report*, for capital.

capital impairment would be sent, and shareholders would need to either correct the deficit through an assessment or close the bank.

The bank's management was not of the highest quality, but at the same time, it did seem committed to supporting the bank. The examination report characterized President J. H. Shaw as "not a banker. He is a cattle man" (Examiner Report, May 16, 1923). Nevertheless, he was viewed as honest: "Mr. Shaw has an enviable reputation for honesty and is well considered in the community, in fact wherever he is known." The vice president, W. S. Davidson, was not quite as well regarded. He was characterized as "inclined not to adhere strictly to the truth. More of a trader than a banker. A good collector when forced but until this examination never realized the necessity of a retrenching policy." Still, the examiner was convinced that they would stand behind the banks: "With Shaw and Davidson rests the responsibility of cleaning up this institution. Both would willingly and have offered to give up their entire worth to protect the depositors."

Thus, FRB Minneapolis was confronted with a challenging situation in the second half of 1923. The liquidity situation of the First National Bank was not improving, and there was every sign that the bank's dependence on the discount window would only increase. However, the bank was regionally important, and its closure would leave a larger city in the area without access to banking services and might cause the closure of other nearby banks. It had clear asset-quality issues, and, while it was not yet insolvent, its condition was not trending in a positive direction. The management seemed committed to the bank, but there were concerns about whether it could be relied on. Federal Reserve officials discussed the situation with the national bank examiners, one of whom reported, "On account of the very small liquidation effected by the Williston bank during the past two years, the Federal Reserve Bank seriously, and in my opinion properly, questioned the advisability of making further advances" (Sims 1923). The short-term resolution to the conundrum was to continue to provide funds but ratchet up the requests for protection that would be provided to the Reserve Bank.

In early August 1923, the First National Bank requested additional funds from FRB Minneapolis to cover a shortfall in its reserve. According to a letter from the chief national bank examiner dated August 3, the Federal Reserve agreed to extend additional funds on the condition that several of the directors provide personal guarantees in the form of bonded commitments to cover losses on some assets and protect against losses on other assets. The decision to continue lending appears to have been strongly influenced by concerns about the impact on the regional banking sector: "Had it failed, the disaster would undoubtedly have caused the closing of a number of banks in adjacent territory, and precipitated a very serious situation throughout the region" (FRB Minneapolis, TBSR).

Shortly thereafter, FRB Minneapolis sent a deputy governor to the bank to monitor the situation and help the bank improve its condition. The cashier of the First National Bank described the Federal Reserve official as assisting in lining up collections which would enable the bank to reduce its borrowing from the Federal Reserve. According to the record of borrowing provided by FRB Minneapolis in its TBSR, the seasonal reduction in discount window use by the bank was slightly greater than had been the case in the preceding two years, though borrowing remained considerable. Even so, this visit gave FRB Minneapolis a better view of the condition of the bank.

At the end of October 1923, the public lost confidence in the bank, and a run occurred: "Funds were withdrawn with great rapidity," according to the bank examiner (Examiner Report, October 20, 1923). The bank's reserve was gone, and it was having difficulty repaying money it had borrowed from others.

At this bleak moment, a buyer for the bank emerged. Otto Bremer—a wealthy, well-known, and well-respected banker—and his associates, Alex Stern and George Nelson, indicated an interest in buying the bank. A series of meetings and proposals followed before a reorganization was agreed to on November 1. Under the plan, the old stockholders surrendered their stock ($75,000) and paid a voluntary assessment of 100 percent (another $75,000). The existing surplus ($25,000) was also written down to zero. Local businessmen and former directors donated $125,000 in cash or acceptable paper.[37] Altogether, $300,000 was contributed to remove losses from the bank. The new stockholders provided $75,000 in new capital and indicated their intention to provide for a new surplus of $25,000.[38]

The new management proved quite successful. With the aid of a good harvest, borrowings from the Federal Reserve were completely repaid by the following November. Problem assets took some time to resolve, but the new management dealt with them steadily and seemed committed to supporting the bank: "The Bremer, Stern, and Fowler interests, as your office is aware, throw their financial strength into the breach at Williston, which we all recognize as a key point in North Dakota, and I am inclined to give assets a lenient treatment in view of their assistance as it is possible to do. These people are squarely behind the bank and they are willing to take their losses in addition to what they have already put into the bank" (Examiner Report, September 15, 1924). By the end of the next year, the examiners were describing the bank as being quite successful.

In this situation, FRB Minneapolis clearly benefited from the injection of new equity into the bank and the installation of new management. Nevertheless, Reserve Bank officials pointed out that they had provided critical support that had kept the bank going and thus facilitated this private-sector solution. Moreover, the discount window lending had prevented a disorderly collapse that could have triggered more widespread regional banking distress: "In this instance, the support of the Federal Reserve Bank not only saved this institution, but doubtless stabilized the banking situation over a large area and prevented the failure of a number of banks not directly involved" (FRB Minneapolis, TBSR).

National Bank of Commerce (Charter 10095), Frederick, Oklahoma—1921 to 1926—FRB Kansas City

Located in the cotton-growing region of Oklahoma, the National Bank of Commerce was swept up in the boom and bust of the early 1920s. In the wake of the bust, the bank held a considerable amount of frozen or slow assets. It was forced to borrow from the Federal Reserve and other banks almost continually from 1921 to 1923 to stay afloat.

As with many other banks, the accumulation of bad assets resulted in the need for an assessment of the shareholders. Across the case studies, the owners' reception of the news of a needed assessment ranged considerably: it was met sometimes with a determination by shareholders to save their bank and at other times with a begrudging admission that the assessment was needed. In the case of the National Bank of Commerce, there was unusual resistance.

One of the shareholders, a Mr. Sims, was a "legal resident" of the state penitentiary as a result of his misappropriation of school district funds. Mr. Sims was the former cashier of the bank, and other bank managers had testified against him at his trial. The twenty-five shares of stock that Mr. Sims owned were currently in possession of his wife, who was described as "antagonistic" toward the bank and the managers who had put her husband in jail. The management of the National Bank of Commerce believed that Mr. and Mrs. Sims would "have created, maliciously, considerable comment which would have proved very disastrous to this institution" (Examiner Report, May 1925). Consequently, the assessment notices had not been sent to either Mr. Sims or his wife. Instead, a few large shareholders contributed some funds beyond what was expected of them, and the school district itself advanced some funds ahead of a judgment against Mr. Sims in favor of the district.

While this assessment was completed in early 1925 and helped considerably, it did not fully address the troubles at the bank. In November, the examiner reported that, of the bank's $860,000 in assets, nearly $300,000 was considered slow or doubtful. Losses at the bank were estimated at nearly $12,000, which would have exhausted the minimal surplus and other loss provisions the bank had on hand and again impaired the capital stock. The regulators and the bank's owners and managers held further discussions about whether the shareholders could make another contribution through an assessment or whether some sort of guarantee of the bank's assets might be provided by larger shareholders. These later discussions appear to have involved working through how to best use the resources of shareholders, without the shareholders offering any resistance to supporting the bank.

Dealing with all the issues the bank faced in the early 1920s took its toll on the management and resulted in turnover. In May 1924, the old, "somewhat weak" management was replaced. The examiner expressed high confidence in the new managers, President Childers and Cashier Case: "I have the utmost confidence in the ability and integrity of the present managing officers, W. W. Childers, and R. L. Case. There is no question but [t]hat they are giving the institution every possible attention and are making every effort to work the institution out of its present precarious condition. As your office well knows, their troubles in this institution were inherited from the former management."

By 1923, the National Bank of Commerce had managed to improve its condition enough that it no longer needed to borrow continually from the Federal Reserve; however, borrowing from FRB Kansas City was still necessary for the bank to meet seasonal needs. FRB Kansas City reported in its TBSR that it provided about $200,000 in discount window credit to the bank in 1925 and 1926 to enable it to meet the seasonal surge in loan demand that coincided with seasonal outflows in deposits. The TBSR reported the size of these seasonal swings: the bank's loan book expanded from $342,000 in April 1925 to $528,000 in September, and at the same time, deposits fell from $853,000 to $532,000. Hence, the discount window loan from the Federal Reserve was key to helping the bank manage these swings. (It is also worth noting that the loan from the Federal Reserve was well in excess of the bank's $55,000 in capital and surplus.) Such were the borrowing needs of the bank that FRB Kansas City reported, "During two of the borrowing seasons, their ordinarily eligible and acceptable paper was exhausted, and it was necessary to advance funds on farmers' paper with no other security than the growing cotton crop."

While at times dealing with the National Bank of Commerce was clearly challenging, it ultimately proved successful. The bank was still operating several years later, at the end of 1928. FRB Kansas City considered its willingness to lend key to enabling the bank to have kept operating. The bank "would undoubtably have been forced to close its doors had it not been for the assistance rendered by the Federal Reserve Bank" (FRB Kansas City, TBSR).

Fourth National Bank (Charter 8365), Macon, Georgia —
1920 to 1921 — FRB Atlanta

The Fourth National Bank of Macon, Georgia, was a relatively large bank with assets of over $17 million (as of the call report in 1920). That made it the fourth-largest bank in the state and the largest bank outside of Atlanta by a considerable margin. The bank was important to the local commercial, industrial, and agricultural interests of the surrounding community. The cotton industry featured prominently in the lending of the bank; when examining the roughly $4.7 million in collateral notes held by the bank in February 1920, the examiner estimated that over one-third involved cotton or cotton products.[39]

This bank was also central in the interbank network and was "the correspondent bank for a large number of banks throughout Georgia and adjoining states" (FRB Atlanta, TBSR). In this role, the Fourth National Bank would typically help other banks manage their seasonal issues both by serving as a repository for surplus funds during quiet periods and by providing liquidity when needed, such as at harvest time. Such liquidity was especially needed in 1920 and 1921. FRB Atlanta reported, "Beginning with the depression of 1920 and 1921, and the invasion of the boll weevil, the subject bank [Fourth National], with its numerous bank accounts, not only sustained declines in deposits but was called upon to extend a large volume of credit to its correspondent banks" (TBSR).

The needs of the Fourth National Bank resulted in the bank borrowing significant amounts from the Federal Reserve. FRB Atlanta reported that maximum borrowings reached $3.9 million in 1920 and $3.6 million in 1921. Those amounts were significant for the bank (representing nearly one-fourth of its total assets and more than twice its capital and surplus). That lending was also large enough to be meaningful for the Reserve Bank itself and amounted to nearly 1.5 percent of the total assets (and 3 percent of total bills discounted) of FRB Atlanta in some weeks. FRB Atlanta noted in its TBSR that decisions about extending these loans were influenced by the Fourth National Bank's importance in supporting other banks and that "the credit extended by the Reserve Bank has been of material benefit to the community served by the subject bank."

When extending this credit, FRB Atlanta was attentive to the risks at the bank. Indeed, Federal Reserve Agent Joseph McCord (1920) reports that in late 1920 the Board of Directors of FRB Atlanta, to fully understand the situation, arranged an interview with the examiner who had just reviewed the bank. The examiner assured the Board that the Fourth National Bank was focused on supporting existing customers, including its respondent banks, rather than expanding its activities and was encouraging the existing customers to repay borrowings where possible; however, because of the challenging circumstances in cotton markets, doing so was very difficult. The examiner also assured the Board that, at that time, the bank had ample loss reserves to take care of problem assets. The examiner further stated that attempts by the Federal Reserve to force the Fourth National Bank to repay outstanding discount loans at that time could seriously damage the bank.

Despite these assurances, and unsurprisingly given the economic difficulties in the area, asset-quality issues surfaced at the bank. In early 1921, slow, doubtful, and otherwise undesirable paper at the bank totaled over $2.6 million. Total losses were still expected to be less than $80,000, and the bank had a buffer surplus and undivided profits of $660,000. Nevertheless, the stock of problematic assets had been increasing rapidly and was affecting the bank's profitability.

Part of the willingness of FRB Atlanta to extend credit (in addition to the importance of the bank in the interbank system) was their perception of the bank management's high competence and responsiveness to issues of asset quality. In his report for August 1919, the examiner reported, "The manner in which the officers and directors have adjusted to the numerous criticisms as shown in report of last examination is worthy of commendation. The management is considered highly competent and it would appear that it is not only the wish but the determination of both the official staff and the board of directors to comply with every requirement of law and to meet the wishes of this department [Examiners Department at the OCC] to the best of their ability." The officers of the bank were also characterized as paying close attention to the quality of the loans that the bank was making.

The provision of credit during 1920 and 1921 was viewed as key for supporting both the banking and cotton industries and was highly consistent with other efforts being made by FRB Atlanta (see appendix 4 as well as White 2015; White and Roberds, 2020). Over time, the cotton situation improved, the health of many banks in the region rebounded, and the size of the borrowing needs of the Fourth National diminished.

However, the Fourth National did continue to borrow regularly. Amid the changing environment, FRB Atlanta began to tighten its approach to lending to this bank. As documented in its TBSR, the Reserve Bank became increasingly concerned about the entanglements of the president with other enterprises that drew more and more of his attention. Problematic assets mounted and put the bank in an "unsatisfactory condition." Conferences were held between the officers of the Reserve Bank, the chief national bank examiner of the district, and a committee of the directors of the Fourth National Bank to discuss the future of the bank and particularly of its management. In January 1927, the president of the bank was ousted, and a new president was elected. It was hoped that the new manager would restore the bank to sound condition.

These efforts were not enough. The bank closed and a receiver was appointed on November 26, 1928. That event proved to be a notable shock. Eight small banks that had used the Fourth National Bank as their correspondent bank closed in the next two days amid a "financial scare" and "heavy withdrawals" (*Atlanta Constitution*, November 28, 1928, 4). Substantial withdrawals were also reported by three member banks in Macon—Macon National, the Continental Trust Company, and the Macon branch of the Citizens and Southern National Bank of Savannah—as well as at several nonmember banks. During the morning of November 30, the member banks contacted FRB Atlanta to request large sums of currency. Further requests came in over the course of the day from other member banks in the vicinity (Newton 1928). The nonmember banks reached out to their correspondent banks. FRB Atlanta officials were determined to support the member banks and the community and, out of concern that the situation in Macon could threaten conditions throughout the region, responded immediately; FRB Atlanta provided discount window loans and rushed $6 million in cash to the city (as described in the minutes of the Board of Directors of FRB Atlanta for December 14, 1928). As a result of this rapid action, there was "more currency in the city of Macon tonight than was ever assembled here at any time in the history of the city" (*Atlanta Constitution*, December 1, 1928, 9). Governor Eugene Black of FRB Atlanta journeyed to Macon to meet with the bankers and issued a statement to the press. Supportive statements came from other quarters as well. The *Atlanta Constitution* reported that local businesses, through the Chamber of Commerce, announced that they would continue to take checks on the banks experiencing the runs; that support might have been quite valuable, as it would have reduced the urgency depositors felt to obtain cash.[40] This energetic response appears to have met the demand, as the situation seems to have calmed with no additional bank closures.

First National Bank (Charter 6130), Hugo, Oklahoma—
September 1923—FRB Dallas

The First National Bank of Hugo was a modest-sized bank in southeastern Oklahoma with about $1.5 million in assets. The area was dominated by cotton agriculture, and the bank's fortunes were deeply tied to the development of that crop. The bank suffered notably during the cotton price collapse and then managed to muddle along for a few years thereafter, without ever really getting back on its feet.

For instance, in March 1922, the bank was considered to be in "a very extended and unsatisfactory condition" (Kane 1922). As of June 1922, over 20 percent of the bank's loans were criticized as slow, doubtful, or likely to be a loss (Examiner Report, June 20, 1922). These loans were typically to local farmers. Many of the bank's loans were tied to crops, and the prospects for repayment, or the extent of partial repayment, were heavily dependent on the harvest. In some cases, the loans were secured by real estate, farm equipment, or farm animals (horses and mules), but even here repayment was almost certainly dependent on the harvest as the bank's ability to realize on the collateral was questionable amid the economic malaise in the area. While the bank did make some progress in addressing these issues during 1922, asset issues remained a problem.

The owner and president of the bank was Mr. Rollin D. Wilbor, who also owned or had substantial interests in six other banks in the area (Examiner Report, March 1923). The operations of this group were centered on the First National Bank, so troubles at the bank were considered likely to generate concerns about the condition of the other banks in the group.

Indeed, to the extent that the First National Bank was a vital source of support and liquidity for these other banks, it is almost impossible that troubles in Hugo would not have affected these other institutions. A collapse of this group, in turn, would likely have had negative spillovers for the regional banking system and economy.

Given the potential for spillovers, Federal Reserve officials intervened to try to right the course of the bank and the banks with which it was affiliated. In a letter to Governor Harding of the Federal Reserve Board, Governor McKinney of FRB Dallas indicated that Mr. Wilbor was "a good man and a capable banker, under ordinary circumstances, but the affairs of these seven banks have more or less gotten away from him and they are requiring a good deal of attention at our hands. At my suggestion, Mr. Wilbor recent employed Mr. Fred Emerson, formerly Vice President of the First National Bank of McKinney, Texas, and one of the best young bankers in the state, to assist him in supervising his chain of banks" (McKinney 1922).

Around the same time, Asa Ramsey, the Federal Reserve agent at FRB Dallas, also wrote to Governor Harding. He indicated that in March 1922, Federal Reserve staff examined, or joined examinations led by others, of all seven of the banks associated with Mr. Wilbor to form a view of this group as a whole, especially since the group was borrowing about $1.25 million from FRB Dallas (Ramsey 1922). Federal Reserve staff found that the group faced challenging conditions although for some of the banks the concern was more of a temporary liquidity challenge than a serious solvency issue. As a whole, the view was that the group could pull through with manageable losses and no capital impairments if proper attention was given.

Agent Ramsey (1922) closed with a thought about the coming difficulties, with the cotton harvest half a year away: "We have got a hard row ahead of us. In that country it is almost six months before any large liquidation, but I think all our Oklahoma friends understand that they must do their part and do it valiantly and intelligently if we are to stay with them. We are keeping these banks, as well as every other weak bank, under a daily surveillance and are making every possible effort to see the thing through without any further substantial advances."

As noted by Mr. Ramsey, the bank had borrowed considerably from the Federal Reserve to fund its operations. In December 1922, the examiner reported that the bank was borrowing over $450,000 from the Federal Reserve. That was down from the over $600,000 that the examiners reported that the bank had been borrowing in March 1922 and June 1922; however, it still represented over one-third of the total liabilities of the bank and was about three times its capital and surplus. Given the extent of the bank's borrowing and concerns about its condition, the bank was a frequent subject of discussions by Federal Reserve officials. The minutes of the Board of Directors of FRB Dallas indicate that developments at the First National Bank were reviewed regularly.

In early 1923, the situation was becoming critical. The bank had once again increased its borrowing from the Federal Reserve. At the time of the May 1923 examination, the bank was borrowing $590,000 from FRB Dallas. The examiner from the OCC viewed these funds as essential to the bank's survival: "The Federal Reserve Bank has been the saviour of the situation." The examiner assessed that the bank was currently solvent, but future solvency was dependent on the cotton harvest. At the time of the May examination, the upcoming harvest was considered likely to be favorable, and the examiner thought that, if so, it would strongly support the bank's health. However, the examiner thought that the bank was unlikely to survive if the harvest were to turn out poorly.

In August 1923, time ran out for the bank. On August 28, 1923, the comptroller of the currency sent a telegram to the Federal Reserve agent in Dallas [Lynn Talley] saying that a "critical situation exists in Hugo." The comptroller encouraged the Federal Reserve to "extend assistance to the extreme limit propriety will permit" as "the disturbing effect of a failure there would be very widespread" (Dawes 1923).

Agent Talley assured the comptroller that the Federal Reserve was taking bold action. A series of letters from Talley described how events unfolded. The first letter (Talley 1923a), dated August 29, 1923, reported that while prospects for the cotton crop had been good for most of the year, hot, dry conditions late in the summer caused those prospects to deteriorate markedly. The realization that the cotton crop would not be good demoralized the population of Hugo and heightened their concerns about the health of their banks. "Indiscrete remarks" by one of the directors of the First National Bank started a silent outflow of deposits. The outflow almost completely depleted the cash resources of the First National Bank and of other banks with which President Wilbor was associated and for which the First National Bank was providing liquidity support.

With the cotton harvest very close and still expected to result in some benefit to the community, Talley reported that FRB Dallas had decided to continue to extend discount window loans to support the bank. He noted that Federal Reserve officials believed that "if the situation at Hugo could be steadied with a small amount of additional funds, it would be well to make reasonable further advances to tide the situation over" (Talley 1923a). There were serious concerns that the collapse of the bank could spread and contribute to a wider loss of confidence. However, the ability of FRB Dallas to extend much more support was limited. Talley (1923b) noted, "A feeling of helplessness is occasioned by the fact that the banks have no more eligible paper." The paper that FRB Dallas had rediscounted was not of the best quality, so the First National was asked to pledge additional collateral. This additional collateral was "far from being satisfactory to us, but represents the best security available to the banks to pledge" (Talley 1923c).

Liquidity pressures at the First National Bank continued to mount as its overall condition showed no signs of improving. On Thursday, August 30, Federal Reserve officials held a late-night conference with the management and board of directors of the First National Bank (Talley 1923b). The members of the commercial bank's board of directors were under significant pressures, and "there was a tendency on the part of the Board to disintegrate and each try to save himself." Talley reports offering encouragement and making an effort to "knit the Board back together." Federal Reserve officials wanted the owners and managers of the member banks to work to take primary responsibility for dealing with the situation, and the officials indicated that they would provide support if an agreement was reached by local bankers to do so. Talley indicated that a deal was made whereby if the directors of the First National Bank could raise funds through a voluntary, 100 percent assessment of existing shareholders (i.e., raise another $100,000 in equity), then the Federal Reserve would find a way to provide additional liquidity and would release some of the excess collateral that it held.

Despite some initial optimism about this plan, it fell through. In his next letter, Talley (1923c) reported that the directors of the bank were unable to raise even half of what they had hoped. A new plan was rapidly developed; at an all-day meeting on September 2, an agreement was reached under which the First National Bank would be consolidated immediately with the Hugo National Bank. Given the considerable indebtedness of the First National Bank to FRB Dallas and the claims that FRB Dallas had to the other assets of the bank, the willingness of FRB Dallas to support this consolidation was key to its success.

The consolidation agreement was described in a memo that accompanied the September 5, 1923, letter from Talley. The agreement was as follows: The Hugo National Bank agreed to take over all liabilities of the First National Bank except the $570,000 loan from the Federal Reserve. The remaining capital of the First National Bank would be used to eliminate existing losses of the bank and write down the worst of the assets. The Hugo National Bank would then select $570,000 of the remaining assets of the First National, presumably the worst of those assets, and sell them without recourse to FRB Dallas to extinguish the loan provided by the Reserve Bank. FRB Dallas would retain an interest in other collateral currently pledged by both banks to the Reserve Bank. An employee of the consolidated bank would be tasked with attending to the collection of paper purchased by FRB Dallas. The agreement was reached over the weekend, to be ready for reopening on Monday, September 3.

In agreeing to this arrangement, FRB Dallas effectively absorbed a considerable amount of the risk associated with the acquisition of the First National Bank by the Hugo National Bank. Agent Talley (1923c) described the motivation for this decision: "We felt that the restoration of confidence in Hugo and the vicinity was quite important and that assuredly if the First National Bank of Hugo were permitted to fail it would cause other failures and greatly add to the already difficult situation." Talley notes that FRB Dallas was already lending to many other banks in the region and that if there were a general disturbance, the Reserve Bank would be called upon to provide considerable additional support. If, however, the situation calmed, then the crop could be brought in, and it would be sufficient to bolster the general liquidity of the banks in southeastern Oklahoma and reduce overall indebtedness to the Reserve Bank.

The Board of Directors of FRB Dallas appear to have had similar thoughts; the minutes from September 13, 1923, report: "The serious trend of affairs at the First National Bank of Hugo, Oklahoma, which seemed likely to result in a catastrophe involving a large portion of southeastern Oklahoma in our district, and affect not only the so-called chain of Wilbor banks but also numerous other banking institutions located in that territory which are badly extended and seriously involved to us and to their other creditors" (FRB Dallas 1920–1929, September 13, 1923).

The OCC had also been concerned about the potential spillovers from a disorderly failure of the First National Bank of Hugo. Chief National Bank Examiner Collier stated in a letter to Comptroller Dawes, "The situation in South-eastern Oklahoma is so bad, precarious . . . if anything happened to his [First National Bank President Wilbor's] own bank, it would undoubtedly seriously affect many others" (Collier 1923). William

Hutt, the field examiner who had examined the First National Bank most recently, in his letter to the comptroller stated that the disorderly failure of the First National Bank would have been a systemic event that caused "an already alarming situation to assume chaotic proportions, affecting the entire banking business of this part of District 11" (Hutt 1923).

Federal Reserve and OCC officials made sure to promote the plan and describe the details to encourage public confidence. The newspaper in nearby Antlers, Oklahoma, reported on the episode, including the action taken by FRB Dallas to absorb the weaker paper: "The move was made, it was said, because of the large amount of doubtful paper burdening the First National Bank, and which has been done away with through purchase by the Federal Reserve Bank of Dallas. Thus the institution starts with a clean slate" (*Antlers American*, September 6, 1923, 1).

Overall, the support provided by the Federal Reserve appears to have accomplished the primary purpose of calming the situation. There were no widespread runs or local panic. Talley (1923c) noted that the immediate reports indicated that confidence in the town of Hugo had been fully restored. The fundamental economic problems remained, but the other banks in the town had been given a chance to deal with these issues over time. Examiner Hutt (1923) considered that the "Federal Reserve has saved the banks here and [in the] vicinity" and that "the fear among the depositing element has been allayed, and expressions from bankers, business men and depositors of considerable amounts lead to justification of the statement that no apprehension is now felt in this regard and an increase is reasonably expected in this bank from depositors who are known to have transferred their deposits from Hugo banks to other points."

Preventing the closure of more banks in the region was important for those communities, as well as for the Federal Reserve. Many of those banks were also borrowers. With the cotton harvest approaching and those banks remaining open, not closed because of a local financial panic, the Federal Reserve expected that farmers would be able to repay their loans and that the banks would in turn be able to repay their discount window borrowing: "[By supporting the consolidation] we could have some assurance that other institutions in that section of our district could remain open and obtain anywhere from $400,000 to $500,000 liquidation out of the present crop, of which we would get practically all the benefit in the reduction of their heavy lines" (Talley 1923c).

This success, however, was not without cost. The assets acquired by FRB Dallas were of truly terrible quality. In its TBSR, FRB Dallas indicated that the paper taken as collateral turned out to be essentially worthless, and the Reserve Bank experienced a $500,000 loss on its loan. Had the Federal Reserve not taken the actions it did, the outcome for southeastern Oklahoma would likely have been considerably darker. The examiner for the Hugo National Bank estimated that the bank would have been unable to absorb such a loss and would itself have become insolvent (Examiner Report, December 1926). The failure of the consolidated entity potentially would have triggered the panic the Federal Reserve was trying to avoid.

McCornick and Co., Bankers, Salt Lake City, Utah—May 1921—
FRB San Francisco

In the case of McCornick and Co., Bankers, in Salt Lake City, Utah, the Federal Reserve again intervened to prevent the failure of a bank from causing a considerable disruption. One of the oldest and largest banks in the city, McCornick and Co. had been founded in 1873 by William S. McCornick, who had overseen operations of the bank ever since. Mr. McCornick was a leading figure in the community and one of the foremost financiers in the state. He had not only built a banking business but also played a prominent role in the economic development of the state and in the development of mining operations in particular (*Ogden Standard*, May 19, 1921, 4). His judgment was described as "barometric in the circles of finance," and "his counsel and advice was constantly sought by leaders of commercial and civic development" (*Salt Lake Telegram*, May 19, 1921, 8).

The stress situation occurred when Mr. McCornick passed away on May 18, 1921, at age eighty-four. He had long played a dominant role in the operations of the bank, reportedly even directing much of its business from a sickbed in the hospital just days before his death (*Salt Lake Telegram*, May 19, 1921, 8). There were concerns about the fate of the bank and its ability to endure without his presence.

The bank was a pillar of Salt Lake City's financial structure. In early 1921, McCornick and Co. was the largest bank in the city in terms of lending volume (according to data from *Rand McNally* 1921). It also held a significant volume of banker deposits; indeed, more than 20 percent of all interbank deposits in the city were held by McCornick and Co. (table 5.2). The bank was a member of the Salt Lake City Clearinghouse. In addition, the bank held a sizable number of individual deposits, which suggests that

TABLE 5.2. **Distribution of assets and liabilities of banks in Salt Lake City**

	Loans ($)	Deposits of other banks ($)	Deposits of individuals ($)	Paid-in capital ($)
McCornick and Company	9,448,410	1,553,700	8,024,480	1,000,000
Continental National	3,107,010	979,880	3,008,260	250,000
Deseret National	3,198,480	1,892,850	3,033,230	500,000
National Bank of the Republic	5,600,000	520,000	4,500,000	300,000
National Copper	3,166,520	843,610	3,691,290	300,000
Utah State National	6,968,190	0	6,389,180	1,000,000
Zions Savings	7,652,240	35,520	8,835,730	1,000,000
Walker Brothers	6,463,690	861,240	9,453,660	500,000
Eight other banks	11,617,570	795,590	10,286,660	1,950,900
McCornick and Co.'s share of city total (%)	**16.5**	**21.4**	**14.0**	**14.7**

Source: *Rand McNally Bankers Directory,* January 1921.

many citizens of Salt Lake City would have been affected in the event of a disruption.

While the bank had a long history and was a substantial presence in the community, it was apparently not in very good shape. FRB San Francisco reported in its TBSR that investigations of the bank had uncovered a notable quantity of bad assets. In 1921, out of total loans of about $9,500,000, examiners rated $2,367,000 as slow, $235,000 as doubtful, and $116,000 as loss. This volume of questionable loans far exceeded the bank's capital of $1,000,000. The bank's earnings had been enough to cover admitted losses on a flow basis, but if more of the slow assets soured at the same time, then the bank would have been in deep trouble. FRB San Francisco further stated that there was a sense in banking circles that McCornick and Co. was not in the best shape, though the extent of the difficulties may not have been widely known and the public seems to have been unaware.[41]

With a deterioration in the confidence in the bank, the loss of its imposing founder, and challenging asset issues, it was unlikely that the bank could continue as a stand-alone institution. However, those issues and the sheer size of the bank made finding a merger partner difficult. Deputy Governor William Day (1921) of FRB San Francisco went to Salt Lake City to help oversee the Federal Reserve's response and assess the situation.

Walker Brothers—the next largest bank in the town—was reluctant to take on McCornick and Co.'s loan portfolio. The Utah State National Bank, the largest national bank in the city, was overseen by senior members of the Church of Jesus Christ of Latter-day Saints who could not meet to approve such a risk within the needed time frame. The Deseret National Bank, one of the best-capitalized banks in the city, was not interested. FRB San Francisco reported that the officers of McCornick and Co. sought to work with the local clearinghouse to find a way to resolve the situation; however, no one wanted to take the lead in organizing a response even though the bankers in the city collectively acknowledged that something needed to be done. McCornick and Co.'s size meant that its disorderly failure could potentially cause a major catastrophe in the city. Moreover, the bank held the deposits of numerous small banks in the region, so its failure would have had impacts throughout the state of Utah.

A meeting between officers of McCornick and Co., the banks that were part of the clearinghouse, and the Federal Reserve began at 8:00 p.m. on May 17 and lasted all night. Eventually they reached an agreement that divided the responsibility for the bank among several parties. Important elements of this agreement are described in the TBSR, in the minutes of the Executive Committee of FRB San Francisco (for May 23, 1921), and by Day (1921). Walker Brothers assumed the deposits and liability for borrowed money other than loans and rediscounts with FRB San Francisco and took over the cash and some other good assets of McCornick and Co.[42] FRB San Francisco agreed to maintain existing rediscounts with Mc-Cornick and Co. and to provide an additional $1 million against the choice of sufficient paper to secure the advance and help wind down the bank. The minutes of the Board of Directors of FRB San Francisco indicate that, altogether, after the agreement, the Reserve Bank had outstanding loans and rediscounts to McCornick and Co. of about $4 million. FRB San Francisco also agreed to release a considerable amount of excess collateral that it acquired from McCornick and Co. to Walker Brothers (which Walker Brothers was allowed to rediscount with FRB San Francisco at its discretion). The local clearinghouse banks provided $1 million in capital to establish an "asset realization company" to liquidate that amount of less desirable assets from McCornick and Co. and to guarantee Walker Brothers and FRB San Francisco against loss.

After this arrangement, there was a prompt announcement that, while McCornick and Co. was closing, depositors would be protected and would suffer no losses. A carefully worded statement provided to the press specified that "Walker Brothers Bankers have purchased McCornick and Co., bankers, taking over all assets and assuming all liabilities to depositors" (*Salt Lake City Telegram*, May 18, 1921, 1). Local newspapers reported a smooth transition, noting that "the changes [the moving of accounts and records] were made with hardly a ripple of excitement and with a minimum of disturbance" (*Salt Lake Tribune*, May 20, 1921, 18). They only hinted at the disquiet in the run-up to the announcement by quoting President John Cutler of the Deseret National Bank as saying, "I consider this the best move that could be made. It at once establishes confidence and settles all rumors that have been afloat in the last few days" (*Deseret Evening News*, May 18, 1921, 1).

In the assessment of FRB San Francisco, this action averted a failure that would have been disastrous not only to local Salt Lake City banks but to some sixty smaller country banks that carried deposits aggregating $600,000 with McCornick and Co. FRB San Francisco suggested that it was not alone in its assessment of the likely repercussions of the collapse of McCornick and Co., noting, "Local bankers have freely stated that had this action not been taken, probably every commercial bank [in Salt Lake City] except one would have suspended; thus placing in liquidation deposits amounting to $40,000,000 out of a total of $65,000,000" (FRB San Francisco, TBSR). FRB San Francisco believed that its intervention "saved also the probable suspension of nearly every bank in an important metropolitan area [Salt Lake City], at a time when such failure would have had a far-reaching effect on an already strained situation throughout the Nation."

This action was not costless to FRB San Francisco. While the Reserve Bank acquired the "choice" assets of McCornick and Co., these were nonetheless not of the best quality. It took some time to liquidate these assets, and even then, FRB San Francisco did so at a loss: "Federal Reserve Bank losses estimated at $200,000. It subsequently proved that the bank's assets were far below quality appraised in all examination over a period of years" (FRB San Francisco, TBSR).

The full wind-down of the McCornick and Co. exposure took over a decade. Along the way, FRB San Francisco acquired some unusual assets, such as two hundred shares of the capital stock of the Bank Realty Company of Pioche, Nevada, and the Barboglio Ranch in Emery County, Utah (the sale of which is discussed in FRB San Francisco 1921–1934, April 1, 1926). The administrative burden of dealing with and liquidating these assets was not inconsequential. The final mention in the minutes of the

Board of Directors of FRB San Francisco regarding the disposition of the assets related to McCornick and Co. appears to have been on February 15, 1934, when approval was given to sell a final piece of real estate that had been acquired as part of the collateral associated with this episode.

Summary

From their responses in these episodes, it is apparent that the factors considered by Federal Reserve officials when intervening and the approaches they used to do so are consistent with the statements they made in their TBSRs and other correspondence as described in chapter 4.

Of particular importance were concerns about the stability of the banking sector. In many of the case studies, policymakers referred to the possibility that other banks might be forced to close as a reason for any extraordinary support provided to a bank at the center of an episode. In some situations, the possibility of contagion reflected direct linkages between the institutions through correspondent balances or through the bank's provision of credit or liquidity to the other banks. In a few situations, overlapping ownership or management provided the linkage. In still other cases, the closure of the bank was viewed as likely to trigger a deterioration of confidence in, and possibly runs on, other banks by signaling that solvency issues were more common or deeper than the public might previously have believed.

The Federal Reserve's efforts to prevent contagion and to respond in situations where there was a risk that a deterioration in confidence might spill over to other institutions are particularly noteworthy. As reported above, bank failures were widespread during the 1920s. Larger numbers of bank failures historically contributed to a loss of confidence in the banking sector and could have triggered local banking panics. Such contagion does not appear to have occurred very often in the 1920s. The case studies presented here provide some evidence that the actions taken by the Federal Reserve to head off contagion may have played a role in preventing more widespread panics.

Federal Reserve officials were also concerned about a second factor: the impact of the bank closure on the community. In several instances, the Reserve Banks noted that the bank was one of a few banks, or the only bank, in the community. In these cases, the need to maintain community access to banking services shaped the approach to either keeping the bank in operation or providing time for the community to make alternative arrangements.

As is consistent with the statement of policymakers in chapter 4, assessments of the quality of management informed lending decisions. Federal Reserve officials indicated in correspondence related to the case studies that confidence in the ability of managers to manage their loan portfolio, manage credit risk, and collect on loans that were due was key to the provision of support. Lending to poor-quality managers was seen as providing more opportunities for mismanagement.

Finally, the case studies indicate that the Federal Reserve Banks were highly attuned to the support being provided to the banks by the shareholders or the community. That support could be demonstrated by a willingness to provide equity injections, to purchase bad assets from the bank, or to provide guarantees against losses on certain assets. The policymakers deciding whether to provide extraordinary support frequently pointed to those measures. By contrast, situations where the managers repeatedly put off the provision of support or found reasons not to fully commit were taken as a warning and resulted in the Federal Reserve deciding not to provide support.

CHAPTER SIX

The Experience of the Early 1920s and Changes in Lending Policies

The Reserve Banks considered that, on the whole, the individual cases described in their TBSRs marked successes and that their lending policies achieved generally beneficial outcomes. Support from the Federal Reserve enabled a number of banks to survive stressful situations and return to conducting a respectable banking business. Communities that had been threatened with the loss of important banks, or in some cases all their banks, continued to receive access to intermediation services. Financial stability was preserved, and potential contagion to other banks and regional banking crises were avoided.

Nevertheless, concerns about some outcomes associated with discount window lending in the early 1920s led Federal Reserve policymakers to adjust some of their lending policies. Reserve Banks became less expansive in the provision of discount window loans and asked more questions of the borrowers. There was an effort to develop among member banks a "reluctance to borrow" too much for too long. These changes were not necessarily stark and did not result in an entirely new approach to discount window lending; rather, they appear to represent a tightening of existing procedures.

Those changes occurred shortly before the onset of the Great Depression. The early 1930s were a period of enormous challenges, and banks faced both solvency issues, as they dealt with a collapsing economy, and liquidity pressures amid several banking panics. As a result of this more restrictive approach to lending adopted in the mid-1920s and policymakers' concerns that they might end up repeating the mistakes they believed they had made in the early 1920s, the Federal Reserve Banks may not have provided as much liquidity in response to the stresses in the banking system as they would have had the early 1920s been different.

Concerns regarding Some Outcomes of Discount Window Lending

A central concern of policymakers was that too-easy access to discount window lending would allow banks to borrow enough to avoid disciplinary pressures from competitors or depositors and continue lax business practices. Moreover, policymakers were concerned that extensive reliance on the discount window had resulted in worse outcomes for the Federal Reserve, depositors, or both.

Banks That Continually Relied on the Discount Window

Reserve Bank officials in this period were troubled by the fact that many banks borrowed continuously from the discount window. In the mid-1920s, the Federal Reserve Board began to collect information on the number of banks that had been borrowing continuously for different lengths of time.

In some of the most concerning instances, banks not only borrowed for a long time but borrowed in substantial amounts for a long time. For instance, statistics on the number of member banks borrowing an amount exceeding their capital and surplus for at least a year are presented in table 6.1, along with total borrowers and total member banks. As shown in the table, as of July 1925, over thirty banks had been continuously borrowing substantial amounts from the Federal Reserve for five or more years. Still more had been borrowing continuously for three or four years. These long-term borrowers were concentrated in the Reserve Districts that experienced substantial economic challenges in the early 1920s.

Even more banks had been borrowing for an extended period of time in smaller amounts. Citing statistics from a variety of internal reports, Shull (1971) reports that, as of the end of 1925, 517 banks had been borrowing continuously for more than a year (though not necessarily in amounts exceeding their capital and surplus). That number represented roughly 10 percent of all the banks that used the discount window in 1925. Moreover,

TABLE 6.1. **Continuous borrowers as of July 1925**

FRB	Number of banks borrowing continuously in excess of capital and surplus for at least			Number of member banks borrowing July 1925	Member banks July 1925
	5+ years	3 to 4 years	1 or 2 years		
Boston				169	420
New York				357	868
Philadelphia			3	401	751
Cleveland		1	6	293	863
Richmond		2	2	327	606
Atlanta		2	5	213	502
Chicago	16	42	51	490	1,407
St. Louis			3	222	624
Minneapolis	5	12	15	144	853
Kansas City		2	6	153	1,046
Dallas				200	853
San Francisco	11	12	12	238	751

Source: Board of Governors of the Federal Reserve System, memo from the Division of Bank Operations, "Member Banks Borrowing in Excess of Capital and Surplus during July 1925," September 15, 1925. National Archives, records of the Federal Reserve, "Bank Credit."

Shull reports that a contemporaneous investigation of these continuous borrowers revealed that 239 had been borrowing since 1920.

Policymakers were troubled by this borrowing for a variety of reasons. For instance, it interfered with healthy competition in the banking sector (see Board of Governors 1926a, 4). If the Federal Reserve was providing stable funding to a bank by continuously rolling over a discount window loan (a practice that was termed "adding to the capital" of the borrowing bank), then that might prevent natural adjustments in the banking sector toward more efficient banks. Without funding from the discount window, competition for deposits might have resulted in less efficient bankers being forced to raise loan rates or losing the ability to make certain loans, and those customers would have moved to more efficient banks. Thus, the efficient banks would have grown larger and the inefficient ones would have shrunk. With sustained discount window funding, the inefficient banks were able to make loans and compete with the more efficient banks. Concerns about such distortions to the competitive environment might have been mitigated by the fact that the discount rate was quite expensive relative to deposits. However, the discount window may not have been especially expensive relative to interbank rediscounts, and, if banks knew that they could borrow continuously for an extended period, then the cost of discount window funding might have been attractive.

Relatedly, but perhaps with more serious implications, allowing longer-term borrowing reduced market discipline that banks might normally experience from deposit funding. Depositors paid attention to the riskiness of their banks (remember that this was the era before widespread deposit insurance) and withdrew their funds from banks about which they had solvency concerns. That would normally force risky banks to either improve operations or shrink. However, the ability to borrow continuously from the Federal Reserve would have cushioned the deposit outflows' impact on bank managers and prevented the needed downsizing of poorly managed institutions. While it is socially valuable to prevent banks from having to sell assets in a fire sale amid rapid deposit withdrawals, it is not helpful to prevent banks from having to downsize to deal with longer-term structural issues. FRB Dallas specifically pointed to the concern that providing ongoing discount window lending might support poor risk-management choices: "The additional credit granted brought about no change in the managerial policies which had originally caused the over-extension, but on the contrary operated to widen the scope of those policies and aggravate the evil consequences following therefrom" (TBSR). Concern that too-easy access to the discount window was enabling bad risk management is consistent with an internal Federal Reserve study that found that quite a number of the continuous borrowers were troubled institutions; of the fifty-three continuously borrowing banks analyzed in the study, twenty-nine were described as being in an unsafe or overextended condition (Division of Bank Operations 1925a).

The Federal Reserve Board's *Annual Report* for 1926 also mentioned that sustained extensions of credit to some banks might limit access to the discount window for other banks. While the Federal Reserve Act did not directly limit the amount of discount window credit that could be extended to banks, the Reserve Banks did have their own reserve requirements, so their ability to lend was not unlimited. As noted by White (2015), the amount of lending conducted by some Reserve Ranks in the early 1920s pushed them up against their reserve requirements and necessitated lending between the Reserve Banks to prevent a breach of those requirements.

An internal staff memo from Smead (1926) reports the most common reason for continuous borrowing in several Reserve Districts. FRB Philadelphia reported that a large portion of the continuous borrowers in that district carried a substantial amount of US securities; banks found it a profitable opportunity to borrow at the discount window and invest in

higher-yielding Treasury securities. (This borrowing was occurring well after the Liberty bond drives and after the end of the preferential rate the
Federal Reserve offered to promote the purchase of US Treasury securities.) For the Chicago and San Francisco Districts, borrowing was reportedly due to "an accumulation of non-liquid assets, based mainly on real estate, during the year subsequent to the closing of the war" (Smead 1926).
This reason is entirely in line with the case studies from chapter 5 where
the Federal Reserve provided long-term support to enable banks and
their customers to deal with the results of the bust in agricultural markets.
FRB Kansas City reported that the withdrawal of deposits was the principal reason that banks were continuous borrowers in that district. Thus,
the reasons for sustained borrowing were wide-ranging, but several could
be viewed as consistent with the concerns of Federal Reserve officials that
too-easy access to the discount window was interfering with the ordinary
market dynamics of the banking sector.

Losses to the Reserve Banks

While the lending conducted by the Federal Reserve was secured, in
some cases with additional collateral, it nevertheless entailed some risk.
The borrowing bank could default, and the Reserve Bank could find that
the collateral used to secure the bank's discount window loans was of
poor quality. In that case, the Reserve Bank could incur a loss on its loans.
These asset-quality issues may have been extremely difficult to forecast;
loans linked to agricultural commodities that looked eminently reasonable at the start of the planting season may have become troubled amid
droughts or insect infestations.

The Federal Reserve Board periodically collected information about
losses on discount window loans. Table 6.2 shows losses incurred in the
early 1920s, including losses resulting from the emergency lending in
the episodes from chapter 5. Different accounting procedures across
the Reserve Banks—whether the losses were booked on an annual basis and then netted against any recoveries or were booked only at final
charge-offs—affected the timing of these losses a bit, but it is clear that
the early 1920s were difficult. To put the losses of $1.4 million incurred in
1925 in perspective, gross earnings of the Federal Reserve that year were
$41.8 million, and net earnings, after salaries and other expenses, were
$9.9 million. Hence, the losses on discount loans represented a modest
share of the Federal Reserve's income. Losses in the 1920s were particu-

TABLE 6.2. **Losses on paper of failed banks, by years from organization of system to December 31, 1925 (determined losses actually charged off)**

	Total losses for all Federal Reserve Banks ($ rounded to the nearest thousand)
1920	38,000
1921	263,000
1922	76,000
1923	1,072,000
1924	1,333,000
1925	1,406,000
Reserve for probable losses as of January 1, 1926	4,615,000

Source: Board of Governors of the Federal Reserve System, memo from Mr. Smead to Mr. Eddy, "Losses on Paper of Failed Banks," March 13, 1926. National Archives, records of the Federal Reserve, "Past Due Paper Held by FRBanks."

larly substantial at FRB Atlanta and FRB Dallas, likely because of the exceptional challenges faced by the cotton industry and the importance of that crop in those Districts, but all the Reserve Banks discussed extensively in this book had some losses on their discount window lending during the decade. In this period, the net earnings of the Federal Reserve were used first to pay a 6 percent dividend to the member banks (which were stockholders of the Reserve Banks), then to add to its surplus account (up to a legally specified amount), and then to pay a franchise tax to the US Treasury.[1] Hence, losses to the Federal Reserve ultimately represented lost income to the taxpayer.

In addition to the losses, dealing with the collateral could sometimes cause considerable headaches and result in added expenses for the Reserve Banks. When banks failed and the loans provided as collateral to the Federal Reserve also soured, the Reserve Banks could end up taking possession of physical assets that had been used to secure the loans originally made by the commercial banks. Examples of the long-run challenges of managing seized assets appeared in the case study regarding McCornick and Co. An additional example comes from FRB Dallas, which ended up owning a substantial amount of cattle after defaults by both banks and ranchers. Managing the cattle involved considerable effort, expense, and staff. Indeed, Kilman (1961, 127) reports that the FRB Dallas's insolvent bank department consisted of "4 office employees, 11 field representatives, and 13 livestock inspectors and caretakers." The cattle holdings of FRB Dallas were apparently sufficiently large that efforts to sell them had a meaningful impact on the local market prices, and Kilman reports that there were a number of complaints from the local cattlemen's associations. In a memo from FRB Dallas to the Federal Reserve Board, Grund (1925) details some of the specific challenges of managing several hundred head of cattle acquired from failing banks in New Mexico and arranging their sale. These additional administrative costs and challenges, along with the negative publicity associated with dealing with the collateral, represented real costs to the Federal Reserve and may well have inspired additional caution regarding the approach to lending to troubled banks and the collateral that the Reserve Banks were willing to accept.

Losses to Depositors

Federal Reserve officials were also concerned that lending on a secured basis could exacerbate the losses to the depositors of failed banks. The Federal Reserve often received the best quality assets as collateral, leaving depositors to be repaid from a smaller and lower-quality pool of assets than would have been in place had those assets not been pledged to the Federal Reserve. Discussions of this concern by FRB San Francisco officials are noted in chapter 4.

The Reserve Banks reported on specific situations where creditors of failed banks argued that the collateral holdings of the Reserve Banks were unfairly reducing what they were likely to receive from their claims. For instance, the Billings (Montana) Credit Men's Association lodged a complaint that the collateral taken by the Reserve Bank had indeed worsened losses to depositors at failed banks in that area; FRB Minneapolis responded by compiling statistics to illustrate that any impact was likely trivial (FRB Minneapolis 1923). Depositors of the First National Bank of Hearne argued that FRB Dallas's holdings of collateral were affecting their claims. Those claims complicated the job of the receiver, as some of the bank's borrowers refused to repay loans because the funds would go to the Reserve Bank (located over a hundred miles away) rather than the depositors (who were the borrowers' neighbors); consequently various arrangements were needed to work things out (Freeman 1921). Some hospitalized World War I veterans sent letters to the Federal Reserve arguing that FRB San Francisco's collateralized claims on a bank in Tucson meant that they would lose even more of their life savings (see Coulter 1923). In several of these cases, the creditors argued that the Federal Reserve should have known that the bank was in danger of closing and refused to lend.

Shull (1971) reports that this topic was of general concern and was discussed at a 1925 meeting of the Federal Reserve Board and the Reserve

Bank policymakers, both the governors and the agents. Participants at that meeting noted that "in borrowing [from the Federal Reserve] ... the bank uses the best assets it has and puts him, the depositor, in a less satisfactory position with regard to the additional assets of the bank" (minutes of the Joint Conference of the Federal Reserve Board with the Governors and Chairman and Federal Reserve Agents of the Federal Reserve Banks, November 4–5, 1925, as cited in Shull 1971). The participants opined that, to protect the depositors, the Reserve Banks should monitor the behavior of borrowing banks and keep them from borrowing excessively.[2]

In 1925, H. Parker Willis and several other scholars prepared a review of the banking situation of the 1920s and of Reserve Bank policies (Willis 1925).[3] This report argues that the fact that the Reserve Banks had been taking high-quality collateral had exacerbated losses to depositors. Moreover, the report argued that the least informed depositors were likely to be most strongly affected by those higher loss rates.

The idea that these actions were increasing losses to depositors troubled policymakers. In addition, concerns that negative public perceptions of the Federal Reserve might impair the central bank's ability to act and to provide support in other situations may have made policymakers more cautious in situations where fights over claims on a failing bank's assets might arise.

Changes in Reserve Banks' Approaches to Lending

Several Reserve Banks indicated in their TBSRs that their experiences during the early 1920s led them to change their discount window lending policies. Similar statements appear in other documents as well. The clearest statement to this effect came from FRB Dallas, which detailed its policy changes. These involved closer scrutiny of the banks' operations and reasons for borrowing:

> For several years prior to 1923, the credit policies of this bank had been framed with the thought in mind that a Federal reserve bank could best assist a weak and overextended member by liberal advance of credit in the hope that improved conditions would enable the member to recover a position of soundness and strength. It subsequently developed, however, that our attempts to serve the banks involved in this way merely had the effect of further overextending them ... several years ago we set about changing in a gradual manner the policies previously followed....

Summed up, the practices of a constructive character that we have developed as a means to this end may be described as follows:

1. The inauguration of more frequent conferences with officers and directors of weak banks, holding them in an unhurried manner and permitting the member banks' representatives to indicate the termination of the conference instead of doing so ourselves.
2. The application of pressure for a closer study and analysis by them of the internal causes of their troubles.
3. The assignment of specially trained analysts from our own staff to visit these banks and assist them to analyze their situation with a view of determining remedial measures, and the best uses of their assets.
4. The policy of volunteering the use of our rediscount facility to assist well-managed member banks in local emergencies arising from suspensions of banks in their community or immediate vicinity. (Acceptances of these proffers have been very few indeed, if any.)
5. A careful and sympathetic consideration of all applications for lines of credit with a view of confining advances to such banks and to such amounts as will safeguard the best interests of both the lending and borrowing institutions. (FRB Dallas, TBSR)

FRB Dallas made clear that it was still willing to lend and provide credit, especially in stress situations. Nevertheless, this shift in tone would have been apparent to prospective borrowers, and the higher level of scrutiny would likely have made banks less willing to use the lending facilities offered by the Reserve Bank.

Further evidence that the experiences of the 1920s resulted in changes at FRB Dallas comes from a memo summarizing discussions between FRB Dallas and the First National Bank of El Paso (FRB Dallas 1926). In a request for more support, the First National Bank of El Paso pointed to the support that had been provided to the City National Bank of El Paso. FRB Dallas responded that the situation had not had the desired outcome (see chap. 5) and that, as a result of that experience, FRB Dallas was attempting to avoid lending in situations that involved attempts to restructure a failing bank:

It was pointed out particularly to Mr. Muchinson that what the Federal Reserve Bank of Dallas did and attempted to do in reference to the support of the City National Bank of El Paso was, insofar as results were concerned, wholly ineffective, and even in the attempt of the Federal Reserve Bank to avoid long drawn out and expensive litigation by the sacrifice of $100,000 of its claim in a compromise settlement, litigation ensued notwithstanding, which litigation developed the preference of the Federal Reserve Bank and its right to a full recovery. It was explained that this circumstance, together with similar experienced in lesser degree, had led us to the conclusion that the resources of the Federal Reserve Bank could not be employed for the purpose of attempting to save banks but that they must be reserved and preserved for and employed in the extension of credit as a purely banking function. (FRB Dallas 1926)

Similarly, FRB Minneapolis stated in its TBSR that it had tightened its policies with respect to discount window lending in response to its experience in the early 1920s:

In reply to your telegram of the 5th instant, regarding our policy and experience in meeting requests for assistance to member banks in weakened condition, I beg to say that I believe our experience has caused us to look upon this subject from a somewhat different viewpoint than a few years ago. . . .

Regarding the question as to whether the assistance given by the Reserve Bank was helpful to the member bank and the community served, it can be stated that in a great many cases the assistance extended to member banks saved the bank from closing, but, of course, all member banks that were assisted were by no means saved from ultimately closing. The assistance rendered by the Federal Reserve Bank in the case of a bank that subsequently closed simply prolonged the life of the institution, and our experience leads us to believe that in a majority of cases it would have been for the best interest of all concerned, including the community and Federal Reserve Bank if the member bank had closed at the time the unsatisfactory condition confronting it became evident. (FRB Minneapolis, TBSR)

This shift in view regarding discount window lending is made even starker when compared to the views expressed in early 1921, shortly after the peak in the amount of discount window credit provided by FRB Minneapolis. At that time, the Reserve Bank had in particular noted that it was willing to provide discount window credit for an extended period to support banks experiencing difficulty:

Some of these banks will not get back into safe condition for several years. In a number of cases I am fully satisfied that it will take two years to clean up, and in some cases longer. In the face of these conditions there have been some members, which we felt have borrowed far in excess of a proper line, who have asked for further accommodation, and we have granted it. We have felt that it was wiser in the long run to prevent a member bank of some consequence at a central point from failing than to permit it to close with the probability that in closing it might drag down a string of other banks with it. I feel that in some cases we have been taking some pretty long chances but that we are justified in our action by reason of the necessity of maintaining banking stability and public confidence in this district. (Rich 1921)

The other Reserve Banks are not as explicit regarding the changes in policy, but there was a general sense of a need to be cautious about discount window lending. The dangers of lending to an overextended bank clearly weighed on the minds of Federal Reserve officials. About this time, Federal Reserve agent John Perrin of FRB San Francisco wrote a memo to the Federal Reserve Board on the topic of "Destructive Effect of Over-lending to Member Banks" (1926). At a conference of Reserve Bank governors in November 1926, a discussion of the steps that Federal Reserve Banks could take to prevent member bank failures included cautions against supporting banks in a weakened condition, with discount window support or other methods, and instead emphasized preventing them from getting into trouble in the first place (Conference of Governors 1926).

Shift to Emphasis on "Reluctance to Borrow"

In its *Annual Report* for 1926, the Federal Reserve Board articulated in more detail what it considered the appropriate (and inappropriate) use of the discount window. The Board also articulated the scrutiny that would be applied to banks making too much use of the discount window.

> In using their influence to discourage member banks from making continuous use of the lending facilities of the reserve banks, the operating officials of the reserve banks are not only protecting the resources of the Federal reserve system as a whole, but are also helping individual member banks to conserve their capacity to borrow at the reserve bank at a time when adverse economic conditions in their localities and among their customers may make additional dependence upon the resources of the reserve system not only justifiable but necessary. (Board of Governors 1926a, 5)

While the *Annual Report* does not explicitly say that the policies had been changed, the unusualness of including a whole section on appropriate discount window use would strongly signal to most readers that a change had taken place.

In his history of discount window lending, Shull (1971) describes this new approach as working to create a greater "reluctance to borrow" on the part of member banks than had been the case previously. He reports that the Federal Reserve imposed restrictions to limit continuous borrowing and heightened the questioning of member banks seeking to borrow, with the goal of dissuading excessive use of the discount window. He also points to a shift in policy guidance from the Federal Reserve Board from referencing the rediscounting of short-term paper (i.e., focusing on the collateral being used) to referencing short-term borrowing by the member banks (i.e., focusing on the length of borrowing).

These shifts in the approach to discount window lending were apparent to others outside the Federal Reserve. Keynes (1930, esp. 239–43) reports that around 1925 or 1926, the Reserve Banks were asking "inconvenient questions" and otherwise seeking to dissuade member banks from borrowing regularly from the Federal Reserve. Friedman and Schwartz (1963) also point to a change toward discouraging continuous borrowing in the approach of the Federal Reserve staff. These shifts seem to have been successful in the sense that a "reluctance to borrow" on the part of the banks became more fully established (Shull 1971; Gorton and Metrick 2013).

Unintended Consequences of This Shift in Policy

These shifts to tighten policy influenced how the Federal Reserve provided discount window credit in subsequent years and likely affected how it responded to the Great Depression just a few years later. Some of these shifts in policy may well have influenced the use and perceptions of the discount window for the next several decades.

Possible Effect during the Great Depression

The Great Depression was catastrophic for the banking sector. Thousands of banks were forced to close. There were several large-scale banking panics: one in late 1930, two in 1931, and a truly nationwide event that led to the temporary shuttering of the banking system with President Franklin D. Roosevelt's banking holiday in early 1933. Numerous local events and collapses in confidence also triggered runs on banks. During these panics and idiosyncratic runs, bank liquidity was strained as depositors withdrew their funds. To shore up their ability to meet unexpected deposit withdrawals, the banks reduced their lending to one another and started to hoard liquid assets.

More expansive lender-of-last-resort policies might have mitigated the effects of the banking panics. One way such policies might have helped was through the direct support of affected banks. For instance, the Federal Reserve could have provided discount window loans to replace funds withdrawn by depositors. Moreover, to the extent that the closure of one bank resulted in a loss of confidence on the part of depositors and triggered withdrawals from nearby banks, Federal Reserve action to prevent the first bank closure might then have prevented subsequent ones as well. Even if the first bank was allowed to close, providing liquidity to the nearby banks affected by the closure might have prevented secondary suspensions.

More expansive discount window lending policies would also have helped by reassuring banks that liquidity would be available when needed. Confidence that they could obtain more cash would have allowed banks to reduce their precautionary cash hoarding. That in turn would have enabled the banks to lend more to one another and to their customers and promoted more favorable credit conditions. This dynamic is very much in line with the thoughts expressed by Representative Beakes during the debates regarding the Federal Reserve Act, as described in chapter 1. Bolstering confidence in the availability of liquidity to dispel fear was also on Congress's mind in the 1930s when it amended the Federal Reserve Act to enhance the Federal Reserve's ability to lend to member banks by expanding the set of assets that could serve as collateral (see Hackley 1973, esp. 84–89).

There is evidence that the more expansive discount window lending policies during this period were beneficial. Richardson and Troost (2009) argue that, when confronted with a banking panic in 1930 after the failure of Caldwell and Company, FRB Atlanta was more willing to use the discount window to provide liquidity than FRB St. Louis. They then look at the experience of banks in Mississippi, a state that was split between the two districts. Richardson and Troost find that banks in the portion of the state located in the Atlanta District were more likely to survive the panic than were the banks in the portion located in the St. Louis District. Ziebarth (2013) finds that these differences in discount window policies and bank outcomes across Mississippi correspond to differences in real economic outcomes, such as output and employment.

The challenge confronting policymakers was that illiquidity was not the only reason that banks closed, and many challenges that had affected bank solvency in the early 1920s were present in the early 1930s. There were once again significant problems in the agricultural sector. Collapsing prices and the environmental shock of the Dust Bowl took their toll on farmers and ranchers and created problems for the banks that had lent to them. Indeed, solvency issues were widespread, and large numbers of bank failures occurred outside the banking panics as tumbling economic activity led to numerous business bankruptcies and borrower defaults. While lender-of-last-resort actions can deal with illiquidity issues, they cannot deal with solvency issues. (Through its lending, a central bank can provide time for other parties to inject equity, but the central bank cannot provide that equity by itself.) Federal Reserve officials may have been concerned that the problems they had experienced in the 1920s of losses to the Federal Reserve (and consequently to the taxpayer) and to depositors would reemerge in force.

Moreover, the solvency and liquidity issues were voluminous and linked. Less financially healthy banks tended to be more exposed to runs. Calomiris and Mason (2003) find that banking-sector fundamentals explain a significant portion of bank closure rates. Policymakers may have viewed the situations in which commercial banks found themselves in the early 1930s as very similar to those of the early 1920s, when, as the case studies make clear, banks were also faced with challenging solvency issues in addition to liquidity issues. As noted above, policymakers viewed their approach to lending in the 1920s as, in some cases, having made the banking problems worse and necessitating a tougher line with respect to liquidity provision at the discount window.

Taking all these considerations into account, in the 1930s Federal Reserve officials may have been more reluctant to provide support to banks that were experiencing problems than they would have if their experiences in the early 1920s had been different. While policymakers believed that their actions had prevented local banking panics from closing banks in the early 1920s, the benefits of doing so were less tangible than the costs of the losses and of some banks becoming dependent on the discount window. An inclination to view the 1930s through the lens of the experiences of the 1920s would also be in line with the tendency to "fight the last war," as described by Grossman and Rockoff (2015). While solvency issues certainly resulted in many bank failures during the 1930s, the "contagion of fear" and the cash hoarding by depositors and by surviving banks that are described by Friedman and Schwartz (1963) and that worried the authors of the Federal Reserve Act may have been at least partly ameliorated by more expansive lending policies.

The Federal Reserve officials' greater reluctance to be expansive in the face of the banking panics would have interacted detrimentally with the member banks' greater reluctance to borrow. The negative connotations associated with the discount window that had been created by the reluctance-to-borrow policy meant that, even in times of stress when there was a systemic liquidity shortage, banks were hesitant to use the discount window to bolster their liquidity position (see Friedman and Schwarz 1963, 318–19; Wheelock 1989). As a consequence, it is likely that the panics were worse than they would otherwise have been and that more banks closed their doors than otherwise would have (Gorton and Metrick 2013). The closure of these banks would have meant a loss of bank-customer relationships and a tightening in the supply of bank credit to the detriment of the economy (Bernanke 1983).

It is worth keeping in mind that more restraint with respect to discount window support did not mean that the Federal Reserve did not provide any support. Indeed, there were certainly instances in which Federal Reserve Banks were quite responsive to financial stresses. As documented by Friedman and Schwarz (1963), FRB New York responded aggressively to the stock market crash of 1929 and made considerable efforts to prevent the failure of the Bank of United States in 1930 and then to cushion any impact on financial markets when that bank did fail. As noted above, Richardson and Troost (2009) show that FRB Atlanta was quite responsive to the panic in 1930, extending credit to member banks and preventing their failure and the failure of nonmember banks in that district. Finally, the use of currency funds to respond to financial strains as reported in appendix 2 also indicates that many Reserve Banks were attentive to financial stresses. Nevertheless, these instances were modest relative to the scale of the shocks that affected the banking system, and they fell well short of the robust response that would have been required to fully offset the financial strains of the panic.

The change in policy regarding discount window lending needs to be viewed in the context of all policies regarding the discount window. The

Reserve Banks' shift toward more restraint with respect to discount window lending was not the only reason that discount window borrowing did not respond robustly to the panics of the Great Depression. Bordo and Wheelock (2013) describe several other reasons, some of which were structural. First, the Federal Reserve Act contained fairly restrictive rules regarding the types of loans and securities that were eligible to serve as collateral. During the Great Depression, many banks exhausted their supply of eligible collateral and were unable to borrow. While the case studies here suggest that, even with that particular constraint, the Federal Reserve Banks figured out ways of providing liquidity—such as through the use of currency funds—it seems unlikely that those strategies would have worked in all cases. The second structural reason was that many banks were not members of the Federal Reserve System and thus were not eligible to use the discount window. While most of the largest banks were members, the panics of the Great Depression hit the small nonmember banks hardest. The large member banks could lend to the nonmember banks and could bolster their own liquidity by borrowing from the Federal Reserve; however, it is unclear to what extent large banks would have been willing to provide that credit to other banks amid widespread solvency issues. Bordo and Wheelock cite a final reason for the lack of a robust response to the banking panics: the policy framework of the Federal Reserve officials. They argue that the high levels of excess reserves in the banking system and the low money market rates convinced Federal Reserve policymakers that there was plenty of liquidity in the financial system. The shift in approach to discount window lending described here should therefore be viewed as an additional factor and not as a substitution for the importance of any factor cited by Bordo and Wheelock.

An economic collapse the size of the Great Depression has numerous contributing factors. Eichengreen (1992) and Eichengreen and Sachs (1985) document the international dimensions of the Great Depression and the harm that efforts to preserve the gold standard did to many economies. Friedman and Schwartz (1963) document the collapse in the money supply, tightening of financial conditions, and as also noted by Wheelock (1991) and Meltzer (2003), the failure of monetary policy to respond with needed vigor. Debt and borrowing in real estate and consumer durables had grown during the 1920s (Olney 1991; White 2009a). With deflation resulting from the collapse in the money supply and tighter financial conditions, households and businesses struggled to repay or refinance these

debts. While the lack of lending of last resort amid the banking panics contributed to the whole of the collapse, it was only one piece among many.

Increased Stigmatization of the Discount Window

The policies meant to increase the reluctance to borrow likely also contributed to the stigma associated with the discount window. As noted in
chapter 3, banks already may have been reluctant to use the discount window in stress situations out of concern that it would send a negative signal
about their condition. Encouraging a reluctance-to-borrow approach to
the discount window may have shifted perceptions and created more concern among bankers that using the discount window would indicate des-
peration and a willingness to endure heightened scrutiny to obtain funds.
That shift in perceptions would reflect increased stigma.

To be sure, greater stigma was not an intended consequence. While the
Reserve Banks did not want banks to borrow too often, they did want
them to be willing to borrow when the need arose. However, as borrowing
became more infrequent, there was a rise in the perception that something was wrong when borrowing occurred. The fact that thousands of
banks still used the discount window in the late 1920s indicates that the
rise in stigma was not extreme, but it seems likely that the change in policies did move perceptions in this direction.

Any increase in stigma would have made the discount window a less
effective crisis response tool. Indeed, Friedman and Schwarz (1963) and
Bordo and Wheelock (2013) argue that stigma did in fact reduce the discount window's effectiveness in responding to crises during the Great
Depression.

Moreover, this aversion to seeking liquidity support could have systemic consequences. Banks may be reluctant to use the discount window
in response to minor stresses, as they may be concerned about being perceived as one of the few banks exposed to that stress or suffering. Instead
of obtaining liquidity support from the central bank, banks may hoard
liquidity, making it difficult for others to obtain. As a result, minor stresses
can persist, liquidity problems can cascade, and minor stresses can turn
into major stresses (Carlson and Rose 2017).[4] Madigan (2009) argues that
this perilous dynamic occurred during the 2008 financial crisis:

> The problem of discount window stigma is real and serious. The intense caution
> that banks displayed in managing their liquidity beginning in early August 2007

was partly a result of their extreme reluctance to rely on standard discount mechanisms. Absent such reluctance, conditions in interbank funding markets may have been significantly less stressed, with less contagion to financial markets more generally. Central banks eventually were able to take measures to partially circumvent this stigma by designing additional lending facilities for depository institutions; but analyzing the problem, developing these programs, and gathering the evidence to support a conclusion that they were necessary took valuable time. (Madigan 2009)

Gorton (2012) and Gorton and Metrick (2013) provide a further discussion of how stigma made the discount window, and other government lending facilities, less effective in crisis situations.

The presence of stigma also makes the discount window less effective as a tool to implement monetary policy. If banks are willing to use the discount window when pressures in money markets push up short-term rates, then that will keep rates closer to the Federal Reserve's target. If the discount window is stigmatized, then banks will not use the window when temporary pressures push money market rates above the levels that the Federal Reserve views as appropriate to meet its monetary policy objectives. Efforts to reduce stigma and make the discount window a more effective monetary policy tool resulted in changes to the discount window in 2003, with the introduction of the current primary credit and secondary credit programs (see Madigan and Nelson, 2002).

CHAPTER SEVEN

Parallels to Modern Times and Lessons for Today

The experiences of the 1920s had a substantial impact on Federal Reserve officials at the time. These episodes also involved approaches and actions that foreshadow those taken by the Federal Reserve in stress situations during more recent times. The parallels in responses reflect the similarities in the issues and challenges faced by policymakers despite the considerable changes in the banking systems. Here, we explore these parallels and the lessons they offer, as well as the implications of some changes in the financial and regulatory system. The lessons are fairly general but are vital nonetheless as they indicate that many of the larger issues involved in crisis responses are universal in nature.

Calming Effect of a Lender of Last Resort Standing Ready as a Backstop

One important lesson is that, in some situations, by making it apparent that ample liquidity is readily available, a lender of last resort can have a considerable impact on the confidence of liability holders and can help ease a crisis and minimize the amount of liquidity that actually needs to be deployed or lent out.[1] These situations tend to be ones where coordination issues or contagion drive the surge in liquidity demand. It is also clear that this publicity needs to be used carefully. Just as the announcement and demonstration of support can be calming in some situations, they can be unsettling and may trigger a run in others.

Bank runs may occur because depositors are concerned about their ability to obtain the full value of their deposits from the bank (because of solvency risk at the bank) or to access those funds in a timely fashion (because of liquidity risk). With solvency risk, depositors are motivated to withdraw because they are concerned that the bank has insufficient good assets to meet all its obligations; the fact that the first depositors to withdraw are paid in full can create a run dynamic (see, for instance, Calomiris and Kahn 1991). With liquidity risk, depositors will withdraw immediately if they know they will need funds in the near future—even if not immediately—because they are concerned that other depositors will exhaust the bank's supply of liquid assets, and the bank will be unable to meet withdrawals promptly even if the solvency of the bank is not in question (Diamond and Dybvig 1983). Solvency concerns and liquidity concerns can interact to create precipitous situations (Morris and Shin 2001; Goldstein and Pauzner, 2005). Where liquidity issues are concerned, the actions of the lender of last resort itself may play a role in the outcome; the extension of credit may allow the bank to survive, while a refusal to extend credit may force closure (Goodhart 1999; Freixas et al. 1999).

There was every reason to think that solvency risk played a part in prompting deposit withdrawals in the 1920s, especially in the absence of widespread deposit insurance. Liquidity risk was likely also a meaningful concern. Upham and Lamke (1934) describe the duties of receivers overseeing closed banks in the period after their appointment; while the receivers were expected to verify the claims of creditors and depositors in the first few weeks, they were not expected to make payouts. If households or businesses feared that a bank closure might make it difficult to obtain funds or to make near-term payments—for example, to purchase necessities or to meet payroll—then that could well have prompted them to hurry to the bank to withdraw funds. Even if some depositors did not need funds immediately, they may have feared that withdrawals by other depositors would force the closure of the bank and freeze the funds there; in that case, the first set of depositors may have sought to withdraw funds as well. In modern times, the Federal Deposit Insurance Corporation (FDIC) ensures not only that covered depositors are protected from loss but also that they will retain timely access to their funds. That protection reduces the incentives to run due to both credit risk and liquidity risk.

Several of the Federal Reserve's emergency responses in the 1920s involved actions to publicly demonstrate that the bank would have ample liquidity to meet withdrawals. This public support appears to have meaningfully contributed to calming situations, sometimes without involving much active liquidity provision by the Federal Reserve. The currency funds used in Boise in 1921 and 1923 are excellent examples of this type of support. The visible presence of the cash appears to have calmed the situation without many discount window loans being required. Similarly, the highly visible manner in which cash was provided to the Park National Bank of Kansas City contributed to calming the situation as much as any other part of the rescue. The calming influence of plentiful liquidity has its limits though. The strains in Tampa in 1929 were severe, and, while the currency fund was helpful, the mere presence of the cash was not sufficient to alleviate the stress.

In the stress situations involving the successful display of ample liquidity, the public nature of that display was key. The fact that all these institutions had access to the discount window to obtain liquidity, and that knowledge of this access was readily available, was not sufficient. It was the prominent public nature of the liquidity support that mattered.

In thinking about the benefits of these public displays, it is helpful to keep in mind the context in which that publicity occurred. The Park National Bank was already under clear pressure when the demonstrations of support were made. When the Federal Reserve established currency funds, it did not identify particular institutions that needed support; instead this extraordinary liquidity provision was portrayed as being general in nature. Hence, the display of liquidity support did not reveal information about challenges faced by any specific banks.

It is equally important to note the situations where support was not made public. In episodes where banks needed longer-term support but there were no sudden pressures, such as the case of the Live Stock National Bank of Sioux City, there were no public statements. Indeed, although the case studies describe certain banks as receiving long-term support, searches of newspapers in the associated communities do not reveal any mention of Federal Reserve support. The lack of news stories is consistent with the idea that indicating support for these institutions might have triggered the sorts of concerns that would have led to a depositor exodus.[2]

In recent times, announcement effects associated with a number of Federal Reserve liquidity support efforts have similarly demonstrated that the availability of liquidity, even before any credit extensions, can have a meaningful supportive effect. A classic example comes from the statement made by the Federal Reserve after the 1987 Stock Market Crash. The statement was simple and straightforward in articulating that the Federal Reserve stood ready to be a liquidity backstop: "The Federal Reserve, consistent with its responsibilities as the Nation's central bank, affirmed today its readiness to serve as a source of liquidity to support the economic and financial system. This announcement reportedly had quite a calming effect and supported market functioning during a turbulent day" (Carlson 2007).

Other situations where the Federal Reserve's presence as a backstop calmed conditions include the 2008 Global Financial Crisis and the financial dislocations in March and April 2020 amid the early days of the COVID-19 pandemic. For instance, announcements about the establishment and expansion of the Term Auction Facility, which provided discount window credit through an auction rather than through a bilateral lending facility, appear to have had beneficial effects even before any loans were made (McAndrews, Sarkar, and Wang 2017; Wu 2011). Similarly, during March 2020, the announcement that the Federal Reserve would provide liquidity through a variety of emergency lending facilities appears to have helped calm markets even before those facilities were fully operational.

Insolvency, Illiquidity, and Collateral

A second lesson is simply that, when providing liquidity support during a financial crisis, a lender of last resort will often find it difficult to fully determine the extent to which the need for support is the result of insolvency versus illiquidity. Some scholars have suggested that making lending decisions based only on the quality of the collateral being posted would be one way of mitigating the concerns about needing to determine whether the borrower is solvent or not. However, when the lender of last resort is providing liquidity on a bilateral basis, such as through loans, the use of collateral can create some difficult issues and have important effects on other creditors of the bank.

The experiences of the Federal Reserve in the 1920s highlight that in some cases it will be impossible to determine whether a bank is solvent at the time it requests funds and whether it will be solvent in the future when the funds need to be repaid. In several of the case studies, the borrowing bank needed funds for an extended period. The solvency of these banks depended on the success of the harvest that would occur several months down the road. Lots of things beyond the banks' control—most obviously the weather—mattered. In the episode involving the Park National Bank of Kansas City, Federal Reserve officials had to make a decision about providing liquidity support while also considering the credibility of an acquisition of the bank. That example further highlights the extreme level of uncertainty under which lending decisions sometimes needed to be made.

In his classic study *The Art of Central Banking*, Hawtrey ([1932] 2005) argues that by focusing on the collateral and only taking good collateral, the central bank can, to a notable extent, avoid making decisions about the solvency of the banks.

> It is not ordinarily possible to examine in detail the entire assets of an applicant for a loan. Demonstration of solvency therefore cannot be made an express condition of the loan, at any rate at a time when the need for cash has become urgent. But the furnishing of security makes scrutiny of the general solvency of the borrower unnecessary. The secured debt being covered by assets more than equivalent to it, there is less need to enquire whether the remainder of the borrower's assets will be sufficient to cover the remainder of his debts. (Hawtrey [1932] 2005, 126–27)

As noted by Freixas et al. (1999), taking collateral can provide protection to the central bank and help mitigate incentive issues that arise because of an asymmetry in the information between the central bank and the commercial bank regarding the true condition of the borrowing bank. They also point out that in these cases, careful margining of the collateral is important to prevent losses.

However, the experiences of the Federal Reserve in the 1920s indicate that this approach is not without its own difficulties. When the Federal Reserve took good collateral, that worsened the position of general creditors such as depositors; if the institution failed, the pool of assets available to repay the depositors would be of lower quality—and would likely have lower recovery rates—than if the lender of last resort had not acted. As noted in chapter 6, depositors of failed banks in the 1920s did indeed claim that the actions of the Federal Reserve had increased the losses they faced.

Additionally, if the depositors are concerned that the lender of last resort will take good collateral and that their claims on the commercial bank will be backed only by lower-quality assets, that might prompt them to hasten to withdraw their funds in advance of any lending by the central bank and worsen the run on the bank. Indeed, Madigan (2009) reports that this dynamic was a concern in 2008. The Federal Reserve authorized the creation of a facility to lend directly to money market funds. However, "representatives of the money fund industry advised the Federal Reserve that money funds would be unwilling to borrow, partly because investors would recognize that leverage would amplify the effects of any fund losses on remaining shareholders and intensify their incentive to run" (Madigan 2009). As a result, this facility was not operationalized.

Disruptive Effects of Bank Failures, the Lender of Last Resort, and the Resolution Regime

A third lesson is that the pressures on the lender of last resort to act depend importantly on the disruptive effects of the bank failures and the presence of a resolution regime to help manage those potential disruptions. The more robust the resolution regime, the less pressure there will be on the lender of last resort.

In the case studies presented in chapter 5, common reasons that Federal Reserve policymakers intervened were related to concerns about the potential disruptive effects of the failure of the commercial bank. Disruptions could occur if the troubled bank was one of the last ones operating in the area or was providing the community with a particularly vital service (as in the cases of the First National Bank of Williston or the Live Stock National Bank of Sioux City). Had the troubled banks been forced to close, the receivership process may have resulted in the loss of important bank-client relationships since that process typically involved winding down the bank (for discussions of the importance of such relationships, see Merwin and Schmidt 1942; Bernanke 1983; Boot 2000). While the case studies describe isolated instances, the challenges in the 1920s were widespread amid the price drops in agricultural markets and the collapse in farm real estate. To prevent the bank failures and the associated disruptions, the Federal Reserve extended liquidity to these banks for considerable periods to enable them to restructure and develop a solid footing. However, doing so appears to have resulted in dependence on the discount window for some banks and in losses to the Federal Reserve. Examples from the case studies include the extended lending to the troubled First National Bank of Shenandoah and lending related to the First National Bank of Hugo, where the Federal Reserve supported a merger and then had to lend at considerable risk to help that new institution survive. In those cases, there may have been better outcomes had regulators had more tools to handle troubled institutions. Indeed, Upham and Lamke (1934) report that additional approaches to bank resolution were developed amid the even more numerous bank failures of the 1930s to reduce problems associated with previous resolution strategies. The tool kit has been expanded further over time as the FDIC has been given additional authority to enable it to resolve banks nondisruptively.

Many of these same issues resurfaced in the late 1980s and early 1990s. During this period, many banks became deeply troubled because of investments in poorly performing commercial real estate (FDIC 1997). In a situation reminiscent of the 1920s, the Federal Reserve provided discount window loans to keep banks afloat while efforts were made to resolve problems in ways that would not cause significant financial disruptions. Schwartz (1992) argues that such lending may have allowed informed and uninsured creditors to withdraw funds from troubled banks; as a consequence, losses at these banks may have increased, which in turn may have increased the losses that had to be borne by the deposit insurance fund. Schwartz draws explicit parallels to the 1920s to argue that central bank lending in situations where troubles are widespread within the banking industry is inherently fraught. Gilbert (1994) notes that the experience of the early 1990s resulted in restrictions on Federal Reserve lending to undercapitalized banks as part of the Federal Deposit Insurance Corporation Improvement Act (FDICIA). Still, it was apparent in this case that the sudden liquidation of all assets of the troubled financial institutions would be disastrous and that longer-term liquidity provision was needed. To allow time to effectively deal with the issues associated with resolving so many troubled institutions without necessitating loans from the Federal Reserve, Congress created a long-term asset management structure in the form of the Resolution Trust Corporation (FDIC 1997).[3]

The disruptive effects of the disorderly failure of a financial institution may be particularly important for highly connected institutions. This was a concern of Federal Reserve officials in the 1920s in the cases of the Stock Yards National Bank of South St. Paul and the Fourth National Bank of Macon. Disorderly failure could also be disruptive if the troubled institution was viewed as a key bank whose collapse would result in a deterioration in confidence in other institutions, as was the case with the City National Bank of El Paso and McCornick and Co. of Salt Lake City. Decisions to provide support to these institutions appear to have been especially fraught, and the pressure to act may have been particularly high, because of the perceived potential spillovers. The Federal Reserve intervened in large part because no other entity could have prevented a collapse.

The decisions to provide liquidity support in these situations are reminiscent of the decision by the FDIC and the Federal Reserve to intervene to support Continental Illinois of Chicago in 1984. That institution was similarly viewed as highly connected, with regulators pointing to its large correspondent banking network and potential spillover effects as a reason to intervene (Conover 1984; FDIC 1997). Moreover, troubles at Continental Illinois appear to have spilled over to other money center banks, as interest rates on the money market funding instruments offered by these other banks increased (Bailey and Zaslow 1984). To keep the bank from failing in a disorderly manner, the Federal Reserve provided substantial discount window support, and the FDIC guaranteed all the bank's liabilities and provided capital support in the form of a preferred equity injection (FDIC 1997, 1998; Carlson and Rose 2019). Thus, while the Federal Reserve was involved in these efforts, the FDIC took the most substantive actions. That meant that the effective resolution of Continental Illinois, and any credit risk associated with the intervention, was handled by a government entity that the legislature had given responsibility for dealing with troubled banks rather than by the lender of last resort.

Concerns about the disruptive failure of large financial institutions, including institutions other than banks, emerged again in the 2008 financial crisis after the failure of Lehman Brothers caused a cascade of problems in financial markets and necessitated an enormous response on the part of central banks globally. In the wake of that crisis, efforts have been made to plan for the orderly resolution of globally systemic financial institutions should one of these institutions become deeply troubled. In the United States, such efforts have involved the establishment of the Orderly Liquidation Authority, under which the FDIC will act as receiver for the entire company, not just the bank, and oversee its restructuring in a way that imposes losses on shareholders while minimizing disruptions to the operations of the firm and its interactions with its customers (see Treasury 2018). These resolution structures should significantly reduce the pressure on a lender of last resort to keep questionable institutions going while everyone races to find solutions.

Issues associated with the disruptive effects of bank failures are particularly relevant when many banks are in trouble at the same time. If only a handful of banks are in trouble, then it may be possible to find buyers who will purchase the banks that have viable business models and who may be able to absorb the profitable parts of the remainder of other banks. When many banks are in trouble, it is considerably more challenging to find a sufficient number of buyers. As a result, there may be situations where many businesses or farmers that are solvent but had dealt with a bank that had made bad loans might find it hard to switch banks or otherwise obtain credit. When this situation arose in the 1930s, Congress established the Reconstruction Finance Corporation (RFC), which ended up injecting equity into banks. In 2008, the Troubled Asset Relief Program (TARP) provided equity support to banks.

In the 1920s, the troubles in the banking system were also widespread. Congress attempted to support the banks by enhancing the ability of the War Finance Corporation to extend loans. As noted by Rieder (2020) and White and Roberds (2020), Congress leaned heavily on the Federal Reserve to support the banks during the hearings of the Joint Commission of Agricultural Inquiry. However, Congress made no provision to provide equity support as it did through the RFC or through TARP. Consequently, the Federal Reserve was put in the position of having to choose between extending longer-term support than it may have preferred (as indicated by subsequent policy changes when conditions recovered) or withholding support and tolerating potentially disruptive bank closures. This challenge was most clearly evident in the case studies involving the Stock Yards National Bank of South St. Paul and the Live Stock National Bank of Sioux City.

Interventions and the Incentives of Private Agents

Another general lesson is the importance of managing moral hazard. The historical experience points to a range of ways that this can be done. Moral hazard issues can arise because of the confidence that the lender of last resort will provide support—the very thing noted above as being important for calming markets. That confidence encourages financial market participants to take more risk than they would otherwise take. Moral hazard could arise because of the existence of a standing liquidity backstop facility (such as the discount window) or because of a statement articulating support from the central bank.

When the lender of last resort provides liquidity assistance, it enables other liability holders to withdraw their funds. If the episode involves a pure liquidity event, then providing emergency liquidity prevents those withdrawals from needlessly disrupting the operations of a valuable financial intermediary. If, however, the institution is insolvent, then the action by the central bank means that certain liability holders can withdraw and that, as noted above, the remaining creditors could be worse off. Moreover, if depositors know that the lender of last resort will provide financing, then they may provide more financing than they would have otherwise and may not demand interest rates related to the credit risk of the financial firm. That in turn may lead the financial firm to use more such financing and to take on more risk. Finally, if the managers know that their institution is troubled and that emergency liquidity support from the central bank is preventing a forced closure, the managers may have some incentive to gamble for redemption and take extra risk if there is a possibility that it would restore solvency.

As discussed by Calomiris, Flandreau, and Laeven (2016), the ability to design interventions to account for the specifics of the situation has a long history in lender-of-last-resort policy and is vital for limiting moral hazard, especially in the presence of potential uncertainty about illiquidity versus insolvency. Managing competing incentives is a significant challenge, but flexibility that allows the lender of last resort to structure its lending program to minimize the moral hazard concerns can promote the long-term robustness of the financial system (see also Kindleberger and Aliber 2005; Goodhart 1999; Tucker 2014).

Efforts to manage these incentives are evident both in how the discount window was managed regularly and how it was used during the episodes reviewed in the case studies. An important part of these efforts included ensuring that managers and shareholders had a considerable stake in the success, or at least solvency, of the bank. That assurance sometimes took the form of the provision of personal guarantees by managers or shareholders on the assets that were being pledged as collateral. In other cases, it took the form of required equity injections by shareholders. The Federal Reserve was more willing to provide extended liquidity support to banks that made these commitments, such as the Stock Yards National, and sometimes withdrew liquidity support from banks where such supports were not forthcoming, such as the First National Bank of Shenandoah.

In some cases where the support for the bank was delayed or impossible, the Federal Reserve appears to have been reassured by broader community support. This support took the form of community investment in the case of the City National Bank of El Paso, where it would have taken some time for the shareholders to come up with the resources to inject additional equity. In the case of McCornick and Co. of Salt Lake City, where the shareholders were unable to provide sufficient resources, the extensive risk- and loss-sharing arrangements with the other banks in the town were key to support provided by the Federal Reserve.

Ensuring that liquidity support involved the careful management of incentives foreshadows various actions taken by the Federal Reserve more recently. For instance, the Term Asset-Backed Securities Loan Facility (TALF) used in 2008 and again in 2020 provided support to the strained asset-backed securities (ABS) market by setting up carefully managed incentives for investors to purchase new ABS (see Meisenzahl and Pence, 2022). In particular, the TALF provided liquidity support in the form of low-cost, long-term funding. The loans offered through the TALF were nonrecourse, but the ABS collateral was subject to very conservative haircuts. Thus, investors had incentive to participate because they could gain from the upside of their ABS purchases but also had incentive not to take too much risk because the haircuts on the collateral ensured that the investors were in a first-loss position.[4]

Rules versus Flexibility in the Response

There is a discussion in the literature about the value of creating rules for how a central bank will act in an emergency versus retaining flexibility to react. As noted by Bagehot (1873) and Tucker (2014), credible and publicly known rules can inspire confidence that in an emergency the central bank will make liquidity available; in doing so, these rules can encourage commercial banks to keep lending and prevent the central bank from needing to lend at all. Meltzer (2003) notes that rules are important in limiting moral hazard by helping clarify when the central bank will not lend and commercial banks need to prudently manage risk.

The experiences of the Federal Reserve in the 1920s highlight the challenges in formulating rules. The events that prompted Federal Reserve responses ranged widely, and it would be difficult to articulate an approach that would have clearly covered them all. The practical challenges would have been compounded at the new and decentralized central bank. Nevertheless, one could view the changes in policy that took place in 1926 and the articulation of policies in the *Annual Report* for that year as an effort to move toward a more rule-based system.

Even so, the experiences of the 1920s illustrate that the extension of emergency liquidity will often require operational flexibility. Gorton (2012) argues that while financial crises tend to occur amid a deterioration in economic conditions, unpredictability regarding how they will unfold and which institutions will be affected makes it impossible to specify in detail what actions the central bank should take in response to a crisis. Indeed, part of what drives financial crisis dynamics is that they are not foreseen by market participants. Consequently, central banks need to be flexible and creative in deciding how to address the particulars of the situation confronting them.

The value in being flexible and creative in delivering emergency liquidity is apparent in the interventions undertaken by the Federal Reserve in the 1920s. The use of currency funds to provide an observable liquidity backstop without actually making loans or using the balance sheet of either the Reserve Banks or the commercial banks certainly stands out. Even when using the discount window, the Reserve Banks were clearly flexible in providing short-term or long-term arrangements depending on what the circumstances seemed to dictate.

The creativity displayed in the 1920s also foreshadows the range of structures used by the Federal Reserve when establishing its emergency lending facilities during the Global Financial Crisis of 2008 and in response to the financial turmoil accompanying the onset of the COVID-19 pandemic in 2020. Those different structures allowed the Federal Reserve to provide credit in ways familiar to participants in a broad range of financial markets while at the same time remaining aligned with the requirements of the Federal Reserve Act.

CHAPTER EIGHT

Conclusion

The 1920s saw a very young Federal Reserve experiment with lender-of-last-resort actions amid challenging economic conditions. Federal Reserve officials provided liquidity to banks to help them manage severe liquidity strains and deal with depositor runs. In a few select cases, they also appear to have been willing to provide loans to failing institutions to help prevent disorderly collapses where there were fears of regional panics. Reserve Bank officials also took a longer view of what was considered a stress event and provided sustained financing to help some banks restructure after the collapse of a credit or agricultural boom.

The early 1920s were a challenging time in the banking sector. More banks closed their doors in each year in the early 1920s than did so in all but the worst financial crises of the preceding fifty years. Despite the widespread banking distress, banking panics—in which numerous banks in close proximity suffered runs or deposit withdrawals that forced them to close their doors—were scarce. In his textual analysis of newspaper articles, Jalil (2015) identifies only a handful of banking panics in the 1920s, mostly centered in Florida. Looking for clusters of bank closures, Davison and Ramirez (2014) find evidence of a few more local panics but still fewer than might be expected given the size of the economic shocks experienced and the concerns about the condition of banks within the system. The deteriorations in economic conditions in the early 1920s were similar to those that had historically led to large-scale banking panics, yet such a panic did not materialize (Gorton 1988). While there might be a variety of possible explanations, the picture of the Federal Reserve that emerges from this book strongly suggests that the actions that Federal Reserve officials took to prevent local panics and keep incidents of instability from spreading helped make panics rare.

This review of the Federal Reserve's experiences with emergency lending in a difficult economic environment in the 1920s provides both insights into the operation of the Federal Reserve during that period and lessons that are relevant today.

Some Things We Learn about the Federal Reserve

We learn quite a lot about the factors that shaped Federal Reserve policymakers' decisions regarding emergency responses. In the examples provided in chapter 5, it is clear how the factors considered by the Reserve Banks fit together to produce successful outcomes. To be sure, these examples are not an unbiased list, and a full review of all the lending (or lack thereof) to all the troubled banks in the 1920s would likely provide a much messier picture. (There were certainly outside commentators who criticized the Reserve Banks for lending too much [H. P. Willis 1925a] or too little [see discussions in Joint Commission of Agricultural Inquiry 1921–1922]). Nevertheless, these examples illustrate how Federal Reserve officials aspired to implement their lending policies.

Risk-Management Practices

One thing we learn about the Federal Reserve is how officials managed the risk of lending in difficult situations. Collateral was an important component of that risk-management strategy. While there appears to have been some variation in the Reserve Banks' interpretation of eligibility criteria and willingness to accept collateral at the margins of eligibility, officials do seem to have been consistent in requiring that collateral be of sufficient quality to provide the Reserve Banks with strong protection from loss in the event that the bank defaulted. Indeed, if Federal Reserve officials had concerns about the quality of either the bank or the collateral itself, it appears not to have been uncommon for them to require additional collateral. At the same time, Federal Reserve officials were conscious that lending on good collateral to troubled institutions risked worsening the losses to other depositors if the bank was put in receivership. That understanding provided a caution regarding continued extensions of credit to troubled banks even if those banks had available collateral.

The second component of the Federal Reserve's risk-management strategy was the use of inside information about the bank, such as from the examiner reports. For instance, Federal Reserve officials were attentive to the quality of bank management. Assessments of the quality of the individuals running the bank required a lot of soft information that typically would only be available to individuals very familiar with the bank or to someone, such as the examiner, who could review the books, see how the parts of the bank lined up, and talk to management. Confidence that the management was operating the bank in a (reasonably) sound manner and had a business strategy that would allow for success in the long term was valuable for determining whether the bank would be able to repay the discount window loan from the Federal Reserve even if, in some cases, that would take some time. Other key inside information included the examiner's assessments of the losses and prospects of the bank going forward. Relying on a disinterested outsider helped mitigate agency problems that would have resulted if the Federal Reserve had been forced to rely only on the management's own assessments. The use of inside information often relied on cooperation with the OCC. While, as described by White (2015), the level of cooperation between the two agencies was not always perfect, the case studies here indicate that in stressful situations there was often good communication and that the insider insights generated by the two agencies were vital in decision-making.

A third component of the risk-management approach was a consideration of how leveraged the bank was. The Reserve Banks (and other regulators) viewed banks as overextended when the banks' loans routinely exceeded their deposits and the bank was relying on funds borrowed from other banks or from the Federal Reserve.[1] Banks that were continually overextended tended to be more vulnerable to shocks and had less capacity to absorb losses on their assets. Because the discount window loans were secured, the extent to which the banks were overextended and relying on Federal Reserve credit heightened concerns about imposing higher losses on depositors if the bank closed. Federal Reserve officials appear to have paid more attention to this component over time, in part as they had negative experiences or as they ended up feeling forced to continue to lend in uncomfortable situations.

Importance of Shareholder Commitment

We also learn that Federal Reserve officials in the 1920s were attentive to the willingness of shareholders to contribute funds to support troubled institutions. The shareholders' contributions took various forms, including voluntary assessments and equity contributions, purchases of poorly performing assets from the banks, or guarantees that the commercial bank would not lose money on certain assets. This support from the shareholders certainly provided additional protection to the Federal Reserve when it was lending and could be thought of as part of the risk-management practices. However, the willingness of shareholders to provide this support was helpful for several other reasons as well.

First, when shareholders were willing to put more of their own funds at risk, it indicated that they believed in the prospects of the bank and its viability in the long run. The shareholders' belief in the prospects of the bank likely reassured Reserve Bank officials that they were not merely propping up a failing bank.

Second, shareholder commitment would have helped mitigate moral hazard issues. The Federal Reserve offered the same discount rate to all banks regardless of their riskiness. If the bank only borrowed from the Federal Reserve when it was in trouble and could not obtain funds in the market at a rate below the discount rate, that would mean that the Federal Reserve was effectively providing funds to insulate the bank from market pressures. The fact that equity holders were making contributions and themselves incurring losses as they wrote down existing equity to purge bad loans from the bank's books would have significantly alleviated concerns that the Federal Reserve's provision of support was incentivizing riskier behavior.

That equity injections were a valuable part of the process of dealing with troubled banks is reminiscent of modern requirements that the globally systemically important banks that may be eligible for government liquidity assistance during resolution also issue securities that can be used as part of a recapitalization. These securities, which constitute part of the banks' total loss-absorbing capacity (TLAC), typically consist of debt that can be converted into equity during a resolution (see, for instance, Financial Stability Board 2015).[2] Requiring that a set of private investors have clear exposures that are subject to loss during a resolution helps promote market discipline, mitigate moral hazard issues that result from the possibility of a backstop, and ensure the repayment of any government funds provided as part of a liquidity backstop during what is likely to be a period of uncertainty.

Importance to Federal Reserve Policymakers of Potential Spillovers from a Bank Failure

A third thing we learn about Federal Reserve officials is that they were concerned about the implications of a bank closure for other banks and for the community and were not just concerned about the bank for its own sake. Concerns about the potential for the closure of one bank to trigger the closure of other banks was frequently pointed to as a reason for intervention, and Federal Reserve officials viewed the prevention of additional failures as one measure of success.

One reason that the closure of a bank might have caused additional closures was the signal it provided. Depositors might well interpret the closure of one bank as indicative of the condition of nearby banks with similar loan portfolios.[3] Hence, Federal Reserve officials were more willing to lend if they believed that the closure of the bank would meaningfully affect local confidence. There was a particular concern about the signal that the closure of a member bank might send. Federal Reserve officials believed that member banks faced lower risks from bank runs because the public had some awareness that the Federal Reserve was providing a backstop. A disorderly collapse might cause public confidence in that backstop to decrease, which might cause withdrawals from other member banks. Thus, the public's confidence in Federal Reserve support would have bolstered the stability of the banking system but also created an obligation on the part of the Federal Reserve to ensure that those beliefs remained credible.

Federal Reserve officials were also concerned about the spillover effects that might result from the closure of key banks that provided liquidity support for other, more remote banks. If the key banks were to fail, then those remote banks would lose access to that support and may be forced to close. Consequently, Federal Reserve officials paid attention to the banks' position in the interbank system and seemed especially willing to provide support to institutions that were in turn lending to other banks. A similar policy appears to have been used in the 1930s by the Reconstruction Finance Corporation, which provided more support for banks with larger numbers of correspondents (see Calomiris et al. 2013).

Finally, Reserve Bank officials were attentive to the negative externalities on communities that might result from the closure of banks and the inability of community members to obtain access to credit and other bank services. For example, officials expressed concern about the closure of a bank that would have left Williston, North Dakota, a town of five thousand people, without access to a bank. Such concerns also appear to have prompted extra effort on the part of the Federal Reserve to provide support. In some cases, concerns about these externalities appear to have encompassed financial markets in which banks were key funding providers even beyond the local community. For instance, as pointed out by White (2015), Governor Wellborn of FRB Atlanta was attuned to the potential for widespread negative impacts on the cotton market had the Federal Reserve not supported the banks amid falling prices and frozen inventories.

The Federal Reserve and Bagehot's Dictum

As noted earlier, Walter Bagehot's 1873 dictum that a lender of last resort should lend freely at a high rate against good collateral to solvent borrowers influenced central bankers in the 1920s and still influences thinking on appropriate lender-of-last-resort policy today. Certainly, the case studies contain a number of episodes where Bagehot's dictum is a reasonable description of the approach used by Federal Reserve officials. During the episodes involving bank runs, such as for the Park National Bank or the Polk County National Bank, the Federal Reserve lent freely. The discount rate was above regular deposit rates and so might be thought of as high; it was less clear that the discount rate was above private rediscount rates, but still the rate appears to have been such that the banks reduced their borrowing as deposits returned. These institutions also appear to have been solvent, as they continued to operate for several years after the Federal Reserve intervened.

There were also situations where it is less obvious that the Federal Reserve followed Bagehot's dictum. As described in some of the episodes and as demonstrated by the losses, the Federal Reserve did not always lend to solvent banks on good collateral. In part, as discussed below, this outcome reflects the challenges of knowing the quality of collateral in real time and of factors beyond the control of either the commercial bank or the borrower whose loan was being used as collateral. At other times, however, the Federal Reserve lent in situations where it knew that losses might be possible because the interconnectedness of the financial system meant that greater losses to the banking system and possibly to the Federal Reserve itself might materialize if action was not taken. Thus, when departures from Bagehot's dictum occurred, at least in the cases studied here, they appear to have been the result of carefully weighed decisions.

Some General Lessons about the Lender of Last Resort

We are also able to draw some lessons about the lender of last resort that are more directly applicable to today. These are general lessons, especially since the financial system is considerably different now than it was in the 1920s. They also may serve more as reminders of existing ideas than as entirely new lessons.

One useful lesson is that the Federal Reserve can alleviate stress by promoting confidence that there is sufficient liquidity available in addition to actually providing that liquidity. Indeed, it was not always necessary for lending to actually occur. Sometimes the Federal Reserve promoted confidence behind the scenes in discussions with bankers about their liquidity needs or the needs of nearby banks. At other times, promoting confidence involved public announcements or prominent displays of cash. The value of publicizing that support depended importantly on the extent to which the public was already acting on concerns about liquidity availability.

A second lesson is that insolvency and illiquidity are frequently interrelated during financial stress. Moreover, there can be enormous challenges in determining whether a borrowing institution will remain solvent if support is needed for some time. While collateral can be useful in protecting the central bank from losses if the borrowing institution turns out to be insolvent, taking collateral can complicate interactions with the other liability holders.

The failure of a financial firm can be very disruptive. Banks have information about their own loan customers based on relationships that can be lost if the bank fails; those customers may be unable to obtain credit elsewhere. Some banks serve as important liquidity providers for other banks, and the loss of these key intermediaries can have sizable spillovers. Given these impacts, the historical experience points to the value of having a robust set of options in place to manage the resolution of key institutions and mitigate the disruptions associated with the failure of a financial firm to reduce the pressure on a lender of last resort to provide liquidity.

Finally, the historical experience points to the value of flexibility in the deployment of tools to respond to stress. The Federal Reserve needed to respond to a variety of stresses: both sudden and short term as well as gradual and enduring. Being able to deploy their tools flexibly allowed policymakers to match the response to the problem.

Being a lender of last resort is one of the most challenging roles for a central bank. Decisions often must made at great speed and under considerable uncertainty. The experiences of the Federal Reserve in the 1920s highlight the value of flexibility and creativity, the importance of information, and the merits of having confidence in the solvency of the borrower — because of either existing equity or shareholder support. These experiences also provide a cautionary tale; policies enacted to address perceived problems associated with past situations might make it more difficult to deal with future situations. Trying to understand the unique features of a newly developing situation can be challenging, but doing so is essential for successfully using the tools of a lender of last resort.

Episodes of Emergency Liquidity Provision in the United States Prior to the Federal Reserve

This appendix discusses some previous episodes of emergency liquidity provision in the United States that may have shaped the thinking of Federal Reserve policymakers. Responding to financial crises was hardly something new when the Federal Reserve was established. Indeed, several Federal Reserve officials were involved in responses to prior financial turbulence. However, some of the tools available to the Federal Reserve and the interactions between the Federal Reserve and member banks were new and different. It is informative to review these prior experiences and discuss how they may have shaped the thinking of Federal Reserve officials, as well as to highlight some of the novel issues confronted by the Federal Reserve.

Clearinghouses

The bank clearinghouses that operated in the United States were a likely source of Federal Reserve officials' ideas on how to respond to financial stress. The clearinghouses were key organizations within the payment-clearing system and therefore played important roles when the banking system was navigating financial crises.

Clearinghouses simplified the payment system. Major banks in major cities had a lot of checks and other payments to process. This was especially true in places like New York, which processed checks on behalf of their respondent banks throughout the country as well as local customers.[1] Rather than having couriers running between all the banks with bags of checks and money, it was more efficient for all the banks to send representatives to a single place. This was the New York Clearinghouse, where, as described by Gibbons (1859), the banks would present all the checks at once, everything could be netted, and the banks would make or receive a single payment. Similar clearinghouses were set up in many other cities that had a sizable number of banks or payments that needed to be cleared; the discussion here focuses on the New York Clearinghouse, which was the most well known and which served as a model for others.

Because all the major banks in a city were members of the clearinghouse, and because the clearinghouses were focused on the liquidity of their members, bankers naturally coordinated responses to financial panics through the clearinghouses.

As the clearinghouses dealt with the processing of payments among member banks, their central focus was on their members' ability to meet their obligations to one another. Problems at one member, such as a loss of public confidence that resulted in a run, could very quickly cascade and affect the condition of other members and public confidence in the clearinghouse. Ensuring that members could meet their obligations in a timely manner meant that each of the member banks and the clearinghouse as a whole were concerned with the solvency and the liquidity of all the member banks. During a crisis, clearinghouses might still be willing to provide liquidity support to member banks whose solvency was questionable; in particular, if the ongoing functioning of the member bank was key to maintaining confidence in the association, the clearinghouse might opt to provide liquidity during the crisis and sort things out once the situation had calmed down (Coe 1884; Gorton and Tallman 2018).

The clearinghouses had a number of tools that they could use to respond to crises and manage the issues they were concerned about. The first of these tools was the examination—a tool that was also important to the Federal Reserve Banks. The clearinghouse employed examiners who could review the conditions of the member banks at any time (Cannon 1910; Moen and Tallman 2000). These examinations were likely to be quite thorough and, since the examiners were local and likely familiar with many of the local businesses, able to provide effective assessments regarding the quality of the banks' assets. They helped ensure that each member of the clearinghouse could be confident that the other members were solvent or were taking the necessary steps to fix any problems.[2] Examinations were conducted regularly during normal times, and special examinations were conducted during stress periods.

Clearinghouses could also mobilize the collective liquidity of their members to support a struggling member. These liquidity provision tools were quite useful, though they were more limited than those of the Federal Reserve. One tool for bolstering liquidity was the issuance of clearinghouse certificates. Clearinghouse certificates were a liquid instrument issued by the clearinghouse to a member bank. Banks could use the certificates to meet demands on their liquidity—for example, by making payments to the clearinghouse to cover obligations associated with clearing checks. By expanding the set of instruments that banks could use to meet payment obligations, the clearinghouse expanded the liquid assets of their member banks (Cannon 1910; Myers 1931; Timberlake 1984). To receive certificates, a bank would have to pledge collateral and typically pay interest to the holders of the certificates. The decision to issue certificates was made by a vote of clearinghouse members, and all members had to be willing to accept these certificates as payment. If a member bank failed with clearinghouse certificates outstanding, then the clearinghouse would first use the proceeds on the collateral to make payments to the holders of the certificates. If that proved insufficient, the clearinghouse would distribute losses proportionally among member banks. The interest payments on the certificates compensated the holders for doing so and also encouraged the retirement of the certificates when the emergency had ended. In New York, the clearinghouse certificates circulated only among clearinghouse members. In some of the smaller cities, clearinghouse notes would circulate among the general public, though only locally (Sprague 1910; Cannon 1910).[3]

Clearinghouses could also provide liquidity to their member banks by lending to them (Gorton 1985; Gorton and Tallman 2018). Funds for these loans would come from the other member banks. The loans would be collateralized, and any losses in the event of the failure of the loan recipient would be borne proportionally by the clearinghouse's member banks. In many ways, these loans were similar to clearinghouse certificates, but the terms of the loan (such as the maturity and interest rate) could be set on a bespoke basis.

The ability of clearinghouses to provide liquidity support appears to have been quite valuable to the members. Jaremski (2018) finds that clearinghouse members were more likely to survive financial panics. Moen and

Tallman (2000) argue that even the perception of liquidity support from the clearinghouse could be critical in supporting banks in stress.

This additional liquidity was helpful but not always sufficient to enable banks to meet the demands put upon them. In these cases, the banks would be forced to suspend paying out deposits, sometimes partially—such as by limiting the size of withdrawals or by limiting payments sent out of town. If an individual bank was forced to suspend, confidence in that institution was damaged, and any reopening required an investigation by the local regulator to confirm solvency. At other times, suspension was coordinated by all the banks in the city—sometimes through the local clearinghouse (Sprague 1910). That created a more complicated dynamic. When the suspension was done collectively, there does not appear to have been a decline in confidence regarding any particular institution. However, if that city was an important hub in the interbank system, then concern that the banks in the hub might suspend payment could lead other banks in the network to preemptively withdraw any deposits held there, and the suspension would become self-fulfilling. Carlson (2015) describes how this dynamic appears to have contributed to the troubles in the banking system during the Panic of 1907. James, McAndrews, and Weiman (2013) find that the widespread city-level suspensions of payments and merchants' inability to carry out trade between cities had a significant negative effect on the economy of the United States. It was this dynamic in particular that the Federal Reserve was set up to prevent.

Finally, and also broadly like the Federal Reserve, the clearinghouses also had tools to manage the flow of information to preserve confidence and help prevent deposit withdrawals. For instance, and unlike the Federal Reserve, the clearinghouses could directly affect the ability of the public to obtain the information about any particular member. During a normal week, the members of the New York Clearinghouse would submit key balance sheet information to the clearinghouse, and the clearinghouse would arrange for all the balance sheets to be published in the New York City newspapers. During stress events, the New York Clearinghouse would continue collecting the balance sheets of the individual banks but only provide aggregate information to the newspapers. This step reinforced the idea that the members of the clearinghouse were a collective and that it was their combined strength that was critical (Gorton 1985). The idea of the clearinghouses as a collective was especially true if the clearinghouse was issuing certificates that facilitated the use of members' liquidity communally.

If certain members were experiencing substantial liquidity issues due to deposit outflows, the clearinghouse would conduct a special examination. (Such an examination would also have been part of the prelude to a loan from the clearinghouse to the member bank.) As discussed by Gorton and Tallman (2018), after such an examination the clearinghouse could announce that the bank had been found to be solvent, with no additional details. Short, simple announcements allowed the clearinghouse to highlight information that supported confidence.

The names of institutions using clearinghouse certificates to settle their balances were not disclosed. Doing so might well have undermined confidence in those institutions, as it might have made them look weak even if their cash was depleted because they were serving as a source of strength for others.

These issues are well articulated in a speech by George Coe that followed the clearinghouse's intervention during the Panic of 1884 to support the Metropolitan National Bank, one of its member banks. Mr. Coe was one of the preeminent financiers of the national banking era, president of the American Exchange Bank, and several-time president of the New York Clearinghouse and was well positioned to articulate the approach taken by the clearinghouse:

Under these circumstances [the suspension of the Metropolitan National Bank], the Clearing-house Committee were summoned together at midnight, to examine the condition of that institution, and to decide what action should be taken respecting it. A fearful responsibility was thus hastily thrown upon that committee. It was impossible in a few short hours, and in apprehension of further possible events, to reach a definite conclusion upon the value of the large and diversified assets of that bank. When we examined its books, this most important fact at once appeared: that it owed some eight to nine millions of deposits, a large proportion of which consisted of the reserves of interior banks, which could not be imperiled or locked up for another day without producing a further calamity of wide-spread dimensions throughout the country. It was also evident that the consequent certain suspension of many banks in the interior cities would occur, and be followed by the suspension of business men depending upon them and by heavy drafts upon those banks here which held similar deposit reserves, and that the immediate danger to our city institutions was great, just in proportion to the extent of such liabilities and to the amount that each bank was expanded relatively to its immediate cash in hand. That should the threatened wild excitement pervade the country, a general suspension of

banks, bankers and merchants was inevitable, and in which case, the magnitude
of the loss to every institution would be incalculable.

The Committee therefore came to the unanimous conclusion that it was
better to confront the risk of losing one or two millions, if need be, by taking
possession of the total assets of that bank, and by paying off its depositors,
rather than by waiting to incur the hazard of an indefinite and greater loss,
by a general financial and commercial derangement throughout the country;
and that it was their manifest duty to promptly accept this grave responsibility,
confidently relying upon their associates for approval and support. On behalf
of the combined capital and surplus of the banks in this Association, amounting
to about a hundred millions, and also to protect the property and assets held
by them together, of more than three hundred millions, your Committee un-
hesitatingly acted, and thus saved the nation from immeasurable calamity. The
Metropolitan Bank was obviously the key to the whole situation. When this
decision was announced the next morning, confidence was instantly restored,
and business resumed its even tenor. (Coe 1884)

This speech points to the essentialness of maintaining overall confidence
in the clearinghouse banks and indicates that the confidence could be lost
if one of them suspended. That is especially true for Metropolitan, which
held the deposits of many other banks and so was key in that regard.
While President Coe makes clear that the clearinghouse was concerned
about the condition of Metropolitan and wanted to know how troubled
the institution was, he also makes clear that the clearinghouse needed to
make a decision about lending even in the absence of full certainty and
that it was willing to take the risk to preserve overall confidence.

As the discussion of clearinghouses and their responses to crises illus-
trates, many of the concerns of clearinghouse officials were quite similar
to those of Federal Reserve officials. Both sets of officials paid close attention to the solvency of the institutions that needed liquidity support
and took advantage of inside information to assess the condition of firms
that were undergoing liquidity risks. Similarly, both sets of officials were
concerned about the position of banks within the interbank system and
the likelihood that suspensions of banks with more interbank connections
would be disruptive, and both believed that that should be considered
when intervening.[4] Concerns about public confidence and the publicity
surrounding support also figured into the thinking of both groups.

One difference in the approach to emergency lending related to the
availability of liquidity support. Liquidity from the clearinghouses through

clearinghouse certificates was only available in a crisis situation with the vote of the clearinghouse. Hence, no institution could depend on it. That limited the moral hazard but also meant that, in the absence of certainty about the provision of emergency assistance, banks had an incentive to pull back and hoard liquidity, which could make conditions worse and create the need for emergency liquidity.

The Federal Reserve's discount window was available at all times. Indeed, the discount window was a regular source of liquidity for many institutions, which enabled the Federal Reserve to mitigate the regular seasonal liquidity issues of the US financial market (as noted in chap. 2). More related to emergency liquidity, the greater availability of the discount window provided greater benefits but also created larger moral hazard risks. The certainty that the discount window was there to provide liquidity if stress ever occurred meant that bank managers should not have had an incentive to hoard liquidity and could more confidently provide liquidity support to their customers. However, this also meant that managers and shareholders with access to the liquidity insurance provided by the Federal Reserve may have had more incentive to take liquidity risks (on this point, see Carlson and Wheelock 2018a). The fact that the discount window was always available also enabled the Federal Reserve to provide longer-term support such that shareholders might have faced less pressure to deal with certain problems quickly. That could be quite beneficial during systemic events, when it might naturally take some time to assemble the resources to deal with the problems; alternatively, it might allow problems to fester longer and result in larger issues. Federal Reserve officials seemed conscious of the moral hazard issues when they discussed the value of shareholders voluntarily providing additional capital or other support for their banks. Of course, the willingness of shareholders to support the banks was almost certainly important to clearinghouse officials as well. However, the constant availability of the discount window meant that Federal Reserve officials needed to consider a greater range of moral hazard issues, and solvency support would have been particularly beneficial in offsetting them.

Aldrich-Vreeland Currency

One other liquidity response, the provision of emergency currency by the Treasury Department, occurred just as the Federal Reserve was being established and may have shaped the thinking of Federal Reserve officials.

Shortly after the Panic of 1907, as efforts to consider the establishment of some sort of a central bank were being developed, Congress passed the Aldrich-Vreeland Act, which enabled the Treasury Department to issue emergency currency to provide liquidity to the financial sector during stress. This emergency currency is often referred to as Aldrich-Vreeland currency after the congressmen who sponsored the act. Up to $500 million in emergency currency could be issued to banks that were part of national currency associations, which were designed to strongly resembled clearinghouse associations. Banks were required to pledge collateral to obtain the emergency currency. Crucially, in addition to the government bonds normally required to obtain ordinary currency, emergency currency could be obtained by pledging other securities, such as municipal securities (Jacobson and Tallman 2015).[5] To encourage its retirement when the emergency was over, the emergency currency was subject to a statutory tax while it was outstanding. The original act was set to expire, but the Federal Reserve Act of 1913 extended the Treasury Department's authority to issue emergency currency until mid-1915 to enable the government to respond to emergencies while the Federal Reserve was commencing operation.

That extension proved prescient, as the start of World War I on July 28, 1914, caused a serious breakdown in the global financial system. There was an exodus of foreign money from the United States. International trade and finance were instantly and substantially disrupted. To prevent large-scale sales of securities and further foreign investment outflows, at the request of the Treasury secretary, the New York Stock Exchange closed on July 31 and stayed closed for more than four months (Silber 2007). It was a long-standing practice of New York City banks to lend a substantial amount of their liquid resources to the stockbrokers on an overnight basis, so the closing of the stock exchange was a serious liquidity shock to these key banks. There were widespread reports of the hoarding of cash and liquidity by banks and individuals throughout the country.

In response to concerns about a possible panic, secretary of the Treasury William McAdoo and other government officials raced to act. Among these officials was Mr. Hamlin, then assistant secretary of the Treasury and soon to be governor of the Federal Reserve Board. He, along with many others, helped organize banks into national currency associations that would enable them to apply to obtain the emergency currency. In the *Annual Report* for 1914, Secretary McAdoo reported that, in anticipation of events, large amounts of emergency currency were distributed to subtreasury offices in New York City and around the country to be ready when banks opened for business on August 3. A considerable amount of this currency was quickly issued to banks. Between August 1 and October 31, 1914, more than $140 million of such currency was issued to banks in New York City. Another $228 million was issued to banks in other parts of the country.[6] Conferences were held with merchants, financiers, and representatives from the agricultural industry; subsequent to those conferences, it was decided that emergency currency would be made available against private securities, including short-maturity warehouse receipts for cotton, in addition to government securities. This substantial liquidity support has been credited with preventing a financial calamity in the United States (Friedman and Schwarz 1963; Silber 2007; Jacobson and Tallman 2015).

Federal Reserve policymakers, such as Mr. Hamlin, were directly involved in the crisis response, and it almost certainly affected their thinking. However, it is uncertain what lessons they may have taken away. The origin of the shock was unusual and not linked to any actions by US banks or depositors. Still, the secretary of the Treasury emphasized the importance of acting swiftly and robustly as well as the value of providing emergency liquidity against a wide variety of collateral. These aspects of the response may have provided lessons to officials at the brand-new Federal Reserve.

Subsequent Use of Currency Funds

Currency funds appear to have been used during the early 1930s in response to some of the banking stresses of the Great Depression.[1] For instance, currency funds were established in the following episodes:

- Bangor, Maine, November 13–15, 1933, at the Merchants National Bank of Bangor. The fund was reportedly established in response to instability stemming from concerns about the Merrill Trust Company (Division of Bank Operations 1934).
- Hartford, Connecticut, January 7–19, 1932, at the Hartford National Bank and Trust Company and in the Phoenix State Bank and Trust Company. The currency fund was established in response to a disturbance that developed after a run on the City Bank and Trust Company of Hartford, a large nonmember bank, which was forced to close its doors. That bank's failure reportedly forced the East Hartford Trust Company and the Unionville Bank and Trust Company, two small institutions closely allied with it, to close the same day. The Federal Reserve agent from FRB Boston reported that the Reserve Bank had opened a temporary currency fund to facilitate the delivery of currency, with officials from FRB Boston going to Hartford to supervise the establishment and operations. The agent further reported that, through the active cooperation of the Hartford Clearinghouse banks, the National Credit Corporation, and FRB Boston, the situation was localized, and within two or three days, the banking situation in Hartford had returned to normal conditions (Curtiss 1933).

- New Haven, Connecticut, July 2–7, 1932, at the Merchants National Bank Building and the New Haven National Bank. The Central Trust Company of Cambridge, a small nonmember bank, closed on May 10. On May 14, the Leominster National Bank, with deposits of $1,500,000, closed. The Mechanics Bank, a large bank in New Haven, after heavy withdrawals from the savings department, was obliged to invoke the law requiring ninety days' notice of withdrawal of savings. On June 29, the National Tradesmen's Bank of New Haven, a member bank with deposits of about $3,000,000, was forced to close. On July 2, the Federal Reserve Bank opened a currency fund, and the daily papers reported that this fund was available to meet any currency situations that might arise. From July 5 on, the situation quieted down and became normal (Curtiss 1933).
- Sacramento, California, from January 21 to February 1, 1933, at the Capital National Bank but later at the Bank of America National Trust and Savings Association. The currency fund was reportedly established because of an emergency arising from bank failures in the area (Division of Bank Operations 1934).
- Charleston, South Carolina, January 4–21, 1932, at the South Carolina National Bank. This currency fund was established at the request of the South Carolina National Bank and was prompted by the suspension of the Peoples State Bank, which had its head office in Charleston and numerous branches throughout South Carolina. At the time of establishment, $1,250,000 was placed in the currency fund (Division of Bank Operations 1934).
- Boise, Idaho, from January 25 to April 15, 1932, splitting $500,000 between the Boise City National Bank and the First Security Bank. This fund was reportedly established in response to public unrest after the failure of several banks in that part of the country and to the challenges of banks in Boise in obtaining currency given their distance from other financial centers.[2]
- Twin Falls, Idaho, from August 31 to September 8, 1932. This fund was reportedly established after the closing of the First National Bank of Boise, Idaho, on August 31, together with nine other affiliated banks scattered though Idaho and Oregon. For that purpose, $200,000 in currency was forwarded on August 31. By September 7, conditions were such that it was felt that there would be no risk in discontinuing the maintenance of the fund (Hale 1932).

APPENDIX 3

Federal Reserve and OCC Officials

TABLE A3.1. **Federal Reserve and OCC officials, Washington, DC**

	Governor of the Federal Reserve Board	Comptroller of the Currency
1919	William P. G. Harding	John Skelton Williams
1920	William P. G. Harding	John Skelton Williams
1921	William P. G. Harding	John Skelton Williams / Daniel R. Crissinger
1922	William P. G. Harding / vacant	Daniel R. Crissinger
1923	vacant / Daniel R. Crissinger	Daniel R. Crissinger / Henry W. Dawes
1924	Daniel R. Crissinger	Henry W. Dawes
1925	Daniel R. Crissinger	Henry W. Dawes / Joseph W. McIntosh
1926	Daniel R. Crissinger	Joseph W. McIntosh
1927	Daniel R. Crissinger / Roy A. Young	Joseph W. McIntosh
1928	Roy A. Young	Joseph W. McIntosh / John W. Pole
1929	Roy A. Young	John W. Pole

TABLE A3.2. **Federal Reserve and OCC officials, Atlanta (Sixth) District**

	Governor	Federal Reserve Agent	Chief Examiner of the District
1919	Joseph McCord / Maximillian B. Wellborn	Joseph McCord	John W. Pole
1920	Maximillian B. Wellborn	Joseph McCord	John W. Pole
1921	Maximillian B. Wellborn	Joseph McCord	John W. Pole
1922	Maximillian B. Wellborn	Joseph McCord	John W. Pole
1923	Maximillian B. Wellborn	Joseph McCord	Ellis D. Robb
1924	Maximillian B. Wellborn	Oscar Newton	Ellis D. Robb
1925	Maximillian B. Wellborn	Oscar Newton	Ellis D. Robb
1926	Maximillian B. Wellborn	Oscar Newton	Ellis D. Robb
1927	Maximillian B. Wellborn	Oscar Newton	Ellis D. Robb
1928	Maximillian B. Wellborn / Eugene R. Black	Oscar Newton	Ellis D. Robb
1929	Eugene R. Black	Oscar Newton	Ellis D. Robb

TABLE A3.3. **Federal Reserve and OCC officials, Chicago (Seventh) District**

	Governor	Federal Reserve Agent	Chief Examiner of the District
1919	James B. McDougal	William A. Heath	Daniel V. Harkin
1920	James B. McDougal	William A. Heath	Silas Cooper
1921	James B. McDougal	William A. Heath	Fred Brown
1922	James B. McDougal	William A. Heath	Fred Brown
1923	James B. McDougal	William A. Heath	Howard Sims
1924	James B. McDougal	William A. Heath	Howard Sims
1925	James B. McDougal	William A. Heath	Howard Sims
1926	James B. McDougal	William A. Heath	Howard Sims
1927	James B. McDougal	William A. Heath	Howard Sims
1928	James B. McDougal	William A. Heath	B. K. Patterson
1929	James B. McDougal	William A. Heath	A. P. Leyburn

TABLE A3.4. **Federal Reserve and OCC officials, Minneapolis (Ninth) District**

	Governor	Federal Reserve Agent	Chief Examiner of the District
1919	Theodore Wold / Roy A. Young	John Rich	Fred Brown
1920	Roy A. Young	John Rich	Fred Brown
1921	Roy A. Young	John Rich	Howard M. Sims
1922	Roy A. Young	John Rich	Howard M. Sims
1923	Roy A. Young	John Rich	Thomas Harris
1924	Roy A. Young	John Rich / J. R. Mitchell	B. K. Patterson
1925	Roy A. Young	J. R. Mitchell	B. K. Patterson
1926	Roy A. Young	J. R. Mitchell	B. K. Patterson
1927	Roy A. Young / William B. Geery	J. R. Mitchell	B. K. Patterson
1928	William B. Geery	J. R. Mitchell	Irwin D. Wright
1929	William B. Geery	J. R. Mitchell	Irwin D. Wright

TABLE A3.5. **Federal Reserve and OCC officials, Kansas City (Tenth) District**

	Governor	Federal Reserve Agent	Chief Examiner of the District
1919	Jo Zach Miller Jr.	Asa Ramsey	Stephen Newnham
1920	Jo Zach Miller Jr.	Asa Ramsey	Luther K. Roberts
1921	Jo Zach Miller Jr.	Asa Ramsey	Luther K. Roberts
1922	Jo Zach Miller Jr. / Willis J. Bailey	Asa Ramsey	Luther K. Roberts
1923	Willis J. Bailey	M. L. McClure	Luther K. Roberts
1924	Willis J. Bailey	M. L. McClure	Luther K. Roberts
1925	Willis J. Bailey	M. L. McClure	Luther K. Roberts
1926	Willis J. Bailey	M. L. McClure	Luther K. Roberts
1927	Willis J. Bailey	M. L. McClure	Luther K. Roberts
1928	Willis J. Bailey	M. L. McClure	Luther K. Roberts
1929	Willis J. Bailey	M. L. McClure	Luther K. Roberts

TABLE A3.6. **Federal Reserve and OCC officials, Dallas (Eleventh) District**

	Governor	Federal Reserve Agent	Chief Examiner of the District
1919	Richard L. Van Zandt	W. F. Ramsey	Richard H. Collier
1920	Richard L. Van Zandt	W. F. Ramsey	Richard H. Collier
1921	Richard L. Van Zandt	W. F. Ramsey	Richard H. Collier
1922	Richard L. Van Zandt / Buckner A. McKinney	W. F. Ramsey	Richard H. Collier
1923	Buckner A. McKinney	W. F. Ramsey / Lynn P. Talley	Richard H. Collier
1924	Buckner A. McKinney	Lynn P. Talley	Richard H. Collier
1925	Buckner A. McKinney / Lynn P. Talley	Lynn P. Talley / C. C. Walsh	Richard H. Collier
1926	Lynn P. Talley	C. C. Walsh	Richard H. Collier
1927	Lynn P. Talley	C. C. Walsh	Richard H. Collier
1928	Lynn P. Talley	C. C. Walsh	Richard H. Collier
1929	Lynn P. Talley	C. C. Walsh	Richard H. Collier

TABLE A3.7. **Federal Reserve and OCC officials, San Francisco (Twelfth) District**

	Governor	Federal Reserve Agent	Chief Examiner of the District
1919	James K. Lynch / Jonathan Calkins	John Perrin	Horace R. Gaither
1920	Jonathan Calkins	John Perrin	Horace R. Gaither
1921	Jonathan Calkins	John Perrin	Harry L. Machen
1922	Jonathan Calkins	John Perrin	Harry L. Machen
1923	Jonathan Calkins	John Perrin	Harry L. Machen
1924	Jonathan Calkins	John Perrin	Thomas E. Harris
1925	Jonathan Calkins	John Perrin	Thomas E. Harris
1926	Jonathan Calkins	John Perrin / Isaac B. Newton	Thomas E. Harris
1927	Jonathan Calkins	Isaac B. Newton	Thomas E. Harris
1928	Jonathan Calkins	Isaac B. Newton	Thomas E. Harris
1929	Jonathan Calkins	Isaac B. Newton	Thomas E. Harris

Actions by FRB Atlanta during the Early 1920s in a More Macroeconomic Context

Chapter 5 focuses on instances in which the Federal Reserve inter-vened in episodes of distress associated with individual institutions. Those case studies deepen our understanding of the details about lending operations and the factors that Reserve Banks considered when making lending decisions in specific instances. Several of these interventions were associated directly or indirectly with the fallout from the economic challenges of 1920–1921, the collapse in agricultural prices, and the stresses on the financial system. A more macroeconomic view of FRB Atlanta's approach to lending during the agricultural bust is provided in White (2015) and White and Roberds (2020). This appendix briefly summarizes that work as it provides a valuable complement and important context for the more microeconomic view presented in this book (though White [2015] and White and Roberds [2020] provide brief descriptions of interventions at a few individual institutions as well).

The Atlanta District was dominated by cotton. A considerable portion of both the real and financial activity of the region was devoted to that crop. In 1910, the key cotton states in this district were responsible for growing about 40 percent of the US cotton crop, which in turn represented about one-fourth of global production. A significant portion of the loans extended by the commercial banks in the Atlanta District were to intermediaries in the cotton sector—cotton merchants, wholesales, or jobbers—and frequently these loans involved the use of bales of cotton as collateral.

When the price of cotton collapsed in the early 1920s, FRB Atlanta responded in a proactive manner and provided a considerable amount of credit to the banks in the district. Indeed, FRB Atlanta extended enough credit that the Reserve Bank would have breached its reserve requirement had it not obtained gold by rediscounting with other Reserve Banks, especially FRB Cleveland.[1]

If the commercial banks had to liquidate their cotton-related loans, many of the intermediaries in the cotton market would have been forced to either liquidate the cotton at already depressed prices or default and turn the cotton over to banks that would then have had to liquidate the cotton at fire-sale prices. To enable the banks to roll over the loans and prevent sales of cotton in a depressed market, FRB Atlanta provided discount window loans to the Federal Reserve member banks in the district. Moreover, under the rules in place at the time, FRB Atlanta was able to rediscount for member banks loans that had been originated by nonmember banks and that the member banks themselves had discounted (see Hackley 1973). The credit provided by FRB Atlanta was key to allowing all the cotton intermediaries to hold their inventories, wait for cotton prices to rise once again, and eventually sell the cotton at prices that would allow them to repay their loans.

In a letter to the Federal Reserve Board, Governor Wellborn stated: "Our policy has merely to given them [member banks and cotton producers] reasonable time to find a market in these disturbed times, in order to keep them from 'dumping' their products on the market at one time. To do otherwise at this critical time would force a disaster upon our agricultural and business interests and might perhaps have the effect of bringing on a state of panic and bankruptcy" (Garrett 1968, 172, reprinted in White and Roberds 2020).

As described in White (2015) and White and Roberds (2020), the policymakers at FRB Atlanta also understood that allowing the financial sector to collapse would have real economic consequences for the Sixth District, as well as spillover effects in many other districts. This thinking is most apparent in letters sent by Governor Wellborn to the Federal Reserve Board defending the actions of FRB Atlanta and is also apparent in discussions contained in the minutes of the Board of Directors of FRB Atlanta. For instance, White (2015) reports that Governor Wellborn stated:

> The commerce of all the states are too closely knit together to permit the confining of the results of financial upheaval to any one particular state or group of

states. The Cleveland District itself, counts this section [Atlanta District] as one of its principal markets. The Sixth District is filled with farm implements, trucks, automobiles, and other manufactured products emanating from the Cleveland District. The commercial banks of the Sixth District have financed the local dealers [of] many of these commodities, that such local dealers might pay cash to the manufacturers in the Cleveland District. To shut off completely, or hamper the buying power of this and other agricultural districts, would bring about a situation which would be felt from the Pacific to the Atlantic.

Such statements clearly indicate that the overall intervention was viewed as key in supporting real economic activity.

Consequently, the descriptions provided in White (2015) and White and Roberds (2020) indicate an effort to promote stability in a stressful episode through a general approach to lending that is entirely consistent with the efforts of the Reserve Banks (as described in chap. 5) to promote stability by intervening in individual instances.

Notes

Chapter One

1. In modern times, institutions eligible to borrow are more fully captured by the term *depository institutions*, which includes some firms, such as credit unions, that are eligible to borrow but that are legally different from banks. In the 1920s, lending was only to banks.

Throughout this book, there are many references to banks, both to the Reserve Banks, which are part of the Federal Reserve System and which hold deposits from and make loans to banks, and commercial banks, which take deposits from households and businesses and make loans to households and businesses. To help distinguish between the two, I capitalize the term *Reserve Banks* and do not capitalize commercial banks.

2. Nor is it clear that some specific actions would be needed given changes to the bank regulatory environment, such as the establishment of the Federal Deposit Insurance Corporation, which provides deposit insurance and has broad powers to resolve failing banks.

3. Thornton (1807) similarly describes how a lender of last resort should behave.

4. As pointed out by Meltzer (2003), Tucker (2014), and others, there may be advantages to having rules regarding lender-of-last-resort operations to manage moral hazard issues or to bolster market confidence in some situations. The episodes discussed below illustrate that it would likely have been challenging for Federal Reserve officials to establish rules that would address the wide range of circumstances they confronted, especially as some circumstances would have been difficult for the newly formed central bank to foresee. This issue is discussed further in chapter 7.

5. Indeed, it is still not a singular institution. While authority became more centralized in Washington, DC, in the 1930s, the Reserve Banks continue to exercise a fair bit of independence, especially with respect to discount window operations.

Chapter Two

1. Of course, prices throughout the economy increased briskly during the war. Relative to these other increases, the rise in agricultural prices is less dramatic but still meaningful, as many agricultural prices rose at a faster pace than did prices generally.

2. However, these financial developments did have implications for financial stability in the early 1930s and may have contributed to the sizable drop in purchases of consumer durables during the Great Depression.

3. Borrowing from other banks is different from accepting deposits from other banks. A key difference is the entity taking the initiative. Deposits from other banks were done at the initiative of those other banks—for example, for the purpose of providing funds that could be used in the payment-clearing process. Thus, those deposits tended to be reasonably stable over time. Borrowing was at the initiative of the borrower and typically took the form of rediscounts or bills payable. Such borrowing covered a defined length of time with no guarantee that future funds would be provided. Thus, funds obtained through borrowing from other banks were less stable. In addition, borrowed funds tended to have higher interest rates and be secured, whereas interbank deposits had fairly low interest rates and were unsecured.

4. All credit extensions to private parties involve some risk. Safe operations mean that the bank is collecting and using information to assess those risks carefully; taking appropriate steps, such as requiring collateral, to protect itself from losses in the event of a default; and charging an interest rate to compensate for the risks that it is taking.

5. This limit was intended as a concentration limit to restrict exposure to any one borrower. It did not limit aggregate lending relative to bank equity.

6. There were also private banks that operated without an official bank charter, as well as a variety of financial institutions similar to banks, such as mutual savings banks and building and loan societies. The statistics in this chapter deal with banks with charters from either the national government or a state government.

7. Though, of course, the number of failures would only increase further in the early 1930s.

8. The fact that troubled loans remained on the books likely impaired the banks' ability to extend better-earning loans and thus would have further weighed down the banks. Helm (1939) suggests that, given the widespread challenges in the banking industry, supervisors may have exercised forbearance to avoid closing all banks in a community at the same time.

9. More comprehensive discussions of the range of rules may be found in Welldon (1910); White (1983, 2013); and Jaremski and Mitchener (2015).

10. Carlson (2015) provides a history of this discussion.

11. These temporary suspensions are not apparent in figure 2.5 because of definitional differences. The counts in the figure relate to suspensions where the decisions were made at the bank level. In 1907, decisions to close all banks were often made by consortia of banks in a town.

12. See, for example, Lowenstein (2016) for a history of the founding of the Federal Reserve.

13. Apparently being a receiver could be quite lucrative. When some banks included in the case studies were put being put into receivership, the Comptroller's office received numerous letters from individuals offering their services as receivers (including from some people the Comptroller's Office flagged with "No!" [underlining and exclamation point in the original]). Vickers (1994) also has stories about some of the earnings of receivers for state banks in Florida.

14. See Grossman (2001) and Mitchener and Richardson (2013) for a discussion of double liability and its impact on bank risk-taking.

15. However, some banks have uninsured liabilities or other exposures, such as through derivatives, where creditor flight might occur. It is important to note that, because depositors have less incentive to monitor the conditions of the banks, bank managers or owners may have an increased incentive to take more risk. That moral hazard increases the importance of prudential regulations and the examination process.

16. In several cases, it was the regulator in charge of the national banks that did not allow them to participate in the deposit insurance programs.

17. For further discussion of these deposit insurance programs, see, for instance, Calomiris and Jaremski (2019); Chung and Richardson (2006); Wheelock and Wilson (1995); and White (1991).

18. See, for instance, Gorton (1985); James, McAndrews, and Weiman (2013); and Jaremski (2018).

19. The reduced seasonality of interest rates and pressures seems to have had broader effects on financial stability. For instance, Bernstein, Hughson, and Weidenmier (2010) find that the reduction in seasonality of interest rates, in combination with the liquidity backstop provided by the Federal Reserve, contributed to a reduction in stock market volatility.

20. Of course, there may also have been other considerations when setting policy. For instance, Wicker (1966) and Chandler (1971) argue that to facilitate the return of other countries, especially the United Kingdom, to the gold standard, the Federal Reserve at times may have kept rates lower than it otherwise would have.

21. The Depository Institutions Deregulation and Monetary Control Act of 1980 enabled the Federal Reserve to extend discount window loans to nonmember banks.

Chapter Three

1. The authority to discount was included in the original Federal Reserve Act in 1913. The authority to make advances was added in 1916.

2. Indeed, when the underlying loan matured, the Federal Reserve Bank would return the loan contract to the bank for collection.

3. The endorsement also had important practical implications. For instance, as noted by Hackley (1973), it meant that the Reserve Bank did not have to initiate

legal proceedings against a commercial firm that defaulted on a paper the bank had discounted at the Federal Reserve; any legal proceedings would instead be the responsibility of the member bank.

4. This maximum maturity prevailed through the 1920s. The maximum maturity was lengthened to 90 days in the 1930s and later to 120 days.

5. The fact that the discounting bank had to endorse the paper and give the Federal Reserve recourse to that bank and that the Federal Reserve would return notes it had rediscounted to the originating bank for collection made the practice of rediscounting fairly similar to the practice of making advances, at least with respect to their credit risk.

6. Of course, a member bank could borrow from the Federal Reserve and then lend to a nonmember bank using different collateral.

7. A similar idea was a "line of credit" (as noted in the first quote in the introduction), whose amount appears to have resulted from discussions between the Federal Reserve and the bank about the amount the bank would likely need to borrow during the upcoming harvest season and the amount the Federal Reserve would be willing to lend on a no-questions-asked basis.

8. The most common formula appears to be $2.5 \times (65\%$ of average reserve balance during the previous calendar month $+ 6\%$ of the commercial bank's paid-up capital stock and surplus). This formula was described in a letter by the Federal Reserve Board to the Reserve Banks asking about their experience with large borrowings (Board of Governors 1920a), but the origins of the formula are not clear, and it may well have been based on practices already in place at some Reserve Banks.

9. An exception to the progressive rate was made if the discount window loan was secured by government obligations actually owned by the member bank. In that case, the discount window loan was provided at the regular posted rate.

10. In the early 1930s, the Federal Reserve Act was changed to considerably expand the types of bank assets that were allowed to serve as collateral for discount window loans.

11. While contemporaries believed that the real-bills approach would not be inflationary, as discussed by Humphrey (1982), this doctrine could result in inflation if businesses raised the prices of the goods involved in the transaction and then borrowed more against them.

12. Two Reserve Banks, FRB Atlanta and FRB Boston, did indicate on the survey that there were times when the collateral acceptability requirements might be tightened, but these seem to have been in response to concerns about credit being too easy rather than stressed conditions. FRB Atlanta reported tightening collateral requirements to limit speculative activity (which would presumably be the opposite of a stress period). FRB Boston reported tightening collateral requirements when it was generally seeking restrictive credit conditions or when it was concerned about the investment policies of an individual bank.

13. The Federal Reserve appears to have taken additional collateral rather than increasing the haircuts on collateral offered by troubled banks. That approach likely reflects the structure of discounting where the Federal Reserve would provide funds equal to the face value of that eligible paper minus the discount rate. In this structure, heightening the haircut would effectively have amounted to increasing the discount rate.

14. Another reason for taking additional collateral appears to have been to manage payment-system risks. Young (1923) reported that FRB Minneapolis sometimes asked for additional collateral to manage additional exposures that the Reserve Bank might gain through payment processing, such as those associated with clearing checks or "wire transfers against deferred credits." (The Reserve Bank would credit a bank's reserve account when that bank presented a check to the Federal Reserve, but it might take a few days for the Federal Reserve to debit the account of the bank on which the check was drawn. This exposure is sometimes referred to as "check float" and results in some credit exposure to the Federal Reserve.) Especially with respect to access to payment-system credit, FRB Minneapolis noted that payments needed to be made "quickly and without hesitance, lest it cause some undue reflection upon a deserving member bank" (Young 1923). If the Reserve Bank had extra collateral, then it could be confident in extending payment-related credit, even to banks about which it might have some concerns, to avoid sending an inadvertent negative signal about the quality of the bank. In modern times, the Federal Reserve maintains a detailed payment-system risk policy; see https://www.federalreserve.gov/paymentsystems/psr_about.htm.

15. This information also tells us something about the challenging economic conditions faced by banks in the early 1920s. The low recovery values indicate the troubled real economic conditions.

16. Such practices appear to have occurred at Reserve Banks other than those that completed the TBSRs. For instance, Burgess (1936, 61–62) reports that FRB New York used the examination results to maintain a list of banks about which it had concerns and to which it gave special scrutiny before lending.

17. These ratings appear to have evolved over time. They were referred to sometimes as "grades" and other times as "classes" of banks.

18. The currency fund in Miami, for instance, required the banks maintaining custody of the Federal Reserve notes to pledge collateral with a market value of $3 million against notes of $2 million (Board of Governors 1926b, August 6, 1926, 6).

Chapter Four

1. Considerations of solvency and risk-taking took into account whether the bank had engaged in speculative lending, as described in chapter 3. However, Federal Reserve officials were also attentive to ratios, such as the bank's loans relative

to its deposits, which are similar to leverage ratios and would indicate riskiness regardless of whether the purpose of the lending was for "speculative activities" or the sorts of real-bills lending that Federal Reserve officials preferred.

2. Interestingly, Agent Perrin indicates that the weight he puts on the bank's preferences for protecting depositors rather than lenders was not necessarily shared by all the other policymakers at the Reserve Bank. He reports that some board members of the Reserve Bank saw greater value in supporting member banks that in turn supported the community and that this had led to debates about the Reserve Bank's approach to lending to particular banks. Thus, views on discount window lending policy differed not only across Reserve Banks but also within Reserve Banks.

3. Jaremski and Wheelock (2020b) find that banks with more interbank connections were more likely to join the Federal Reserve System. That would have made it easier for the Federal Reserve to extend credit to interconnected banks.

4. The years 1920–1922 on the West Coast appear to have met FRB San Francisco's definition of a national crisis. P. B. Willis (1937, 182) describes the response by Reserve Bank officials as having three phases, with a first, extremely aggressive response followed by gradually more restrained phases as conditions stabilized: "(1) No selection of banks or paper. The [Reserve] bank admitted everything in an attempt to allay a panic. (2) After the panic, it still discounted freely, even taking real estate loans, ignoring the principles of eligibility. (3) Eventually its policy selected banks and paper admitted to discount privileges. This policy has been developed conservatively ever since. The seriousness of the situation at that time is reflected in the reserves of 1¼ millions of dollars set up against possible loss on paper rediscounted."

5. The willingness of FRB Chicago to extend a discount window loan to this bank was likely bolstered by the apparent health of the bank. The TBSR reported that the bank had few suspect loans, that the Reserve Bank had confidence in the bank's management, and that the bank held a large volume of government securities.

6. In the first case, the bank ended up being closed. In the second case, the management was changed. In both cases, FRB Atlanta reported that it considered the outcome to be in the long-term interest of the community.

7. Note that FRB Dallas does not rule out all lending to banks with poor management but instead refers in its statement to "continuous lending." Short-term extensions of credit in which there was a clearly defined end point would still be permissible. It should be remembered that a number of communities in the Dallas District were experiencing droughts or other challenging economic situations. In these cases, the quality of the management was most important in balancing the needs of the community with the maintenance of the bank's soundness.

8. After it had been fully repaid, the Federal Reserve would return any additional proceeds to the receivership. Hence, the impact of the Federal Reserve's

collateral policies on other creditors depended on the recovery rates of the assets taken as collateral.

9. A similar point is made in the annual report of the Federal Reserve Board for 1926 (4).

10. This dynamic in particular is associated with a "stigma" regarding discount window borrowing and a reluctance by banks to use the discount window for assistance.

Chapter Five

1. The bank was successfully reorganized and reopened.

2. In a letter dated December 13, 1921, Mr. Perrin, a Federal Reserve agent and the chair of the Board of Directors of FRB San Francisco, formally requested approval of the currency fund as an emergency matter. The board approved the request shortly thereafter.

Local banks lobbied for the establishment of the fund and, in addition to FRB San Francisco, contacted the governor of Idaho and US Senator W. E. Borah. Both the governor and the senator expressed their support for the establishment of the currency fund.

3. This was not the first use of a currency fund in Florida. Previously, such funds had been used intermittently in Miami to address high payment-flow needs in the city. The first instance appears to have been established in August 1925 and discontinued in October 1926. Another had been established in March 1928 and discontinued in January 1929 (see Board of Governors 1938).

4. Moreover, owing to the stress situation, special authorization was given to enhance Citizens Bank's ability to use its connection to the Federal Reserve to provide liquidity to other banks. In particular, FRB Atlanta was authorized by the Federal Reserve Board to rediscount for Citizens Bank eligible and acceptable paper that Citizens Bank had acquired from selected nonmember banks (Board of Governors 1929, June 17, 1929). See chapter 3 for more detail on this mechanism and the rules around it.

5. It was also explicitly stated that "the funds will not be utilized for the purpose of supplying till money to the banks in the localities" (Board of Governors 1929, July 16, 1929). The currency fund that had been set up in Miami in 1925 had been discontinued when Federal Reserve officials determined that the banks serving as custodians were misusing it as a substitute for holding cash on their own and that the currency fund was giving an unfair advantage to these banks.

6. The Federal Reserve Board authorized the currency fund on July 16, 1929 (Board of Governors 1929, July 16, 1929). CMR (2011) report that the cash was shipped to Tampa on July 17, 1929, and was available to be distributed to the banks. The legal arrangements for the currency fund to remain in place as a standing fund

NOTES TO CHAPTER FIVE

for the next six months were not complete until August 18 (Board of Governors 1938).

7. As noted in chapter 2, balances maintained at correspondent banks could be used to settle payments or facilitate the provision of other services. These balances constituted an important part of the plumbing of the financial system and facilitated the flow of cash around the banking system to where it was needed most. As banks drew down these balances and held cash, that reduced the availability of cash generally in the system.

8. Also of note, in their resolution establishing the currency fund, the directors of FRB Atlanta specifically indicated that, in their opinion, establishing this currency fund would not create a precedent or induce requests for similar funds (Board of Governors 1929, July 16, 1929).

9. See also New York Times, "Wild Run on Banks by Cuban Depositors Ended by Machado," April 11, 1926, 1.

10. It is informative to understand a little about the accounting of such a transaction. For instance, if National City Bank of New York wanted to send cash to Havana, it bought a cable transfer from FRB Boston with funds from its reserve account at FRB New York that would be payable in Havana. FRB Boston would then alert FRB Atlanta so that FRB Atlanta would have sufficient cash at the Havana agency to satisfy the cable transfer (though if the amount was for a small payment, such an alert should not have been necessary). Transactions between the Reserve Banks could be settled through the Gold Settlement Fund. FRB New York would see a debit in its reserves (a liability) when National City used those funds to buy the cable transfer from FRB Boston. The decline in reserves would be associated with a decrease in FRB New York's gold settlement fund balance in favor of FRB Boston. FRB Boston would see a temporary increase in its gold settlement fund as resources came from FRB New York but then an offsetting decrease as FRB Boston sent resources to FRB Atlanta to cover the currency that FRB Atlanta would be providing to cover the cable transfer. FRB Atlanta would see an increase in its Federal Reserve notes (currency) outstanding, a liability item, and its gold settlement account, an asset. Indeed, according to the Federal Reserve's weekly balance sheet (the H.4.1 statistical release), the amount of notes outstanding at FRB Atlanta increased from $163 million on April 9, 1926, to $197 million on April 16, 1926, a sizable one-week adjustment.

11. While on board the vessel, the Cuban postmaster also offered a dinner where alcohol was provided. Accusations regarding the consumption of alcohol by FRB officials while on duty, especially during Prohibition in the United States, caused a notable controversy. See Garrett (1968) and Gamble (1989) for details.

12. These actions also highlight that when the US dollar plays a prominent role in offshore markets, the Federal Reserve may be called on to provide emergency liquidity to those markets. In that regard, this episode may, in a very broad sense, foreshadow the use of the dollar swap lines to support offshore dollar funding mar-

kets, as was the case in the 2008 financial crisis (see https://www.federalreserve.gov
/monetarypolicy/bst_liquidityswaps.htm).

13. A formal notarized statement of the amount of equity provided, dated February 16, 1926, is available in the National Archives, records of the OCC, alongside the 1926 examination report for this bank.

14. Todd (2008, 150) also provided a narrative of the run and FRB Kansas City's response.

15. As a warning of the challenges of formulating statements in the moment, some newspapers reported that Governor Bailey had indicated that the Federal Reserve was guaranteeing the bank's deposits. That caused a minor kerfuffle; some nonmember banks sent indignant letters to the Federal Reserve asking them to issue a statement clarifying that the Federal Reserve did not in fact guarantee deposits. After some internal discussion, Federal Reserve officials decided that the newspapers had misinterpreted Governor Bailey's words, that they did not need to respond to each and every newspaper mischaracterization of statements by Federal Reserve officials, and that the nonmember banks would likely use any statement by the Federal Reserve on this matter in their own ads (possibly through selective interpretation of the statement). So officials sent a carefully worded letter to the complaining nonmember banks but made no public statement.

16. Vickers (1994) provides a detailed history of this episode, complete with a review of some of the seedier and more corrupt elements.

17. The word *safe* reflects the terminology used in the examination reports at this time to denote management that was not taking excessive risks.

18. Descriptions of the history of the economic situation around El Paso were prepared as part of a meeting on August 31, 1926, between FRB Dallas officials and representatives of the First National Bank of El Paso amid troubles at that commercial bank (see FRB Dallas 1926).

19. This account of the acquisition follows the overview provided in the bank examiner report started on November 8, 1923, and concluding in February 1924. This examination report was interrupted by other emergencies and was added onto several times, including with descriptions of the events of late January. For clarity about the timing, this report is referred to as the examination report of February 1924.

20. For instance, the May 1923 examination report indicates that slow paper, doubtful paper, and otherwise undesirable paper were $886,533.37, $89,735.56, and $62,233.96, respectively. Much of this paper was secured with collateral, and earnings were expected to be sufficient to allow any defaulting paper to be written off gradually.

21. Kilman (1961) is slightly ambiguous about which bank he is referring to, pointing only to the "City National Bank of ___" while noting that the response was coordinated through the El Paso branch. The details of his description exactly align with the descriptions in the examination report for the City National Bank of El Paso, so it is assumed that he is referring to that bank.

22. The telegram sent by Examiner Longmoor (1924) read:

> Ratan Quasi jibe plans for regal thus far asylum harp and sermon
> stop am reader here to redwood and awl pecan jocose joking to
> obelisk arsenal for work out stop revival weapon closet just as
> soon as parasol stop cockade very loop distill now from cockade
> aggrieve my laurel.

This was translated as:

> Regarding 7514 [charter for City National Bank El Paso] Plan
> for reorganization thus far has failed and situation serious. Am
> remaining here to render all possible assistance and await ar-
> rival President 2532 [the First National Bank, El Paso, Texas] to
> obtain assistance for working out. Report of examination will be
> completed just as soon as possible. Condition very little different
> now from condition advised my letter. This office feels that there
> is some way this bank can be saved. Think advisable for you to go
> to El Paso and take charge situation.

23. Consequently, when the bank was closed a few months later, the citizens accused the bank officials of fraud and claimed that the Federal Reserve had in fact purchased the assets and did not have other claims on the bank. The claims regarding the Federal Reserve were firmly rejected by the courts.

24. The legal arrangement under which the funds were provided is a bit murky. The resolution agreed to by the bank officers and by Governor McKinney refers to this as a deposit (McKinney 1924a). The bank ended up closing with this arrange- ment still in place, and it resulted in some discussions between lawyers for the re- ceiver and the Federal Reserve. It was determined by the regulators, and affirmed by the courts, that the funds provided to the bank by FRB Dallas constituted an advance (see Wyatt 1926).

25. Earlier in the day, President McNary had sent a telegram requesting that the Federal Reserve Board urge Governor McKinney to purchase bad assets from the City National Bank.

26. This amount notably exceeds the deposit to which Governor McKinney agreed. The newspaper may have provided an incorrect figure, or it may have joined the Federal Reserve's and the citizens' contributions and rounded up.

27. The governor of New Mexico ordered a holiday to commemorate the pass- ing of Woodrow Wilson (who died on February 5, 1924). The banks and regulators reportedly used this time to regroup and plan their response (McKinney 1924b).

28. However, a short while later, the Border National Bank of El Paso was forced to suspend. That bank was subsequently able to reopen and resume operations.

29. In the examination report of February 1924, the examiner reported that, as of November 20, 1923, City National Bank had rediscounted over $1.1 million

of loans with FRB Dallas. The report of the Insolvent Banks Department of FRB Dallas states that, at the time it closed, City National still owed the over $1.1 million (Insolvent Banks Department 1924). (It is not clear whether that includes the $500,000 deposit). Given the size of the overall losses, there are many scenarios in which losses to FRB Dallas could have been considerably worse. These interventions' impact on the depositors is less clear, but it is likely that they benefited, though at the expense of the new equity holders.

30. Some of these exposures were acquired through the affiliated financial institutions: the Stock Yards Mortgage & Trust Company and the St. Paul Cattle Loan Company. The stockholders of the Stock Yards National Bank had a controlling interest in those institutions. These affiliations gave the combined entity an even larger footprint in the livestock industry of the Ninth District. An examination of St. Paul Cattle Company was conducted by national bank examiners in July 1922 to assess the joint solvency of the firms. This examination found that, while the operations of the two enterprises were quite intertwined, the books, collateral, and interactions were appropriately managed, and the two institutions were jointly well run.

31. A notarized statement of this decision, dated January 19, 1922, is included alongside the examination report for the bank.

32. The OCC bank examiner also viewed the support provided by FRB Minneapolis as key to the bank's survival. In the February 1921 report, he noted, "The bank has been able to continue its operations largely by a liberal use of the facilities of the Federal Reserve Bank, and the generous deposits made in periods of most stress by the packers who have large interests in the bank."

33. The examiner reported that there had previously been problems as the prior management of the bank had switched assets between the two firms to keep the bank free of criticism and undesirable assets.

34. In addition, the minutes of the Executive Committee of the Federal Reserve Bank of Chicago from January 1921 indicate that there were challenges regarding the condition of another bank in Sioux City, Iowa. Support for the Live Stock National may thus have reflected efforts by Federal Reserve officials to prevent a deterioration in local confidence in the banking system.

35. This belief proved prescient. In the June 3, 1925, report, the examiner wrote, "At the time of the previous examination, the Reads requested time to arrange to remove the losses personally rather than to use any more of the surplus, and since such a policy was desirable, they were given what was supposed to be a reasonable length of time to do it. However, they either acted with mental reservations or their plans did not develop wherein they were to get the money, and consequently, I found them at this time without having carried out their agreement."

36. The bank did also have a surplus fund of $25,000 and undivided profits that in 1923 were about $30,000. Still, borrowing from the discount window significantly exceeded the bank's net worth on a regular basis.

37. The size (and existence) of these contributions is striking, as there was no legal requirement for them. They provide an indication of the value that the community placed on retaining a bank.

38. Details of this plan are described in the examiner report started on October 20, 1923. (This examination was paused amid the reorganization and was not completed until a few months later.)

39. The examiner also noted a large number of "speculative loans" secured by Coca-Cola stock.

40. In addition, and exercising a particular form of moral suasion, the bishop of a prominent diocese in the city reportedly urged the crowd outside one of the banks to disperse and return to business as usual (*Atlanta Constitution*, December 1, 1928, 9).

41. Moreover, there appears to have been some recent evidence of employee theft from the bank. Not long before Mr. McCornick passed away, there had been a $250,000 shortage in a former cashier's account (FRB San Francisco, TBSR). This deficit was covered by voluntary contributions from the directors, but its existence would not have promoted confidence on the part of other banks in the city regarding how the bank was being run.

42. Consistent with this, the *Salt Lake City Telegram* (May 18, 1921, 3) reported that, according to a financial statement from March 31, 1921, McCornick and Co. had owed bills payable and rediscounts to the Federal Reserve totaling over $3,100,000. On its June 30, 1921, statement, Walker Brothers reported only $425,000 in bills payable with the Federal Reserve (as published in the *Salt Lake Tribune*, July 8, 1921, 16).

Chapter Six

1. There are some nuances to this waterfall. The surplus requirement was specific to the individual Reserve Banks, and a small fraction of earnings was still paid as the franchise tax even if the surplus was still being built up. The distribution of earnings was described in Section 7 of the Federal Reserve Act. See also the *Annual Report* of the Federal Reserve Board for 1926 (21) for a cogent discussion.

2. This concern also appears in Board of Governors (1926, 4).

3. This seven-volume report was prepared by H. Parker Willis in cooperation with B. H. Beckhart, John Chapman, W. H. Steiner, A. H. Stockder, and Mary McCune and was titled "Report of an Inquiry into Contemporary Banking in the United States." This report was not published, but copies are available in the library of the Board of Governors of the Federal Reserve and among the papers of H. Parker Willis at Columbia University. H. Parker Wills was an academic who also served in policy positions—for instance, by serving as the first secretary to the Federal Reserve Board. The writings in this report would not have reflected the views of Federal Reserve officials but may have influenced them.

4. Indeed, during the 2007–2008 financial crisis, the Federal Reserve established the Term Auction Facility (TAF) as a way to get around the stigma problem. This facility auctioned a specified amount of discount window credit to commercial banks and other depository institutions. Among the features of TAF, bidders were limited with respect to the amount of auctioned credit they could receive; that meant there had to be multiple winners, which reduced the likelihood that any particular institution would be singled out. Other features included delayed settlement, so that the facility was less useful for banks in immediate trouble, and a market (auction-determined) rate. McAndrews, Sarkar, and Wang (2017) and Wu (2011) find that the TAF was effective in reducing pressures in funding markets.

Chapter Seven

1. Of course, a backstop may also create moral hazard and an incentive to take more risk. Moral hazard and efforts to manage it are described further into this chapter, in the subsection titled Interventions and the Incentives of Private Agents.

2. See Shin (2009) and the description of the run on Northern Rock for an instance in which news stories of government support triggered a bank run.

3. Interestingly, in testimony before a joint congressional committee in the 1920s, Mr. Silver of the American Farm Bureau Federation argued that what holders of the cotton crop really needed was some sort of long-term financial instrument outside of the Federal Reserve and the banking system that could sustain them until prices recovered (Joint Commission of Agricultural Inquiry 1921, 1:350). It should also be noted that Congress did expand the powers of some other agencies, such as the War Finance Corporation, to help address the situation.

4. In addition, the TALF loans were structured such that there were no other creditors that would face increased risks because of the Federal Reserve taking collateral or imposing conservative haircuts.

Chapter Eight

1. This approach of comparing (presumably steady) deposits to the bank's (presumably less liquid) loan portfolio is reminiscent of the modern regulation regarding the net stable funding ratio (NSFR). The NSFR compares the available stable funding, which includes some deposits, to the required stable funding needed to fund the longer-maturity and less liquid portions of the bank's balance sheets (see Bank for International Settlements 2014).

2. These equity injections are also broadly in line with proposals for contingent convertible securities such as those described by Flannery (2016).

3. See Freixas et al. (1999) for a further discussion about such signaling effects.

Appendix One

1. For example, if a bank in Minneapolis was presented with a check drawn on a bank in New Orleans (perhaps as a result of trade along the Mississippi River), it could be expensive to send the check back to New Orleans and seek to have the cash to cover it sent to Minneapolis. Instead, the bank in Minneapolis could send the check to New York, where both banks had a correspondent. The check would be settled by moving funds from the New Orleans bank's account with its correspondent in New York to the Minneapolis bank's account with its correspondent in New York (for further details, see James and Weiman 2010). Moreover, if the Minneapolis bank received checks from Cleveland and San Francisco in addition to New Orleans, rather than send the checks back to all these different cities, it could send all of them to New York. This clearing system was notably more efficient. Similar operations to clear local checks occurred at the regional city hubs.

2. In addition, members of clearinghouses typically faced capital and liquidity requirements that were more stringent than those imposed by the chartering authorities (Jaremski 2018). Those tighter requirements would have ensured that there was more time to correct any issues before the bank failed.

3. The issuance and use of clearinghouse certificates was probably not strictly legal, but since it was well understood that they would be used only during the crisis and were vital for managing the crisis, no one raised serious questions about them (Andrew 1908; Timberlake 1984).

4. Another similarity is related to concerns about the fueling of speculative activity. Federal Reserve officials were concerned about banks borrowing at the discount window to facilitate their lending to the stock market or in real estate bubbles. New York Clearinghouse officials were concerned that banks in New York City were paying rates that were too high, or any interest rate at all, on bank deposits that were attracting funds to invest in speculative activities and drawing funds away from "more productive" lending; Coe (1884) makes this point.

5. Before the establishment of the Federal Reserve, paper currency consisted (mainly) of national bank notes. To issue these notes, national banks needed to deposit US government securities with the Treasury. See Friedman and Schwarz (1963).

6. Jacobson and Tallman (2015) find that clearinghouse certificates were also issued about this time and played a secondary, but meaningful, role in providing liquidity and preventing a panic.

Appendix Two

1. Several of these funds were extremely short term in nature. Consequently, it was determined that collateral was not required but instead that the currency was covered by the Reserve Banks' insurance policies.

2. Excerpt from the examination report of the FRB San Francisco, April 2, 1932, and part of a collection of documents in the National Archives on currency depots compiled by the Division of Bank Operations, Board of Governors of the Federal Reserve System, "Currency Funds."

Appendix Four

1. As described by White (2015) and White and Roberds (2020), this rediscounting was the source of some friction.

References

Books and Journal Articles

Alcorn, Edgar. 1908. *The Duties and Liabilities of Bank Directors*. Columbus, OH: Financial Publishing.

Alston, Lee. 1983. "Farm Foreclosure in the United States during the Interwar Period." *Journal of Economic History* 43 (4): 885–903.

Alston, Lee, Wayne Grove, and David Wheelock. 1994. "Why Do Banks Fail? Evidence from the 1920s." *Explorations in Economic History* 31:409–31.

Anbil, Sriya, Mark Carlson, Christopher Hanes, and David Wheelock. 2021. "A New Daily Federal Funds Rate Series and History of the Federal Funds Market, 1928–1954." *Federal Reserve Bank of St. Louis Review* 103 (1). https://doi.org/10.20955/r.103.45-70.

Anderson, Clay. 1971. "Evolution of the Role and the Functioning of the Discount Mechanism." In *Reappraisal of the Federal Reserve Discount Mechanism*, 1:133–64. Washington, DC: Board of Governors of the Federal Reserve System.

Andrew, A. Piatt. 1908. "Substitutes for Cash in the Panic of 1907." *Quarterly Journal of Economics* 22:497–516.

Bagehot, Walter. (1873) 1909. *Lombard Street: A Description of the Money Market*. New York: Charles Scribner's Sons.

Bailey, J., and J. Zaslow. 1984. "Continental Illinois Securities Plummet amid Rumors Firm's Plight Is Worsening." *Wall Street Journal*, May 11, 1984, 3.

Bank for International Settlements. 2014. "Basel III: The Net Stable Funding Ratio." Basel Committee for Bank Supervision publication number 295.

Bernanke, Ben. 1983. "Nonmonetary Effects of the Financial Crisis in the Propagation of the Great Depression." *American Economic Review* 73:257–76.

Bernstein, Asaf, Eric Hughson, and Marc D. Weidenmier. 2010. "Identifying the Effects of a Lender of Last Resort on Financial Markets: Lessons from the Founding of the Fed." *Journal of Financial Economics* 98:40–53.

Boot, Arnoud. 2000. "Relationship Banking: What Do We Know?" *Journal of Financial Intermediation* 61:7–25.

Bordo, Michael, and David Wheelock. 2013. "The Promise and Performance of the Federal Reserve as a Lender of Last Resort 1914–1933." In *The Origins, History, and Future of the Federal Reserve: A Return to Jekyll Island*, edited by Michael D. Bordo and William Roberds, 59–98. Cambridge: Cambridge University Press.

Boyle, James E. 1928. *Farm Relief: A Brief on the McNary-Haugen Plan*. New York: Doubleday, Doran.

Burgess, W. Randolph. 1936. *The Reserve Banks and the Money Market*. New York: Harper and Brothers.

Calomiris, Charles W., and Mark Carlson. 2022. "Bank Examiners' Information and Expertise and Their Role in Monitoring and Disciplining Banks before and during the Panic of 1893." *Journal of Money, Credit, and Banking* 54 (2–3): 381–423

Calomiris, Charles W., Marc Flandreau, and Luc Laeven. 2016. "Political Foundations of the Lender of Last Resort: A Global Historical Narrative." *Journal of Financial Intermediation* 28 (October): 48–65.

Calomiris, Charles W., and Matthew Jaremski. 2019. "Stealing Deposits: Deposit Insurance, Risk-Taking, and the Removal of Market Discipline in Early 20th-Century Banks." *Journal of Finance* 74 (2): 711–54.

Calomiris, Charles W., and Charles Kahn. 1991. "The Role of Demandable Debt in Structuring Optimal Banking Arrangements." *American Economic Review* 81:497–513.

Calomiris, Charles W., and Joseph R. Mason. 2003. "Fundamentals, Panics, and Bank Distress during the Depression." *American Economic Review* 93 (5): 1615–47.

Calomiris, Charles W., Joseph R. Mason, Marc Weidenmier, and Katherine Bobroff. 2013. "The Effects of Reconstruction Finance Corporation Assistance on Michigan's Banks' Survival in the 1930s." *Explorations in Economic History* 50 (4): 526–47.

Cannon, James G. 1910. *Clearing Houses*. S. Doc. No. 61-491 (National Monetary Commission).

Carlson, Mark. 2007. "A Brief History of the 1987 Stock Market Crash with a Discussion of the Federal Reserve Response." *Finance and Economics Discussion Series 2007–13*, Board of Governors of the Federal Reserve System, Washington, DC.

———. 2015. "Lessons from the Historical Use of Reserve Requirements in the United States to Promote Bank Liquidity." *International Journal of Central Banking* 11 (1): 191–224.

Carlson, Mark, and Kris James Mitchener. 2009. "Branch Banking as a Device for Discipline: Competition and Bank Survivorship during the Great Depression." *Journal of Political Economy* 117 (2): 165–210.

Carlson, Mark, Kris James Mitchener, and Gary Richardson. 2011. "Arresting Banking Panics: Federal Reserve Liquidity Provision and the Forgotten Panic of 1929." *Journal of Political Economy* 119 (5): 889–924.

Carlson, Mark, and Jonathan D. Rose. 2017. "Stigma and the Discount Window." FEDS Notes, December 19, 2017. https://doi.org/10.17016/2380-7172.2108.

———. 2019. "The Incentives of Large Sophisticated Creditors to Run on a Too Big to Fail Financial Institution." *Journal of Financial Stability* 41:91–104.

Carlson, Mark, and David Wheelock. 2015. "The Lender of Last Resort: Lessons from the Fed's First 100 Years." In *Current Policy under the Lens of Economic History: Essays to Commemorate the Federal Reserve System's Centennial*, edited by Owen Humpage, 49–101. New York: Cambridge University Press.

———. 2018a. "Did the Founding of the Federal Reserve Affect the Vulnerability of the Interbank System to Contagion Risk?" *Journal of Money, Credit, and Banking* 50, no. 8 (December): 1711–50.

———. 2018b. "Furnishing an 'Elastic Currency': The Founding of the Fed and the Liquidity of the U.S. Banking System." *Federal Reserve Bank of St. Louis Review* 100 (1): 17-44.

Chandler, Lester. 1971. *American Monetary Policy 1928–1941*. New York: Harper and Row.

Chung, Ching-Yi, and Gary Richardson. 2006. "Deposit Insurance Altered the Composition of Bank Suspensions during the 1920s: Evidence from the Archives of the Board of Governors." *Contributions to Economic Analysis and Policy* 5 (1): article 34.

Coe, George. 1884. Speech regarding Banking Reform in New York. *Banker's Magazine*, July, 44.

Davis, Joseph, Christopher Hanes, and Paul Rhode. 2009. "Harvests and Business Cycles in Nineteenth-Century America." *Quarterly Journal of Economics* 124 (4): 1675–1727.

Davison, Lee, and Carlos Ramirez. 2014. "Local Banking Panics of the 1920s: Identification and Determinants." *Journal of Monetary Economics* 66:164–77.

Diamond, Douglas, and Philip Dybvig. 1983. "Bank Runs, Deposit Insurance, and Liquidity." *Journal of Political Economy* 91 (3): 409–19.

Eichengreen, Barry. 1992. *Golden Fetters: The Gold Standard and the Great Depression, 1919–1939*. New York: Oxford University Press.

Eichengreen, Barry, and Jeffery Sachs. 1985. "Exchange Rates and Economic Recovery in the 1930s." *Journal of Economic History* 45: 925–46.

Financial Stability Board. 2015. *Total Loss-Absorbing Capacity (TLAC) Principles and Term Sheet*. Basel: Financial Stability Board. https://www.fsb.org/2015/11/total-loss-absorbing-capacity-tlac-principles-and-term-sheet/.

Flannery, Mark. 2016. "Stabilizing Large Financial Institutions with Contingent Capital Certificates." *Quarterly Journal of Finance*, 6 (2): 1–26.

Freixas, Xavier, Curzio Gianini, Glenn Hoggarth, and Farouk Soussa. 1999. "Lender of Last Resort: A Review of the Literature." *Financial Stability Review*, November, 151–67.

Friedman, Milton, and Anna Schwartz. 1963. *A Monetary History of the United States, 1867–1960*. Princeton, NJ: Princeton University Press.

Gamble, Richard. 1989. *A History of the Federal Reserve Bank of Atlanta, 1914–1989*. Atlanta: Federal Reserve Bank of Atlanta. https://www.atlantafed.org/about/publications/atlanta-fed-history/first-75-years.aspx.

Garrett, Franklin. 1968. "A History of the Federal Reserve Bank of Atlanta, Sixth District." Unpublished manuscript, December 31, 1968. https://fraser.stlouisfed.org/title/6028.

Gibbons, J. S. 1859. *The Banks of New York, Their Dealers, the Clearing House, and the Panic of 1857*. New York: D. Appleton.

Gilbert, R. Alton. 1994. "Federal Reserve Lending to Banks That Failed: Implications for the Bank Insurance Fund." *Federal Reserve Bank of St. Louis Review*, January/February, 3–18.

Goldstein, Itay, and Ady Pauzner. 2005. "Demand Deposit Contracts and the Probability of Bank Runs." *Journal of Finance* 60 (3): 1293–1327.

Goodhart, Charles. 1999. "Myths about the Lender of Last Resort." *International Finance* 2 (3): 339–60.

Gorton, Gary. 1985. "Clearinghouses and the Origin of Central Banking in the United States." *Journal of Economic History* 45:277–83.

———. 1988. "Banking Panics and Business Cycles." *Oxford Economic Papers* 40:751–81.

———. 2012. *Misunderstanding Financial Crises: Why We Don't See Them Coming*. New York: Oxford University Press.

Gorton, Gary, and Andrew Metrick. 2013. "The Federal Reserve and Financial Regulation: The First Hundred Years." National Bureau of Economic Research Working Paper 19292. Cambridge, MA.

Gorton, Gary, and Ellis Tallman. 2018. *Fighting Financial Crises: Learning from the Past*. Chicago: University of Chicago Press.

Griswold, John A. 1936. *A History of the Federal Reserve Bank of Chicago*. St. Louis: J. Mulligan.

Grossman, Richard. 2001. "Double Liability and Bank Risk Taking." *Journal of Money, Credit, and Banking* 33 (2): 143–59.

Grossman, Richard, and Hugh Rockoff. 2015. "Fighting the Last War: Economists on the Lender of Last Resort." National Bureau of Economic Research Working Paper 20832. Cambridge, MA.

Hackley, Howard. 1973. *Lending Functions of the Federal Reserve Banks: A History*. Washington, DC: Board of Governors of the Federal Reserve System.

Harding, W. P. G. 1925. *The Formative Period of the Federal Reserve System*. Cambridge, MA: Riverside.

Hawtrey, R. G. (1932) 2005. *The Art of Central Banking*. Milton Park: Frank Cass.

Helm, Florence. 1939. *Banking Developments in Missouri, 1920–1939*. Fulton, MO: Ovid Bell.

Horton, Donald C., Harald C. Larsen, and Norman J. Wall. 1942. *Farm Mortgage Credit Facilities in the United States*. Miscellaneous Publication 478. Washington, DC: United States Department of Agriculture.

Humphrey, Thomas. 1982. "The Real Bills Doctrine." *Federal Reserve Bank of Richmond Economic Review*, September/October, 3–13.

Jacobson, Margaret, and Ellis Tallman. 2015. "Liquidity Provision during the Crisis of 1914: Private and Public Sources." *Journal of Financial Stability* 17:22–34.

Jalil, Andrew. 2015. "A New History of Banking Panics in the United States, 1825–1929: Construction and Implications." *American Economic Journal: Macroeconomics* 7:295–330. Online appendix available at https://assets.aeaweb.org/asset-server/articles-attachments/aej/mac/app/0703/2013-0265_app.pdf.

James, John. 1978. *Money and Capital Markets in Postbellum America*. Princeton, NJ: Princeton University Press.

James, John, James McAndrews, and David Weiman. 2013. "Wall Street and Main Street: The Macroeconomic Consequences of New York Bank Suspensions 1866–1914." *Cliometrica* 7 (2): 99–130.

James, John, and David Weiman. 2010. "From Drafts to Checks: The Evolution of Correspondent Banking Networks and the Formation of the Modern U.S. Payments System, 1850–1914." *Journal of Money, Credit, and Banking* 42 (2–3): 237–65.

Jaremski, Matthew. 2018. "The (Dis)Advantages of Clearinghouses before the Fed." *Journal of Financial Economics* 127:435–58.

Jaremski, Matthew, and Kris Mitchener. 2015. "The Evolution of Bank Supervisory Institutions: Evidence from American States." *Journal of Economic History* 75 (3): 819–59.

Jaremski, Matthew, and David Wheelock. 2020a. "Banking on the Boom, Tripped by the Bust: Banks and the World War I Agricultural Price Shock." *Journal of Money, Credit, and Banking* 52 (7): 1719–54.

———. 2020b. "The Founding of the Federal Reserve, the Great Depression, and the Evolution of the U.S. Interbank Network." *Journal of Economic History* 80 (1): 69–99.

Kemmerer, Edwin. 1910. *Seasonal Variations in Demands for Currency and Capital: A Statistical Study*. National Monetary Commission. Washington, DC: Government Printing Office.

Keynes, John M. 1930. *A Treatise on Money. Vol. 2*. London: Macmillan.

Kilman, Herman W. 1961. *A History of the Federal Reserve Bank of Dallas*. Dallas: Federal Reserve Bank of Dallas. https://fraser.stlouisfed.org/title/6859/item/627773.

Kindleberger, Charles, and Robert Aliber. 2005. *Manias, Panics, and Crashes: A History of Financial Crises.* 5th ed. Hoboken, NJ: John Wiley and Sons.

Lowenstein, Roger. 2016. *America's Bank: The Epic Struggle to Create the Federal Reserve.* New York: Penguin Books.

Madigan, Brian. 2009. "Bagehot's Dictum in Practice: Formulating and Implementing Policies to Combat the Financial Crisis." Speech at the Annual Economic Symposium of the Federal Reserve Bank of Kansas City, Jackson Hole, WY, August 21, 2009. https://www.federalreserve.gov/newsevents/speech/madigan20090821a.htm.

Madigan, Brian, and William Nelson. 2002. "Proposed Revision to the Federal Reserve's Discount Window Lending Program." *Federal Reserve Bulletin*, July, 313–19.

McAndrews, James, Asani Sarkar, and Zhenyu Wang. 2017. "The Effect of the Term Auction Facility on the London Interbank Offered Rate." *Journal of Banking and Finance* 83:135–52.

Meisenzahl, Ralf, and Karen Pence. 2022. "Crisis Liquidity Facilities with Nonbank Counterparties: Lessons from the Term Asset-Backed Securities Loan Facility." *Finance and Economics Discussion Series 2022-021*, Board of Governors of the Federal Reserve System, Washington, DC.

Meltzer, Allan. 2003. *A History of the Federal Reserve. Vol. 1, 1913–1951.* Chicago: University of Chicago Press.

Merwin, Charles, and Charles Schmidt. 1942. "Capital and Credit Requirements of Federal Reserve Bank Industrial Loan Applicants." Unpublished manuscript. Available at the Federal Reserve Board Research Library.

Miron, Jeffrey A. 1986. "Financial Panics, the Seasonality of the Nominal Interest Rate, and the Founding of the Fed." *American Economic Review* 76:125–40.

Mitchener, Kris. 2005. "Bank Supervision, Regulation, and Financial Instability during the Great Depression." *Journal of Economic History* 65:152–85.

Mitchener, Kris, and Gary Richardson. 2013. "Does 'Skin in the Game' Reduce Risk Taking? Leverage, Liability and the Long-Run Consequences of New Deal Banking Reforms." *Explorations in Economic History* 50:508–25.

Moen, Jon, and Ellis Tallman. 2000. "Clearinghouse Membership and Deposit Contraction during the Panic of 1907." *Journal of Economic History* 60:145–63.

Morris, Stephen, and Hyun Shin. 2001. "Rethinking Multiple Equilibria in Macroeconomic Modeling." *NBER Macroeconomics Annual 2000*, 15 (1): 139–61.

Myers, Margaret. 1931. *The New York Money Market, Origins and Development.* Vol. 1. New York: Columbia University Press.

Olney, Martha. 1991. *Buy Now, Pay Later: Advertising, Credit, and Consumer Durables in the 1920s.* Chapel Hill: University of North Carolina Press.

———. 2013. "The 1920s." In *Routledge Handbook of Major Economic Events in Economic History*, edited by Randall Parker and Robert Whaples 105–18. New York: Routledge.

Owen, Robert. 1919. *The Federal Reserve Act: Its Origins and Principles*. New York: Century.

Rajan, Raghuram, and Rodney Ramcharan. 2015. "The Anatomy of a Credit Crisis: The Boom and Bust in Farm Land Prices in the United States in the 1920s." *American Economic Review* 105 (4): 1439–77.

———. 2016. "Local Financial Capacity and Asset Values: Evidence from Bank Failures." *Journal of Financial Economics* 120:229–51.

Richardson, Gary, and William Troost. 2009. "Monetary Intervention Mitigated Banking Panics during the Great Depression: Quasi-experimental Evidence from a Federal Reserve District Border, 1929–1933." *Journal of Political Economy* 117 (6): 1031–73.

Rieder, Kilian. 2020. "Financial Stability Policies and Bank Lending: Quasi-experimental Evidence from Federal Reserve Interventions in 1920–21." European Systemic Risk Board Working Paper 113. Frankfurt am Main.

Riefler, Winfield. 1930. *Money Rates and Money Markets in the United States*. New York: Harper and Brothers.

Schwartz, Anna. 1992. "The Misuse of the Fed's Discount Window." *Federal Reserve Bank of St. Louis Review* 74 (5): 58–69.

Shin, Hyun Song. 2009. "Reflections on Northern Rock: The Bank Run That Heralded the Global Financial Crisis." *Journal of Economic Perspectives* 23 (1): 101–19.

Shull, Bernard. 1971. "Report on Research Undertaken in Connection with a System Study." In *Reappraisal of the Federal Reserve Discount Mechanism*, 1:27–75. Washington, DC: Board of Governors of the Federal Reserve System.

Silber, William L. 2007. "The Great Financial Crisis of 1914: What Can We Learn from Aldrich-Vreeland Emergency Currency?" *American Economic Review* 97 (2): 285–89.

Sprague, Oliver M. W. 1910. *History of Crises under the National Banking System*. S. Doc. No. 61-491 (National Monetary Commission).

Thornton, Henry. 1807. *An Inquiry into the Nature and Effects of the Paper Credit in Great Britain*. Philadelphia: James Humphreys.

Timberlake, Richard. 1984. "The Central Banking Role of Clearinghouse Associations." *Journal of Money, Credit and Banking* 1:1–15.

Todd, Tim. 2008. *Confidence Restored: The History of the Tenth District's Federal Reserve Bank*. Kansas City: Federal Reserve Bank of Kansas City.

Tucker, Paul. 2014. "The Lender of Last Resort and Modern Central Banking: Principles and Reconstruction." Bank for International Settlements Working Paper 79. Basel.

Upham, Cyril, and Edwin Lamke. 1934. *Closed and Distressed Banks: A Study in Public Administration*. Washington, DC: Brookings Institution.

Vickers, Raymond. 1994. *Panic in Paradise*. Tuscaloosa: University of Alabama Press.

Wall, Norman J. 1937. "Agricultural Loans of Commercial Banks." US Department of Agriculture Technical Bulletin 521; and supplement, "Recent Agricultural Credit Developments Relating to Commercial Banks." Washington, DC: US Department of Agriculture.

Warburg, Paul. 1914. "A United Reserve Bank of the United States." *Proceedings of the Academy of Political Science in the City of New York* 4 (4): 75–115.

———. 1916. "The Reserve Problem and the Future of the Federal Reserve." Speech before the Convention of the American Bankers Association, Kansas City, MO, September 29, 1916.

Welldon, Samuel. 1910. *Digest of State Banking Statutes*. S. Doc. No. 61-353 (National Monetary Commission).

Westerfield, Ray. 1932. "Margin Collateral to Discounts at the Federal Reserve Banks." *American Economic Review* 22 (1): 34–55.

Wheelock, David. 1989. "The Strategy, Effectiveness, and Consistency of Federal Reserve Monetary Policy, 1924–1933." *Explorations in Economic History* 26:453–76.

———. 1991. *The Strategy and Consistency of Federal Reserve Monetary Policy, 1924–1933*. Cambridge: Cambridge University Press.

Wheelock, David, and Paul Wilson. 1995. "Explaining Bank Failures: Deposit Insurance, Regulation, and Efficiency." *Review of Economics and Statistics* 77:689–700.

White, Eugene. 1983. *The Regulation and Reform of the American Banking System, 1900–1929*. Princeton, NJ: Princeton University Press.

———. 1991. "State-Sponsored Insurance of Bank Deposits in the United States, 1907–1929." *Journal of Economic History* 41:537–57.

———. 2009a. "Lessons from the Great American Real Estate Boom and Bust of the 1920s." National Bureau of Economic Research Working Paper 15573. Cambridge, MA.

———. 2009b. "The Merger Movement in Banking, 1919–1933." *Journal of Economic History* 45 (2): 285–91.

———. 2013. "'To Establish a More Effective Supervision of Banking': How the Birth of the Fed Altered Bank Supervision." In *The Origins, History, and Future of the Federal Reserve: A Return to Jekyll Island*, edited by Michael D. Bordo and William Roberds, chap. 1, [1]–58. Cambridge: Cambridge University Press.

———. 2015. "Protecting Financial Stability in the Aftermath of World War I: The Federal Reserve Bank of Atlanta's Dissenting Policy." National Bureau of Economic Research Working Paper 21341. Cambridge, MA.

White, Eugene, and William Roberds. 2020. "Central Banks, Global Shocks, and Local Crises: Lessons from the Atlanta Fed's Response to the 1920–1921 Recession." Federal Reserve Bank of Atlanta Policy Hub 15-2020.

Wicker, Elmus. 1966. *Federal Reserve Money Policy, 1917–1933*. New York: Random House.

———. 1996. *The Banking Panics of the Great Depression*. Cambridge: Cambridge University Press.

Willis, H. Parker. 1925a. "Contemporary Phases of the Banking Problem in the United States." In "Report of an Inquiry into Contemporary Banking in the United States," vol. 1, edited by H. Parker Willis, B. H. Beckhart, John Chapman, W. H. Steiner, A. H. Stockder, and Mary McCune. Unpublished manuscript. Available at the library of the Board of Governors of the Federal Reserve System.

———. 1925b. "Reserve Bank Policy towards Borrowers." In "Report of an Inquiry into Contemporary Banking in the United States," vol. 3, edited by H. Parker Willis, B. H. Beckhart, John Chapman, W. H. Steiner, A. H. Stockder, and Mary McCune. Unpublished manuscript. Available at the library of the Board of Governors of the Federal Reserve System.

Willis, Parker B. 1937. *The Federal Reserve Bank of San Francisco: A Study in American Central Banking*. New York: Columbia University Press.

Wu, Tao. 2011. "The U.S. Money Market and the Term Auction Facility in the Financial Crisis of 2007–2009." *Review of Economics and Statistics* 93 (2): 617–31.

Ziebarth, Nicolas. 2013. "Identifying the Effects of Bank Failures from a Natural Experiment in Mississippi during the Great Depression." *American Economic Journal: Macroeconomics* 5:81–101.

Federal Reserve Letters, Memos, Reports, and Official Publications

Bailey, Willis. 1927. Letter to the Federal Reserve Board, February 23, 1927. National Archives, Records of the Federal Reserve, "Bank Credit, FRBank Kansas City, Discount Rates—Operations of FRBanks."

Blair, John. 1928. Letter to the Federal Reserve Board, April 24, 1928. National Archives, Records of the Federal Reserve, "Bank Credit 1928."

Board of Governors of the Federal Reserve System. 1920a. Letter to the Federal Reserve Agents, "Discounts for Member Banks in Excess of Basic Line [St. 1133]," May 5, 1920. National Archives, Records of the Federal Reserve, "Statement of Comparison of Borrowing of Member Banks with Basic Discount Line."

———. 1920b. *Bulletin*. Washington, DC: Board of Governors of the Federal Reserve System.

———. 1922. *Bulletin*. Washington, DC: Board of Governors of the Federal Reserve System.

———. 1923. *Annual Report*. Washington, DC: Board of Governors of the Federal Reserve System.

———. 1926a. *Annual Report.* Washington, DC: Board of Governors of the Federal Reserve System.

———. 1926b. *Minutes of the Meeting of the Federal Reserve Board.* Washington, DC: Board of Governors of the Federal Reserve System. Minutes of the April 30, 1926, meeting are available at https://fraser.stlouisfed.org/title/minutes -board-governors-federal-reserve-system-821/meeting-minutes-april-30-1926 -30580.

———. 1927. *Telegram to Reserve Banks.* February 5, 1927. National Archives, Records of the Federal Reserve, "Policy of FR Banks with Regard to Member Banks in Weak or Extended Condition."

———. 1929. *Minutes of the Federal Reserve Board.* Washington, DC: Board of Governors of the Federal Reserve System.

———. 1937. *Bulletin.* Washington, DC: Board of Governors of the Federal Reserve System.

———. 1938. *The Establishment and Operation of Branches, Agencies, and Currency Funds of Federal Reserve Banks.* Report prepared in Division Examinations. Washington, DC: Board of Governors of the Federal Reserve System. https://fraser.stlouisfed.org/title/establishment-operation-branches-agencies -currency-funds-federal-reserve-banks-239.

———. 1943. *Banking and Monetary Statistics, 1914–1941.* Washington, DC: Board of Governors of the Federal Reserve System.

———. 1959. *All Bank Statistics United States, 1896–1955.* Washington, DC: Board of Governors of the Federal Reserve System.

Conference of Governors. 1926. Transcript of remarks at the Conference of Governors, Washington, DC, November 8, 1926.

Coulter, William. 1923. Letter to the Federal Reserve Board, October 9, 1923. National Archives, Records of the Federal Reserve, "Bank Suspensions 1918–1925."

Crissinger, Daniel. 1924. Telegram to First National Bank of El Paso President McNary. January 27, 1924. National Archives, Records of the Federal Reserve, "Bank Suspensions, FRBank Dallas (May 1920–Mar 1924)."

Curtiss, Frederic. 1933. Letter to the Federal Reserve Board, February 14, 1933. National Archives, Records of the Federal Reserve, "Currency Depots."

Day, William. 1921. Letter to Federal Reserve Agent Perrin, June 3, 1921. National Archives, Records of the Federal Reserve, "Bank Suspensions, FRBank San Francisco."

Division of Bank Operations, Board of Governors of the Federal Reserve System. 1925a. Internal memorandum, March 26, 1925. National Archives, Records of the Federal Reserve, "Bank Credit."

———. 1925b. "Member Banks Borrowing in Excess of Capital and Surplus during July 1925," internal memorandum, September 15, 1925. National Archives, Records of the Federal Reserve, "Bank Credit."

———. 1934. "Currency Depots," memorandum, July 13, 1934. National Archives, Records of the Federal Reserve, "Currency Depots."

Federal Reserve Bank of Atlanta. 1927. Survey response regarding dealing with weak and overextended banks [TBSR]. National Archives, Records of the Federal Reserve, "Policy of FR Banks with Regard to Member Banks in Weak or Extended Condition."

———. 1929. *Minutes of the Board of Directors.*

Federal Reserve Bank of Chicago. 1919. *Report of Business Conditions in the Seventh Federal Reserve District*, June 25, 1919. https://fraser.stlouisfed.org /title/5562#574403.

———. 1927. Survey response regarding dealing with weak and overextended banks [TBSR]. National Archives, Records of the Federal Reserve, "Policy of FR Banks with Regard to Member Banks in Weak or Extended Condition."

Federal Reserve Bank of Dallas. 1920–1929. *Minutes of the Board of Directors.* Dallas, TX.

———. 1926. "Memorandum of Conference [with the First National Bank of El Paso]," August 31, 1926. National Archives, Records of the Federal Reserve, "Bank Credit, FRBank Dallas, Discount Rates—Operations of FRBanks."

———. 1927. *Survey response regarding dealing with weak and overextended banks* [TBSR]. National Archives, Records of the Federal Reserve, "Policy of FR Banks with Regard to Member Banks in Weak or Extended Condition."

Federal Reserve Bank of Kansas City. 1927. *Survey response regarding dealing with weak and overextended banks* [TBSR]. National Archives, Records of the Federal Reserve, "Policy of FR Banks with Regard to Member Banks in Weak or Extended Condition."

Federal Reserve Bank of Minneapolis. 1920–1924. *Minutes of the Board of Directors*, Minneapolis, MN.

———. 1921. Table showing selected balance sheet items of principal banks of Minneapolis and St. Paul. National Archives, Records of the Federal Reserve, "Bank Credit."

———. 1923. Letter to A. C. Miller of the Federal Reserve Board, December 8, 1923. National Archives, Records of the Federal Reserve, "Bank Credit (April 1922–1923)."

———. 1927. Survey response regarding dealing with weak and overextended banks [TBSR]. National Archives, Records of the Federal Reserve, "Policy of FR Banks with Regard to Member Banks in Weak or Extended Condition."

Federal Reserve Bank of San Francisco. 1921–1924. *Minutes of the Executive Committee*, San Francisco, CA.

———. 1921–1934. *Minutes of the Board of Directors*, San Francisco, CA.

———. 1927. Survey response regarding dealing with weak and overextended banks [TBSR]. National Archives, Records of the Federal Reserve, "Policy of FR Banks with Regard to Member Banks in Weak or Extended Condition."

———. 1931. "Response to Questionnaire." In *Operation of the National and Federal Reserve Banking Systems: Hearing before a Subcommittee of the Senate Committee on Banking and Currency*, 71st Cong.

Freeman, E. W. 1921. Memo to the Federal Reserve Board, September 27, 1921. National Archives, Records of the Federal Reserve, "Liquidated of Banks, National Banks (1915–1954)."

Grund, Val. 1925. Letter to the Federal Reserve Board, April 1, 1925. National Archives, Records of the Federal Reserve, "Bank Credit, FRBank Dallas, Discount Rates—Operations of FRBanks."

Hale, W. M. 1932. Letter to the Federal Reserve Board, September 14, 1932. National Archives, Records of the Federal Reserve, "Currency Depots."

Heath, William. 1929. Letter to Edmund Platt, Vice Governor, February 21, 1929. National Archives, Records of the Federal Reserve, "Bank Credit, FRBank Chicago, Discount Rates—Operations of FR Banks 1929–1933."

Insolvent Banks Department. 1924. Report of the Insolvent Banks Department of the Federal Reserve Bank of Dallas for June 1924. National Archives, Records of the Federal Reserve, "Bank Suspensions, FRBank Dallas (May 1920–Mar 1924)."

McCord, Joseph. 1920. Letter to Governor Harding, November 19, 1920. National Archives, Records of the Federal Reserve, "Bank Credit, FRBank Atlanta, Discount Rates—Operations of FRBanks (1914–1920)."

McKinney, Buckner. 1922. Letter to Governor Harding, March 27, 1922. National Archives, Records of the Federal Reserve, "Bank Credit, FRBank Dallas, Discount Rates—Operations of FRBanks."

———. 1924a. Extract from report to Board of Directors of Federal Reserve Bank of Dallas, February 7, 1924. National Archives, Records of the Federal Reserve, "Bank Suspensions, FRBank Dallas (May 1920–Mar 1924)."

———. 1924b. Telegram to Governor Crissinger, February 6, 1924. National Archives, Records of the Federal Reserve, "Bank Suspensions, FRBank Dallas (May 1920–Mar 1924)."

Newton, Oscar. 1928. Letter to the Federal Reserve Board, November 30, 1928. National Archives, Records of the Federal Reserve, "Bank Credit, FRBank Atlanta, Discount Rates—Operations of FRBanks."

———. 1930. Letter to the Federal Reserve Board, "Tampa Revolving Currency Fund," August 9, 1930. National Archives, Records of the Federal Reserve, "Currency Depots."

Perrin, John. 1921. Letter to Governor Harding, December 13, 1921. National Archives, Records of the Federal Reserve, "Currency Depot."

———. 1926. "Destructive Effect of Over-lending to Member Banks," Memo to the Board of the Federal Reserve Bank of San Francisco, February 26, 1926. National Archives, Records of the Federal Reserve, "Bank Credit, FRBank San Francisco, Discount Rates—Operations of FRBanks."

Ramsey, W. 1922. Letter to Governor Harding, March 22, 1922. National Archives, Records of the Federal Reserve, "Bank Credit, FRBank Dallas, Discount Rates—Operations of FRBanks."

Reordan, Dwight. 1922. Letter to Federal Reserve Agent Ramsey, "Cattle Conditions in New Mexico," September 26, 1922. National Archives, Records of the Federal Reserve, "Bank Credit, FRBank Dallas, Discount Rates—Operations of FRBanks."

Rich, John. 1921. Letter to Governor Harding, April 27, 1921. National Archives, Records of the Federal Reserve, "Bank Credit."

———. 1924. Letter to Governor Crissinger, February 15, 1924. National Archives, Records of the Federal Reserve, "Bank Suspensions, FRBank, Minneapolis."

Smead, Edward. 1924. Memo to Mr. Hamlin, regarding bank borrowing, July 18, 1924. National Archives, Records of the Federal Reserve, "Bank Credit."

———. 1926. Letter to the Federal Reserve Board, "Banks Borrowing from the Federal Reserve Banks Continuously during the Year 1925," July 22, 1926. National Archives, Records of the Federal Reserve, "Continuous Borrowers."

———. 1927. Memo to Mr. Cunningham, "The Maturity of Bills Discounted by Federal Reserve Banks," November 29, 1927. National Archives, Records of the Federal Reserve, "Bank Credit."

Talley, Lynn. 1923a. Letter to Comptroller of the Currency Dawes, August 29, 1923. National Archives, records of the Comptroller of the Currency, examination report material for the Hugo National Bank.

———. 1923b. Letter to Comptroller of the Currency Dawes, August 31, 1923. National Archives, records of the Comptroller of the Currency, examination report material for the Hugo National Bank.

———. 1923c. Letter to Comptroller of the Currency Dawes, September 5, 1923. National Archives, records of the Office of the Comptroller of the Currency, examination report material for the Hugo National Bank.

Vest, George. 1925. "Establishment of an Agency for the Distribution of Currency at Boise, Idaho," memo to the Federal Reserve Board, April 25, 1925. National Archives, Records of the Federal Reserve, "Currency Funds."

Wellborn, Maximillian. 1921. Letter to Federal Reserve Board Governor Crissinger, December 14, 1921. National Archives, Records of the Federal Reserve, "Bank Credit, FRBank Atlanta, Discount Rates—Operations of FRBanks."

———. 1923. Letter to Federal Reserve Board Governor Crissinger, December 19, 1923. National Archives, Records of the Federal Reserve, "Bank Credit, FRBank Atlanta, Discount Rates—Operations of FRBanks."

Wyatt, Walter. 1924. Memo to Federal Reserve Board member Hamlin, "Failure of City National Bank El Paso, Texas," [1924]. National Archives, Records of the Federal Reserve, "Bank Suspensions, FRBank Dallas (May 1920–Mar 1924)."

———. 1926. "Opinion of Circuit Court of Appeals in Crowell v. Federal Reserve Bank of Dallas," memo, April 1, 1926. National Archives, Records of the Federal Reserve, "Bank Suspensions 1918–1925."

Young, Roy. 1923. Letter to A. C. Miller, Federal Reserve Board, December 8, 1923. National Archives, Records of the Federal Reserve, "Bank Credit (Apr 1922–1923)."

Examiner Reports, Correspondence, and Other Records
of the Office of the Comptroller of the Currency

City National Bank of El Paso. 1924. Letter to shareholders, February 13, 1924, National Archives, records of the Office of the Comptroller of the Currency, examiner reports for the City National Bank of El Paso.

Collier, Richard. 1923. Letter to Comptroller of the Currency Dawes, August 31, 1923. National Archives, records of the Office of the Comptroller of the Currency, examiner reports for the First National Bank of Hugo.

Comptroller of the Currency. 1924. Letter to the management and Board of Directors of the First National Bank of Shenandoah, IA, April 25, 1924. National Archives, records of the Office of the Comptroller of the Currency, examiner reports for the First National Bank.

Dawes, Henry. 1923. Telegram to Agent Talley, August 28, 1923. National Archives, records of the Office of the Comptroller of the Currency, examination records of the First National Bank of Hugo.

Examiner Reports. National Archives, records of the Office of the Comptroller of the Currency.

    City National Bank of El Paso, TX (charter 7514).

    First National Bank, Shenandoah, IA (charter 2363).

    First National Bank of Hugo, OK (charter 6130).

    Hugo National Bank of Hugo, OK (charter 7747).

    Live Stock National Bank, Sioux City, IA (charter 5022).

    National Bank of Commerce, Frederick, OK (charter 10095).

    Park National Bank, Kansas City, MO (charter 9382).

    Polk County National Bank, Bartow, FL (charter 4627).

    Stock Yards National Bank, South St. Paul, MN (charter 6732).

First National Bank. 1924. Letter from the First National Bank of Shenandoah, IA, to Comptroller, March 27, 1924. National Archives, records of the Office of the Comptroller of the Currency, examiner reports for the First National Bank.

Hutt, William. 1923. Letter to Comptroller of the Currency Dawes, September 6, 1923. National Archives, records of the Office of the Comptroller of the Currency, examiner report for the First National Bank of Hugo.

Kane, Thomas. 1922. Letter from the Acting Comptroller to the Board of Directors of the First National Bank of Hugo, April 8, 1922. National Archives, records of the Office of the Comptroller of the Currency, examiner report for the First National Bank of Hugo.

Live Stock National Bank. 1920a. Letter to Deputy Comptroller Kane, July 14, 1920. National Archives, records of the Office of the Comptroller of the Currency, examiner reports for Live Stock National Bank.

———. 1920b. Letter to Deputy Comptroller Kane, October 23, 1920. National Archives, records of the Office of the Comptroller of the Currency, examiner reports for Live Stock National Bank.

———. 1921. Letter to Deputy Comptroller Kane, November 17, 1921. National Archives, records of the Office of the Comptroller of the Currency, examiner reports for Live Stock National Bank.

Longmoor, S. A. 1924. Telegram to Chief Examiner Collier, January 26, 1924. National Archives, records of the Office of the Comptroller of the Currency, examiner reports for the City National Bank of El Paso.

McNary, James. 1924. Letter to Comptroller of the Currency, May 13, 1924, Available in the National Archives, Records of the Federal Reserve regarding "Bank Suspensions, May 1920-March 1924"

Northcutt, V. H. 1926. Telegram to the Comptroller of the Currency, August 3, 1926. National Archives, records of the Office of the Comptroller of the Currency, examiner reports for the Polk County National Bank.

Office of the Comptroller of the Currency. 1917, 1920, 1921. *Annual Report*. Washington, DC: US Government Printing Office.

Roberts, L. K. 1926a. Letter to the Deputy Comptroller of the Currency, January 7, 1926. National Archives, records of the Office of the Comptroller of the Currency, examiner report for Park National Bank of Kansas City.

———. 1926b. Letter to the Comptroller of the Currency, September 2, 1926. National Archives, records of the Office of the Comptroller of the Currency, examiner report for Park National Bank of Kansas City.

———. 1926c. Letter to the Comptroller of the Currency, November 30, 1926. National Archives, records of the Office of the Comptroller of the Currency, examiner report for Park National Bank of Kansas City.

———. 1927. Letter to Governor Crissinger, February 25, 1927. National Archives, Records of the Federal Reserve, "Bank Credit FRBank Kansas City."

Sims, Howard. 1923. Letter to the Comptroller, July 27, 1923. National Archives, records of the Office of the Comptroller of the Currency, examiner reports for the First National Bank of Shenandoah, IA.

———. 1924. Letter to the Comptroller, November 14, 1924. National Archives, records of the Office of the Comptroller of the Currency, examiner reports for the First National Bank of Shenandoah, IA.

Stock Yards National Bank. 1921a. Letter to the Deputy Comptroller of the Currency, April 4, 1921. National Archives, records of the Office of the Comptroller of the Currency, examination reports for Stock Yards National.

———. 1921b. Letter to the Deputy Comptroller of the Currency, May 21, 1921. National Archives, records of the Office of the Comptroller of the Currency, examination reports for Stock Yards National.

Other Government Sources

Beakes, Samuel. 1913. 50 Cong. Rec. 4906.

Conover, C. Todd. 1984. Statement and comments of C. T. Conover, comptroller of the currency. In *Inquiry into Continental Illinois Corporation and Continental Illinois National Bank: Hearing before the House Subcommittee on Financial Institutions Supervision, Regulation, and Insurance of the Committee on Banking, Finance and Urban Affairs*, 98th Cong., 2d Sess.

Federal Deposit Insurance Corporation. 1997. *History of the Eighties: Lessons for the Future*. Vol. 1, An Examination of the Banking Crises of the 1980s and Early 1990s. Washington, DC: Federal Deposit Insurance Corporation.

———. 1998. *A Brief History of Deposit Insurance in the United States*. Washington, DC: Federal Deposit Insurance Corporation.

Joint Commission of Agricultural Inquiry. 1921–1922. *Agricultural Inquiry: Hearings before the Joint Commission of Agricultural Inquiry*, 67th Cong., 1st Sess., under Senate Concurrent Resolution 4 (1921). https://fraser.stlouisfed.org/title/959.

Secretary of the Treasury. 1914. *Annual Report of the Secretary of the Treasury on the State of the Finances*. Washington, DC: US Government Printing Office.

Senate Hearings. 1931. *Operation of the National and Federal Reserve Banking Systems: Hearings before a Subcommittee of the Senate Committee on Banking and Currency*, 71st Cong., 3d Sess.

Treasury Department of the United States. 2018. *Orderly Liquidation Authority and Bankruptcy Reform*. Report to the president of the United States pursuant to the presidential memorandum issued April 21, 2017. Washington, DC: Treasury Department.

Other Reference Materials

Carter, Susan B., Scott S. Gartner, Michael R. Haines, Alan L. Olmstead, Richard Sutch, and Gavin Wright. 2006. *Historical Statistics of the United States: Earliest Times to the Present*. New York: Cambridge University Press.

Rand McNally Bankers Directory. 1921. Chicago: Rand McNally.
———. 1922. Chicago: Rand McNally.
———. 1929. Chicago: Rand McNally.

Newspapers (Alphabetical by State, City)

Atlanta Constitution, Atlanta, GA
Burley Bulletin, Burley, ID
Filer Record, Filer, ID
Daily Star-Mirror, Moscow, ID
Mountain Home Republican, Mountain Home, ID
Kansas City Star, Kansas City, MO
La Plata Home Press, La Plata, MO
Sedalia Democrat, Sedalia, MO
Star-Journal, Warrensburg, MO
Alamogordo Daily News, Alamogordo, NM
Commercial and Financial Chronicle, New York, NY
New York Times, New York, NY
Antlers American, Antlers, OK
El Paso Times, El Paso, TX
Pecos Enterprise, Pecos, TX
Ogden Standard, Ogden, UT
Deseret Evening News, Salt Lake City, UT
Salt Lake Telegram, Salt Lake City, UT
Salt Lake Tribune, Salt Lake City, UT

Index

Italic page numbers refer to figures and tables. The term "bank" by itself refers to a commercial bank. The abbreviation "FR" stands for "Federal Reserve," and "FRB" stands for "Federal Reserve Bank."